Surviving your DIVORCE

A Guide to Canadian Family Law

Surviving your DIVORCE

A Guide to Canadian Family Law

FOURTH EDITION

Michael G. Cochrane, LL.B.

BICENTENNIAL
BICENTENNIAL
1807
WILEY
2007
BICENTENNIAL
BICENTENNIAL

John Wiley & Sons Canada, Ltd.

National Library of Canada Cataloguing in Publication Data

Cochrane, Michael G. (Michael George), 1953-
   Surviving your divorce : a guide to Canadian family law / Michael G. Cochrane.—4th ed.

Includes index.
ISBN-10: 0-470-83952-X
ISBN-13: 978-0-470-83952-2

   1. Divorce—Law and legislation—Canada—Popular works. I. Title.

KE569.2.C63 2006   346.7101'66   C2006-905922-5
KF510.ZA2C63 2006

Production Credits
Cover design: Jason Vanderberg
Interior text design: Interrobang Graphic Design Inc.
Typesetter: Pat Loi
Wiley Bicentennial Logo: Richard J. Pacifico
Printer: Tri-graphic

John Wiley & Sons Canada, Ltd.
6045 Freemont Blvd.
Mississauga, Ontario
L5R 4J3

Printed in Canada
1 2 3 4 5 TRI 10 09 08 07 06

CONTENTS

Acknowledgements... *ix*
Author's Note.. *xi*
Introduction.. *1*

Chapter 1 – Taking a Look at Ourselves:
The Emotional Stages of Marriage Breakdown... **11**
    The Five Emotional Stages of Marriage Breakdown....................................13
    Marriage: A Note 17
    Marriage Counselling...18
    Transition People 19

Chapter 2 – Taking a Look at Lawyers: Take Charge of the Relationship........ **23**
    Family Law Lawyers 24
    Hiring a Lawyer 24
    The Ideal Lawyer..24
    Family Law and Legal Aid...26
    The Retainer (or What Everyone Else Calls a Contract) 27
    Confidentiality...29
    If You Are Dissatisfied with Your Lawyer 30
    Firing Your Lawyer..32
    What to Do When You Are Unhappy about Your Lawyer's Bill.................35

Chapter 3 – Taking a Look at the Process: Understanding Family Law
and the Legal System... **39**
    The Legal System...41
    Family Law and the Courts 43
    The Personnel of the Courts..43
    The Rules of Court..47

Chapter 4 – Divorce: Dissolving the Marriage Vows **57**
    Grounds for Divorce 58
    Reconciliation..62
    The Procedure for a Divorce 63
    Uncontested Divorces 64
    Joint Application for Divorce...65
    Contested Divorces..65
    Bars to Divorce..66
    Marriages of Convenience..67
    Legal Fees for Divorce..68

**Chapter 5 – Dividing the Family's Property: Get Your Fair Share
from the Marriage Partnership**.. **71**
    What is "Property?"...73
    What is Divided?...74
    What is Not Divided? Exempt Property............................74
    How is Value Determined?..75
    Date of Valuation 78
    Unequal Division of Property Values 78
    The Matrimonial Home 79
    Pensions...80
    Financial Statements...83
    Paying the Judgement...84
    Some Tax Considerations 84
    Some Strategic Considerations 86

Chapter 6 – The Children: Every Parent's Top Priority **91**
    Custody and Access...92
    Who Is a Child?..93
    The Child's Best Interests..94
    Other Considerations...95
    Assessments 99
    Custody 100
    Joint Custody and Child Support 102
    Advice on Joint Custody 104
    Conditions on Sole Custody...104
    Access 106
    Strategic Considerations 107
    Paternity...111
    Paternity Agreements...113
    What Will We Tell the Children? 114
    Stepfamilies..121
    A Warning...122

Chapter 7 – Support: Financial Assistance After Separation **125**
    Child Support..127
    When Is a Child Eligible for Support?...132
    Spousal Support...138
    Parental Support 147

Chapter 8 – Common-Law Spouses Have Rights, Too **151**
    The Meaning of "Common Law"..151
    Children in Common-Law Relationships...153
    Spousal Support...153
    Property Division for Common-Law Couples 155
    Federal Legislation...159
    Cohabitation Agreements..160
    Legal Advice 160

Chapter 9 – Settling Your Differences: Avoiding the Courtroom **163**
    Offers to Settle...165
    Minutes of Settlement 167
    Orders on Consent 168
    Separation Agreements 168

Chapter 10 – Not Settling Your Differences: Going to Court.......................... **177**
    The Courtroom 179
    The Paper Chase...181
    The Trial Itself..181
    Appeals 188

Chapter 11 – Alternatives to Court: Mediation, Arbitration and
Collaborative Family Law **191**
    Mediation..192
    Arbitration 198
    Mediation/Arbitration...199
    Religious Arbitration..199
    Collaborative Family Law...200
    Strategic Considerations for Alternatives to the Court..................................201

Chapter 12 – Enforcing Family Law Orders: Making an Order Stick............. **205**
    Custody Enforcement..206
    More on Abductions...209
    Canada Customs and Travelling Outside Canada 210
    Access Enforcement..212
    Support Enforcement 214
    The Support Enforcement Offices 216
    Property Enforcement...218
    Personal Restraining Orders 220
    Contempt 221

Chapter 13 – Grandparents and "Other Interested Persons" **225**
    Grandparents 226
    Strategic Considerations 231
    "Other Persons" 233

Chapter 14 – Domestic Violence: A Problem that Just Won't Go Away **235**
    Violence: The Myths 237
    Why Are Women Assaulted? 238
    Why Do Men Do It? 239
    What Can Be Done? 240
    Strategic Considerations and Domestic Violence 242

**Chapter 15 – Marriage Contracts and Cohabitation Agreements:
Managing Your Relationship—Contractually** **247**
    Marriage Contracts 248
    Cohabitation Agreements 251
    Setting Aside Domestic Contracts 252

Chapter 16 – Family Law and Your Will **257**
    Making a Will 257
    Divorce and Your Will 260

Chapter 17 – Self-Help Advice: Going It Alone? **265**
    How to Complain 265
    How to Do Your Own Research 266
    How to Represent Yourself: Eyes Wide Open 269

Appendix A – Some Important Paperwork **275**
    The Retainer Form 275
    A Separation Agreement 277
    The Family Law Client History Form 297

Appendix B – Canadian Child Support Guidelines **299**

Glossary *305*
Index *313*

ACKNOWLEDGEMENTS

I find it hard to believe that this book has now been on bookshelves in Canada for fifteen years. The number of changes to family law and the ways in which these changes are affecting Canadian families continue to grow with each passing year.

In this fourth edition, I would like to again acknowledge the very positive responses I have had from readers. They continue to share the details of their own difficult separations and divorces with me. Their stories, along with my own experiences in the family law system with my clients, continue to deepen my understanding of family law in Canada and its impact on families.

I would also like to thank and acknowledge again the Law Foundation of Ontario, which provided a grant 15 years ago to assist me in the preparation of the first edition of this book.

Thank you once again for all of your feedback. Read on.

AUTHOR'S NOTE

The goal of this book is to make you a more informed consumer of legal services in the family law area. It is designed as an overview and guide to Canadian family law.

Each family law case is different and the law varies from province to province, so the book's applicability to individual cases is limited. I cannot guarantee that the laws described will apply in your particular case. If you have a family law problem, please consult an experienced family law lawyer to determine how your circumstances may be affected by the law of your province.

My goal is not to help you avoid lawyers, but rather to help you deal with them confidently. Having said that, I am personally alarmed at the number of Canadians who have been forced to represent themselves in our justice system. Perhaps they are representing themselves because they have lost confidence in their own lawyer, they can no longer afford to pay for legal services and do not qualify for legal aid, or they simply feel that they are in the best position to speak for themselves or their family. Regardless of their reason, self-represented people are presenting a major challenge to the family law system in Canada.

More than ever, you may find this book of assistance if you have been forced into self-representation. I wish you good luck. As you will see from some of the new commentary in this fourth edition, the family law system in Canada is not only in serious trouble, but it has become increasingly hostile to self-represented individuals.

In this book I have used factual situations to illustrate some of the problems people encounter. While all of the circumstances described are real, names, places and some facts have been changed to protect people's privacy and the confidentiality clients enjoy with their lawyers.

I invite you to check out my website for regular updates on things of interest to people struggling with separation, divorce and other legal problems: www.michaelcochrane.ca

Michael G. Cochrane, B.A., LL.B.
Partner, Ricketts Harris LLP, Toronto, Ontario
www.rickettsharris.com

INTRODUCTION

REALITY CHECK: BECOME AN INFORMED CONSUMER

The increasing number of marriage breakdowns, common-law relationships, single-parent families, the recognition of domestic violence, the mobility of families and now the rights of same-sex couples have all contributed to a growing complexity in family relations. Newspapers, magazines and television, as well as the Internet, provide us with the most intimate details of family disputes—"Grandparent seeks access to grandchild," "Mother loses custody of children," "Father refuses to pay support," "Wealthy couple fights over family business," and let's not forget the many cases of violence.

A great deal of information is now available to families and individuals undergoing family crises. The Internet in particular has made many resources available to Canadians, but the information is often inaccurate and unreliable. Self-help books are plentiful. Yet many people still get what little information they can secondhand from the experiences of friends and acquaintances who have "gone through the mill." Other people go directly to a lawyer and pay for a potentially expensive lesson in basic family law.

This means that people experiencing family crises can be among the least informed of consumers. They head into the marketplace of legal services without the foggiest idea about the family law system. They are powerless and because of it they are taken advantage of by "the system." (More on that in a minute.)

On the basis of my experiences as a lawyer in private practice, as a lecturer at universities and law schools, as a policy advisor to the Attorney General and as someone who has talked directly to thousands of consumers about this issue, *I believe that ordinary people with family law questions want more than gossip and anecdotes, but often require less than a lawyer's advice before they start to make informed decisions about their personal lives and the lives of their children.*

This book is designed as a handbook for anyone who wants to know more about Canadian family law. Who will benefit from reading it?

- People who are separated and involved in legal proceedings
- People who are thinking about separating
- People who are living common law—or thinking about it
- People who are thinking about getting married
- People who want Marriage Contracts
- People who are involved in violent marriages
- People who have already been through the legal mill but are still wondering what happened
- Students studying law will find this book of assistance as well.

A quick glance at the table of contents will give you an idea of some of the areas that I try to demystify for you, areas like the following:

- The emotional stages of marriage breakdown
- Hiring and firing lawyers
- The family law court system
- The division of family property
- Custody and access
- Support
- The rights of common-law spouses
- Domestic violence
- Marriage contracts and more

When I described this project to a family law lawyer friend of mine 20 years ago, he said, "You're giving away all the secrets." He was right.

Take a quick look at Appendix A for some examples of the paperwork that you may face in a family law dispute, a glossary of legal terms to guide you through the legal mumbo-jumbo and other "insider" secrets previously known only to the lawyers.

The information is provided in a way that makes it useful in all provinces (except Quebec) and the territories. While the specific names of documents, courts and procedures can vary from province to province, the broad principles and guidelines are very similar. I have tried to organize these guidelines by subject area and in a way that makes the most sense.

SMARTER, SAFER AND SANER

My goals in writing the book are fairly straightforward: I want you to become an informed consumer of family law legal services and to be able to protect yourself. If you do,

- you will save thousands of dollars in legal fees,
- you will have a great deal more control over your life,
- you will make better decisions for you and your family and
- you will be smarter, safer and saner after the whole experience.

Will reading this book save you a thousand dollars in legal fees? If you read this book and apply some of the information before going to a lawyer about a family law matter, you will save at least $1,000. In some cases, you will save much more. The reason is simple: After reading this book, you will be a more informed consumer. You will know how to pick the right lawyer for your needs and how to tell the lawyer what you want for yourself and your children. You will have a good understanding of what our laws actually say about family problems and how "the system" works. You will even learn when *not* to see your lawyer—a significant saving in itself.

I am especially concerned about people who are self-representing in family law cases. Lawyers themselves often struggle to understand this crazy system of family law that has developed in Canada. I honestly do not know how self-represented people can cope with the pressures. I do understand that many self-represented people simply cannot afford to pay lawyers' fees. I urge these people in particular to take the time to develop a big-picture view of how the family law system works, or at least of how it is supposed to work. The system is in big trouble and it is not serving Canadians particularly well right now. No one is in the system by choice. When I have met individuals who are representing themselves, one comment that they have made about this book is that they had to read sections of it a couple of times in order to appreciate what was happening to them. You will certainly benefit from reading the book if you have a lawyer or intend to hire one, and you will benefit even more so if you are intending to go it alone.

The best way to illustrate the potential savings in being an informed consumer is through some examples. The following situations are all drawn from cases I knew about while in private practice or while participating in the reform of our family laws.

THE BATTERED CLIENT

An older woman arrived in a lawyer's office early one Monday morning still bearing the marks of a beating she had received more than a week earlier. She was accompanied by three lovely children who had finally persuaded her to leave their father, her abusive husband of 30 years. She had finally had enough and had left him the previous week. Where had she been for the past week? The first lawyer she had consulted was the real estate lawyer who had helped with the purchase of their home and occasional refinancing. He didn't "do" family law, but agreed to see her. After two interviews, the collection of some of her important documents, after telephone calls to the husband, who was holed up in the family home on an alcoholic binge, and after taking care of some other clients' important real estate deals, the lawyer gave his advice: He suggested she try to "work things out," especially since legal proceedings would be slow and expensive. A court order, he said, couldn't be obtained for over a month. With this priceless advice she received a bill for $1,000.

She nearly took the advice until her eldest daughter encouraged her to get a second opinion from an experienced family law lawyer. Twenty-four hours after she arrived in that lawyer's office, she had an interim order for exclusive possession of the home, a restraining order against the husband, interim custody of the youngest child and a temporary support order. *Getting the right lawyer from the start makes a big difference.*

THE CLIENT IN THE DARK

A 36-year-old man who had divorced two years earlier consulted a lawyer about enforcing an order that gave him access to his eight-year-old son on specific days of the week. He had started a new relationship recently and was accompanied by this woman when he went to pick up his son one Friday evening. His former spouse didn't approve of this new development and denied access. (This was wrong, but she did it anyway.) His lawyer said, "Leave it with me."

After a preliminary phone call, a court proceeding was started involving a sworn affidavit from the man reporting what had occurred. The proceeding asked that the wife be found in contempt of court and that she be jailed or fined for denying access. Court papers were served on the former wife and the case was scheduled to be in court three weeks later (the first available court date). When the day arrived, the case was adjourned to allow the former wife to file a sworn affidavit too. Then it was adjourned to allow both lawyers to ask the clients questions under oath in front of a court reporter. Then each party waited for the transcript of the cross-examination to be prepared. Then it was adjourned because the lawyers were detained in other courts on other cases.

Finally, nine weeks after the proceeding was started, the matter was actually going to be dealt with by a judge. The woman's lawyer suggested that it be settled by giving the child's father an extra weekend to make up for the time lost. It was also suggested that both clients pay their own lawyer's fees. The husband's lawyer recommended that the offer be accepted because contempt motions are rarely, if ever, successful anyway.

The client wanted to know why he hadn't been told that in the first place. Cost? $5,500 and he hadn't seen his child regularly during those nine weeks. *Knowing how the system works before you go into it makes a big difference.*

THE ANGRY CLIENT

When an older, childless couple separated, the wife was beside herself with anger. After years of devotion to her husband, he had become distant and then suddenly left her for another woman. She hired the "toughest" family law lawyer. The husband hired the other toughest lawyer in town. Property division and support were the only issues and even those were not very complicated. Her instructions? She wanted what she was entitled to by law and she wanted to teach him a lesson. The lawyer took her instructions seriously and a battle began that allowed the lawyers to show each other just how good they were in court.

Two years and over a dozen court appearances later, she got exactly (well, almost) what she wanted, a judgment for half of the family's property and spousal support, as well as a lawyer's bill. However, the court did not order the husband to pay all or even part of her legal fees, which were $100,000. The court didn't make such an order because the husband had offered to settle the case for the same amount that the judgment specified. She actually netted less than she was entitled to simply because of the cost of legal fees. *Don't let anger be the only motivator in your divorce proceedings—it can cost you in the end.*

THE BLINDSIDED CLIENT

A young couple went to their respective lawyers to get a Separation Agreement. They were on relatively friendly terms and knew what they wanted, except for a couple of small concerns about their two children. Both suddenly found themselves being told not to discuss the matter with each other—to avoid "confusion" during the settlement discussions.

His lawyer suggested that legal proceedings be commenced, as a precaution, and held in the file. If negotiations didn't go well, they could serve the proceedings and gain "strategic advantage." Discussions continued but suddenly the proceedings were served on her at work in front of her friends. The papers said that her husband wanted custody, so she instructed her lawyer to file for custody, too. They were in court before they knew what hit them. The matter was adjourned to allow everybody to cool off. Cost? $3,500—each.

She heard from a friend that mediation (where an objective third person facilitates settlement discussions between the couple directly) should be tried. With a little help, they found a mediator, the original problem was solved and an agreement was reached for joint custody of the children.

The mediator's fees were $1,500. The clients wanted to know why the lawyers had not told them about mediation. His lawyer's answer? You didn't ask about it. Her lawyer's answer? She didn't believe in mediation.

The $7,000 in lawyer's fees was a waste, particularly in a year when finances were tight due to the separation and the new expense of maintaining two households. *Knowing all of your options can make a big difference.*

I could fill a book with similar examples of uninformed clients watching money slip away in the lawyer's office or in the legal system. This would be less likely to occur if people had a good idea of what awaited them and played a more active role in deciding what was going to happen to them, their children or their hard-earned property.

Clients in these cases could have saved a lot more than the thousand dollars I mentioned earlier if they had gone to a family law specialist, if they had asked for written retainers and opinions before proceeding, if they had understood that instructions given in anger are invitations for disaster, if they had understood that the "toughest" lawyer may not be the best, and if they understood that there is more to family law settlements than fighting it out in the courtroom.

Read the book. Save a thousand dollars—maybe more. But, more importantly, gain some control over what will be a difficult time for you emotionally and financially.

WHAT'S WRONG WITH FAMILY LAW?

In trying to explain what I think is wrong, I divide our system of family law into three general parts:

1. the angry, hurt, "unwell" and uninformed people who come to the system with their problems,
2. the process of family law—the rules and methods of problem solving and
3. the lawyers who should act as guides through the system.

The Angry, Hurt, "Unwell" and Uninformed People

Let's consider for a moment the people who must use the family law process—people undergoing separation and divorce. This group is largely uninformed or worse, misinformed, about what is about to happen and the decisions that will be expected of them. To make matters worse, at the time they are expected to make these decisions, they are angry, broken-hearted, depressed, mentally unwell at times, victims of violence, or despairing and frequently unaware of their future needs. We are seeing more and more people in the family law system who have problems with alcohol, drugs, mental health and other disorders.

The Process

We then take these poor souls and make them resolve their problems in a process that is adversarial, slow, often illogical, expensive, inflexible and filled with people who are often very cynical and may not have any interest in family law cases. I have seen an increasing attitude from people in the system amounting to "if you're here, you get what you deserve." At the same time, there is little or no emotional support in the system for the people who are looking for help.

You will notice a theme in this fourth edition and I will be repeating it from time to time—the Canadian family law system is in crisis. As I did my research for this edition, an experienced family law lawyer related to me an incident that he had seen in court where a terribly insensitive judge brought a self-represented individual to tears. The individual was simply pursuing his rights in the system and did not deserve the harsh treatment. Was the judge's attitude caused in part by his frustrations with the system? Perhaps.

You would be hard-pressed to find someone in Canada who is familiar with our family law justice system who would be prepared to stand up and defend it as doing anything approaching an adequate job for Canadian families. It is not good for women, it is not good for men and it is certainly not good for children. Those who administer justice—whether they be judges, court staff or lawyers—are equally dissatisfied with the system. In my view, it is a billion-dollar drag on the Canadian economy and families' resources are devastated unnecessarily because of the way in which our family law system is currently operating.

Here is the really bad news: no one is doing anything about it and it will in all likelihood get worse. What does this mean for you? It means that you have even more reason to understand what you are in for as you go forward with a separation and divorce. Read on.

The Lawyers

Who is best placed to help people through this maze? Lawyers, of course. But even this important decision—the selection of a personal guide to take people through the system—is often left to chance. I am always shocked to find that some people have actually selected their lawyers simply by looking in the Yellow Pages. I think if you do anything as a result of reading this book, it should be to select a competent lawyer who is sensitive to your needs. That decision alone can be half the battle. My goal is to make you an informed consumer of legal services who is able to exercise control over yourself as a user of the system, control over the lawyers and, finally, control over the process itself. Smarter, safer, saner.

It is not a goal of this book to convince you to go it alone, without a lawyer. (Although I know many of you have to go it alone and have no choice.) There is too much at stake to tinker with your own case. Support, property division and, most importantly, the best interests of your children are all at risk. You should realize that by informing yourself, you are doing your part, but there is still a part for your lawyer to play. By becoming an informed consumer, you are helping your lawyer do a better job for you. *Remember, lawyers should not just listen to your opinion, they should respect it.* Your knowledge and confidence will undoubtedly speed up the process, save time and expenses, as well as narrow the issues in dispute and facilitate a solution.

If there are any lessons to be learned from this introduction, they are as follows:

- Don't be an accident waiting to happen—inform yourself about your rights.
- Accept and deal with the system as it is—inform yourself about your options.
- Get an experienced, affordable family law lawyer who respects and appreciates you as an informed consumer.

1

TAKING A LOOK AT OURSELVES

~

The Emotional Stages of Marriage Breakdown

L awyers love to go to court. That's where all the real drama is played out—witnesses cross-examined, exhibits shown, legal arguments made and, almost anti-climactically, a judgment or some order is arrived at by the court. But as dramatic as that setting may be, lawyers also love to settle cases outside of court. They can often be found around courthouses leaning on walls, talking with pride about "the one they just settled," as if they had just mounted some trophy.

I had a chance to eavesdrop before a meeting one day as a couple of family law lawyers—one senior, one very junior—traded banter about their recent settlements. The junior lawyer was bemoaning the fact that his client had just accepted a settlement that was, in his opinion, satisfactory. That's right—satisfactory—and the lawyer was unhappy.

"I can't figure it," he said. "I could have got her that settlement six months ago. Suddenly one morning my client waltzes into my office, instructs me to accept the offer of settlement that had been made months earlier. I couldn't believe my ears. After six months of vicious motions and really testy discoveries, six months of bloodletting, she wants to settle. She was like a different person . . . the same settlement was available six months ago . . ." The lawyer's voice trailed off in disbelief. He was totally baffled by the about-face of his client.

The senior lawyer nodded knowingly but added an observation. "Maybe she was a different person."

"No, it was her alright," the junior lawyer added with a laugh.

"I'm serious, maybe she was a different person; maybe she had changed." The senior lawyer bore down a little on her pupil. "Maybe she had moved into that stage of acceptance where she felt comfortable restructuring her life."

"Stage? What stage?" The junior lawyer looked uncomfortable.

I thought to myself, *Uh oh—this lawyer is trying to help people involved in family problems and does not understand the first thing about the emotional stages that most people move through during marriage breakdown.*

Not only must lawyers themselves understand these stages, but they also have an obligation to explain them to their clients at the very outset. I believe lawyers have an obligation to provide their clients with some perspective on where the clients are, emotionally, and where they may be headed emotionally, not just legally.

This poor young lawyer was destined to a never-ending string of family law clients who would constantly surprise him with seemingly unpredictable mood changes and apparently conflicting opinions and instructions. The lawyer's only explanation? "Wow, clients in family disputes sure are crazy!" His clients probably went away feeling that he was right, not knowing how or why their feelings could change so dramatically over a relatively short period of time.

Well, they are not crazy at all. They are simply being asked to make some of the most important decisions of their lives under the most painful and stressful of circumstances. It is difficult to be reasonable and sensible under such pressure. However, with a little help and perspective on the emotional changes, these difficult times can run considerably smoother.

Understanding people undergoing family breakdown is possible if one understands some of the general stages through which they may pass. I say that they *may* pass through them because there are no guarantees that they will do so. I still have vivid memories of clients who never quite got on with their lives. Some stayed stalled for five, even ten, years after the separation, not really wanting or needing to reconcile with their spouse, sometimes seething with a vague anger, but at the same time not knowing what to do next.

Others, of course, move quickly and smoothly through all the emotional stages and emerge after just a few months, ready for career changes, new loves and new families. I can't help but wonder whether having an "emotional perspective" on the family breakdown contributed in some way to them having a better sense of direction and control.

THE FIVE EMOTIONAL STAGES OF MARRIAGE BREAKDOWN

In 1969, Elisabeth Kübler-Ross, then Medical Director of the Family Service and Mental Health Center of South Cook County in Illinois, published a book entitled *On Death and Dying*. *Life* magazine described it as a "profound lesson for the living." Her observations on death and dying were formed on the basis of her experiences with terminally ill patients. She identified a number of distinct phases through which the terminally ill will pass.

Many experienced family law practitioners and mental health professionals have been struck by the parallels between the experiences of those who are dying and those undergoing a marriage or family breakdown. While these stages will not apply to every case, they provide a useful framework to understand where a person may be, emotionally. This understanding is invaluable because it may provide clues to a person's motivation when instructing his or her lawyer.

Kubler-Ross identified the following stages:

1. Denial and Isolation
2. Anger
3. Bargaining
4. Depression
5. Acceptance

What follows is a modest attempt to adapt her analysis of terminally ill patients to those undergoing the breakdown of a relationship or family. Based on my 26 years of doing this work, it is a very reliable way of looking at our emotional selves.

Denial and Isolation ("It's not happening to me . . . something else is wrong.")

Kubler-Ross identified a tendency to deny the fact of the illness when learning that one is terminally ill. This, she speculated, was meant to "act as a buffer after the unexpected shocking news," allowing the patient to collect himself or herself and to mobilize defences.

Our expectations of our marriages are not unlike our expectations about life—we expect to be immortal in both. These expectations are somewhat understandable given the rather spectacular pledges made at weddings. This is not to suggest that we should be more cynical about wedding vows, but rather that we should recognize the extremely high expectations with which couples begin their marriages and live-in relationships. It is these huge expectations that come crashing down at separation. This appears to be true, regardless of the number of marriages the individual enters into. I have frequently encountered people who have married three and four times, each time with renewed confidence that this one is "the right one."

It is not surprising, therefore, that the first reaction to marital strain, marriage breakdown or many other problems in a family is denial. Something (his job's too much lately) or someone else (her family) must be to blame. A typical response is "If I ignore this problem, it will blow over." This denial, more likely than not, occurs or begins to occur well in advance of the actual separation. Some spouses report knowing something was wrong months or even years in advance of separation. They admit denying there was a problem—"Please let it be something else," "He'll change," "She promised it would never happen again," "She's just depressed." Sometimes it works and the problem appears to blow over. Of course, sometimes it is "something else." But many times it is just plain old denial of a fundamental challenge to the relationship or family.

If the marriage has indeed ended for one partner but not the other (as is usually the case), denial can be a powerful obstacle to a lawyer attempting to assist in the orderly severing of the knot. "Denying" clients may move from lawyer to lawyer in search of someone who will share their view, someone who will keep them in the marriage, someone who will keep the family together. It is not unlike the terminally ill patient who seeks a second, a third, even a fourth medical opinion. They search for someone who will keep their original expectation of immortality alive. I myself have met clients who have listened patiently as we worked through their issues, thanked me, paid their bill . . . and gone right back to the troubled marriage or relationship and were only able to separate many years later.

So we should understand that for those experiencing marital difficulties or other family problems, a likely first response is to deny, deny, deny. This can be both tragic and painful for the people involved. Imagine the difficulty in resolving any issue between spouses in such a predicament. One person is not ready to discuss a settlement because they don't even know or agree that there is a major problem. I remember one client who asked me to delay a divorce so that his wife would have time to "snap out of it." She was remarried by the time he clued in.

Anger ("It is happening to me . . . and I hate it.")

The denial stage is often followed by a partial acceptance of what has occurred. The issue or problem between them can no longer be avoided, perhaps because the other partner has taken unmistakable steps to confront the issue, like moving out or starting divorce proceedings. The "patient" finally accepts the diagnosis, perhaps after multiple consultations with other "doctors." However, while the diagnosis is finally accepted, denial may be replaced with anger because the client doesn't like what he or she hears and feels. The anger may be directed against the other spouse, family members, oneself (the harshest perhaps) or the lawyers who may now be involved. Sometimes, these angry clients talk of being made to look "foolish," of being "blind" or "stupid." Suddenly the other spouse has been taking advantage of him or her, apparently laughing all the while. The anger becomes white-hot.

Once the awful truth is accepted, a spouse may be left with little else but his or her anger at a frustrating, possibly humiliating, predicament (with a lot of "I told you so's" not really helping the situation). It is at this stage that people consult their lawyers. The other spouse may have forced the issue into the open by consulting a lawyer and having letters sent (see Chapter 4—Divorce), and the truth is finally accepted by the denying spouse.

It is also at this stage that lawyers frequently receive their instructions to start legal proceedings, to go to court, to be tough and, in short, to vent the angry client's venom. These proceedings the lawyer and client can ill afford because they are not designed to advance the client's interests, nor will they make the client happy. If anything, such proceedings may produce only regrets. The client who offers instructions to a lawyer while in such a state of mind will never be happy and will later blame his or her lawyer for wasting time and money. With the client in this angry stage, we may be left with a person who no longer denies there is a problem but now confronts the issue with what is never a scarce resource—unproductive anger.

Beware—this stage has been known to last a long time. In my experience, this stage can also make people sick. Family law lawyers see clients with all manner of physical complaints caused by the stress of their anger.

Bargaining ("If I do this, maybe you will do that.")

Kubler-Ross describes this next phase as an attempt to postpone the inevitable. The anger has not produced anything and subsides partially. But now promises, often unrealistic ones, are made in the hope of buying more time. The patient has accepted what is happening but now negotiates to postpone it. The same can be true of people in family breakdown.

The bargaining may manifest itself in overly generous settlement proposals—"She can have everything," or "I'm the one who left; he can keep the house." Sometimes the offer is no more than a weak attempt to ease guilt or to prove to the other spouse that "I'm not so bad after all." For some reason, men do this more often than women. Unfortunately, but not surprisingly, such promises are rarely wise or kept. The client's interests have not been advanced; in fact, they may have been harmed.

At this stage, we have a client whose anger may be subsiding but whose instructions are nonetheless tainted by unreal feelings. Lawyers and clients alike must be alert to these motivations and recognize that instructions during this phase of false bargaining are unlikely to produce lasting settlements. They will, however, produce a legal bill . . . and you will wonder later what you are paying for. A "settlement" achieved during this phase can be a waste of money. I have met many clients who were filled with resentment for having entered into an unwise settlement for all the wrong reasons.

Depression ("I'm losing my past and I have no future.")

This next phase is identified by Kubler-Ross as one in which the terminally ill patient's sense of anger subsides, the false bargaining has ended unsuccessfully (as it had to) and a sense of great loss sets in. She identifies this depression as being two-edged—a reactive depression and a preparatory depression. Reactive depression is a reaction to the past loss. What the patient once had is now gone or is slipping away. Preparatory depression anticipates impending losses.

For the couple undergoing marriage breakdown, this "double depression" is understandable. Their reactive depression may be in response to the loss of things such as "their best friend," "their life partner," a sense of family, time with their children, the family home, the cottage, valued possessions and so on. At the same time, they must face the losses yet to come—the companionship of the spouse, the old network of friends and the plans that were made but will never materialize. Discovering that there will be no more anniversaries can hurt. In many cases both spouses must lower their expectations financially. A standard of living once taken for granted is gone.

Few clients in this state of mind are equipped to provide balanced instructions to their lawyer. Not only does the past generate feelings of sadness, but prospects for the future seem bleak as well. Sadness and loss of hope suddenly overwhelm everything. Negotiating on behalf of these clients is pointless for a lawyer. These clients do not care what happens.

Acceptance ("I've got things I want to do.")

From the foregoing, it may appear that people are virtually never able to provide instructions to their lawyers. If they are not denying the problem, angry or depressed, they are engaged in false bargaining. However, there *is* a time when clients are best equipped to make decisions, although lawyers may not always have the luxury of awaiting that moment (if it actually arrives). This stage is described by Kubler-Ross as a time when the patient is "neither depressed or angry about his fate." It is a time of contemplation and almost void of feelings. The dying patient at this time has found some peace and acceptance.

In the case of marriage breakdown, the spouse at this stage will have accepted the end of the marriage and will not see the dispute or court process as offering a meaningful or desirable link with the other spouse. It is as if everything has suddenly become clear. Settlement proposals suddenly seem worthy of consideration. If the marriage is truly over, then the final loose ends should be tied up. The chapter of life that was the marriage must be closed. Suddenly, planning seems worthwhile, new events have meaning and the past is just that—past. What is also important at this stage is the client's willingness to reconstruct or start again. What is ahead is what is important. As corny as it sounds—what is past truly is prologue.

It is at this stage of acceptance that clients are best equipped emotionally to settle. (Please understand that by "settle" I do not mean "give up.") For the first time, perhaps in months or years, emotions are not obstructing their powers of reason. They are able to describe what is best for their children, what they need and what they want.

This is the stage at which, in my anecdote, the junior lawyer's client "suddenly" arrived. She had denied, she had been angry, she had been depressed. She had even tried a little false bargaining, too. But she ultimately accepted what had occurred and was ready to move on.

No one should be embarrassed about this experience because it is a natural evolution of feelings. I would be worried if it didn't occur. Of course, you should be angry and depressed—you are going through something that is awful. The best you can do sometimes is to just understand it, roll with it and recognize that it will all pass and you will move on.

MARRIAGE—A NOTE

I could easily devote an entire book to the subject of marriage in Canada. Most Canadians heading into marriage spend more time thinking about where they will hold the ceremony, who will take the pictures, what kind of flowers will be at the wedding and what will be served for dinner than they do actually thinking about the marriage. In other words, they spend more time thinking about the *wedding* than they do about the realities of marriage. In my view, we should not give people marriage licences unless they have taken some kind of course to prepare them for marriage. These courses would teach them about the meaning of having a mature love and about the realities of challenges presented to marriages, and it would equip them to have dispute-resolution skills so that when a reality leaps up and bites them, they would have the skills to tackle the problem and develop a solution. Many Canadian marriages break an axle the first time they hit a pothole because they are not equipped to deal with a crisis.

As we see marriages at the point of separation and divorce, we hear people saying such things as "marriage is an economic partnership." Yet we see people spend very little time doing due diligence on their future business partner in advance of the marriage. Canadian marriages would be much more successful if more due diligence was performed. What is your future partner's track record with money? If he or she has gone bankrupt two or three times, brace yourself. If he or she has criminal convictions for domestic violence, fraud or other serious crime, brace yourself. If your future partner has a history of health problems, mental or physical, then you had better brace yourself. All of these realities should be known in advance. If you still choose to marry someone who has a terrible financial record, a history of criminal convictions and propensity to mental health issues, then you are at least going in with your eyes wide open. (Stay tuned for my next book on how to get married properly.)

MARRIAGE COUNSELLING

It can be tough going through all of these stages. Many of the male clients that I have met over the years deal with the breakdown of their relationship in stereotypical isolation. Their colleagues at work are often stunned when the separation is announced. Meanwhile, women have shared their problems with friends, family, co-workers, the grocer . . . Two extremes—he tells no one; she tells everyone.

Men have said to me, "My God, I can't believe it. The whole neighbourhood knows!" And their wives shake their heads, "He refuses to talk to anyone. Even his family doesn't know!"

I suggest a little understanding of these ways of coping. Women typically have a wider circle of friends than men. Men don't share much with the few friends they have. For male readers, find someone to share your situation with. I don't mean somebody who will just say, "Yeah, I know what you mean . . ." For the women, be sensitive to the limits that may be need to be respected when sharing details of the relationship.

Why not get some help? Have you tried marriage counselling? If one more person tells me that they want to try marriage counselling but their spouse won't go . . . I am speaking to the reluctant spouse directly: What exactly do you think will happen if you go? No one has died from marriage counselling. No one is stigmatized or shunned. It is confidential. Marriage counselling is always a help unless, of course, you can't speak the truth or hear the truth.

If you are afraid of the unknown, let me try to help. Imagine having a wise friend that both you and your partner like and trust. Neither of you is any closer to this friend than the other. You join your friend in a comfortable room and discuss the situation that you face or that you think you face. You take turns explaining it. The friend asks questions. Probes. Makes you think. Challenges you. Makes you think some more. Helps you identify some mistakes. Some strengths. Helps you say you're sorry. The friend keeps all of this in confidence and sends you off to work on some things. You can check in as often as you need.

I have never heard of a marriage counsellor making a couple stay together. Or break up. I have heard of marriage counsellors saving marriages that were headed for a split. I have also heard of counsellors who have helped a couple come to a realization that it is over but then helped them to deal with that reality.

Go to marriage counselling. Go now. Keep going. Don't let a relationship die because you wouldn't work at it. Go down swinging. You won't regret it—no matter how it turns out.

If you are worried about the expense, don't be. It is much less expensive than a lawyer is. Rates range from $50 to $300 per hour.

TRANSITION PEOPLE

What is a transition person? Sometimes when a marriage is in trouble or over, you will meet someone. This person may be a great listener, fun and attractive. They are able to make you forget about all the problems in the marriage or the separation. Maybe they have already been through it themselves and can really empathize. The relationship may become one where the people in it are more than "just friends."

Do these people cause the marriage to break down? Not really, though they can make a marriage breakdown happen faster. The marriage may already be in trouble, but the transition person helps you to make the move out of the marriage—at least emotionally or psychologically.

But suddenly you are out of the relationship and this supportive person may start to look different. They have served their purpose. However, the transition person may have expectations about where the both of you will go now together, in a new relationship, but you may have a different plan that doesn't necessarily include them.

I mention this for three reasons:

1. If you have a transition person in your life, be careful about feeling obligated to him or her. He or she may have been a great friend during a tough time, but that doesn't mean you have to be together for the rest of your lives.

2. If your spouse has "used a transition relationship" to exit the marriage, be aware of the role it played for him or her. In other words, don't blame the transition person for something that may have been happening anyway. Your issue is with your spouse.

3. If you are a transition person, go into these situations with your eyes open. It can be tough for you, too, if things don't evolve the way you expected.

CHECKLIST

We have seen the five stages (denial and isolation, anger, bargaining, depression and acceptance) but knowing of them is of little use unless they are applied to your own circumstances.

1. How do you feel about the predicament in which you find yourself?
2. Are you in any of these stages? In more than one?
3. What has been your motivation in hiring a lawyer?
4. Have you provided instructions to your lawyer out of anger? Out of guilt? Out of fear?
5. Have you been trying to bargain for time?
    a) Why? What do you expect to gain?
6. What do you really want?
7. Can you realistically have that? If not, why?
8. Would you be happy getting what you wanted?

9. Are you unhappy with what occurred?

10. Are you anxious about the future?

11. Are you filled with second thoughts?

12. Are you secretly relieved that it may be over?

13. Are you ready to start living again?

14. Are you making plans?

15. Have you tried marriage counselling? If not, why?

16. Is there another person on the scene?

    a) If so, is it a transition relationship?

You are not the first person to have asked themself many or all of these questions. You are one of the very few who have looked at themselves emotionally in the context of their legal problems. You are on the way to becoming an informed consumer of legal services and a very powerful client. You are taking care of yourself and your family. You are getting smarter, safer and saner.

2

TAKING A LOOK
AT LAWYERS

~

Take Charge of the Relationship

On the subject of lawyers, it is difficult to know where to begin. No trade or profession has been so vilified in recent times as this group. Lawyers have been called everything in the book and then some. Do we deserve it? A little bit. But it does not change the fact that at some point in time you are going to need one of us. This chapter will provide a few insights into the legal profession, with a view to helping you make intelligent decisions about which lawyer to use and how to deal with him or her.

The criticism of lawyers ignores two important things. First and foremost there are many excellent family law lawyers. I know dozens of lawyers who genuinely care about their clients, their clients' families and their futures. Second, you must understand that clients can be largely responsible for much of their own misfortune in dealing with lawyers. I am not blaming these clients. They are hurt and angry and want to do something about it. However, generally people are very poorly informed and very undemanding consumers of legal services. They set themselves up for problems. So, rather than debate whether all lawyers are vipers or not, let's focus on how to find a good family law lawyer and what to demand as an informed consumer once in his or her office.

FAMILY LAW LAWYERS

The selection of your lawyer could be the single most important decision you make about your own case, so take some time to make it properly. It is not uncommon to hear non-family law lawyers remarking to family law lawyers, "How can you do that stuff?" or "If I wanted to be a social worker or psychiatrist, I wouldn't have gone to law school" or "Family law? It's not challenging enough—every case is decided on the facts, not the law," and so on. While lawyers recognize that a family law case is a legal matter and can be quite lucrative, they do not flock to this area of practice. Lawyer "burnout" is common because family law is emotionally charged. Files are injected with added intensity, stress, emotion and, too frequently, violence.

HIRING A LAWYER

Ontario has established a method of accrediting lawyers as specialists in fields such as family law, criminal law and so on. This represents a quantum leap for consumers who before had to rely on word-of-mouth, the Yellow Pages and "hit and miss." The lawyer who handled granddad's will, Aunt Mary's car accident and Mom and Dad's real estate deal often inherited the family's first divorce. When the economy is in bad shape, lawyers from real estate law or commercial work with little or no experience in family law often move into family law cases. Contact your provincial law society and ask if they have an accreditation system for family law lawyers and a list of those in your community.

In addition, some provincial law societies have established Lawyer Referral Services. These free services list lawyers in the province by city and preferred area of practice. It lets you pinpoint family law lawyers in your community. These referral services can also give you information about the availability of legal aid, which we will discuss in more detail shortly. In Ontario, a lawyer who receives a client through this service will give the first half hour for free—not a bad deal if you are shopping around.

With systems such as accreditation and lawyer referral services, clients have a fighting chance to at the very least find an experienced family law lawyer. Assuming that you have found your way to a lawyer, let's consider in more detail what makes a lawyer "good."

THE IDEAL LAWYER

In my opinion, the ideal family law lawyer is experienced, honest, a good listener, has a sense of humour and is respected by his or her peers. This person does not lose sight of people, especially children, in the heat of practice. He or she is punctual, considerate and professional.

The ideal lawyer lets you participate in a discussion about your situation and is not afraid to tell you, at the outset, things you may not want to hear. After spending 30 minutes with this lawyer you can answer three questions:

1. Do I feel comfortable with this person?
2. Do I respect his or her opinion?
3. Does he or she respect mine?

Do not be influenced by designations such as Q.C. (Queen's Counsel). Ignore lawyers who bluster about past "wins" or "big cases" and have a hired-gun attitude. If somebody comes across as a stuffed shirt, they probably are.

You do not need the most expensive lawyer in town. He or she is not necessarily the best. You do not need the biggest law firm in the city, either. Do not pass over lawyers who may appear too young or too old. Both may have special skills. It is experience, not age, that counts.

Some clients have preferences for a lawyer of a particular sex. More women than men seem to practice family law, but all that matters is that men or women can serve you equally well. I have met male clients who feel they need a female lawyer because

• they can control her,

• they want their ex-spouse to see how "enlightened" they really are or

• the judge will like them more if they have a woman lawyer. (Oh, brother! Now we know why the marriage had trouble.)

On the other side of the coin, we have the female client who thinks that she must have the toughest male lawyer to intimidate her husband and earn his respect. So the male lawyer becomes a personal gladiator. These kinds of clients end up having fascinating conversations like, "My lawyer says your lawyer . . ." or "My lawyer has never heard of your lawyer and . . ." They are ignoring the fact that they should be picking their own lawyer, not letting their spouse pick for them.

Family law has also become a bit of a battleground for the "rights" movements—fathers' rights, mothers' rights, grandparents' rights, women's rights and men's rights. There are lawyers out there who are fighting causes while they practise law, lawyers who describe themselves as a "father's rights lawyer" or lawyers who practise with a "feminist perspective." This is not to say that these lawyers do not fulfill a role or make some important contributions to the law through, for example, test cases. If you want to be a test case and are prepared to pay for it, then that is your choice. But I believe that these people have an admitted bias and should be avoided. Their cause becomes your cause—at your expense. You have enough to worry about without getting tangled up in someone else's agenda.

In a similar vein, you do not want a lawyer who says things like "I never send anybody to mediation . . ." or "I don't approve of joint custody . . ." or "I never agree to . . ." Their straightjacket probably doesn't fit you. You want more choice, not less.

You do want a lawyer who is going to actually *be* the lawyer. You do not want someone who meets you at the initial interview, sniffs the file and then passes it to a junior lawyer without consulting you, and the junior lawyer then proceeds to do all the work, including meeting with you, going to court and negotiating the issues. Know who you are actually hiring. It is one thing to have lawyers work as a team. It is another thing to have the work done by lawyers that you did not actually hire.

Get the names of several experienced family law lawyers and take the time to meet at least three of them. For the first interview, make a list of questions about the important issues. (See suggestions at the end of the chapter.) In preparation for the interview, you may want to prepare your own written history of the relationship. Collect as many important documents as you can (marriage certificate, financial records, mortgage papers, previous orders or agreements, and so on). See the Family Law Client History form in Appendix A.

During the interview, be as complete and as frank as possible. The lawyer needs to know everything to be able to provide an objective analysis. Resist the temptation to colour the facts in your favour.

You should also be aware of any potential conflict of interest when hiring a lawyer. Do not use a lawyer who has previously done work for your spouse or your spouse's family. The lawyer may have information from these sources that will put him or her in a difficult position. Similarly, the lawyer should never act for both of you. It is impossible to provide objective advice to two people at the same time when they have opposing interests. If the lawyer is aware of a potential conflict, he or she should alert you to it and decline to act for either of you.

FAMILY LAW AND LEGAL AID

Every province has a form of legal aid for people who cannot afford legal services. This usually involves applying for the aid, passing a "means test" (they judge your neediness) and receiving a "Certificate of Legal Aid." The lawyer to whom you present this certificate then renders his or her accounts to the provincial legal aid plan. The amount that can be charged for particular steps is restricted by a tariff, so lawyers receive less for their work on an hourly basis than if you hired them directly. On the other hand, payment of the account is guaranteed. If you own property, in many cases legal aid will take a lein on your home. You then either pay legal aid when that home is sold or you have a repayment scheme.

THE RETAINER (OR WHAT EVERYONE ELSE CALLS A CONTRACT)

The word "retainer" can mean a number of different things. It can mean the amount of money you give a lawyer up front. He or she may request the money to cover disbursements that will be incurred, such as couriers, court filing charges or similar relatively small expenses. The amount of such a "retainer" can range from a few hundred dollars up to 10 thousand dollars or more. "Retainer" can also mean the actual contract the client signs to hire the lawyer to do the work. It is this type of retainer we will examine.

It never ceases to amaze me that a person will go into a lawyer's office, discuss the most intimate details of his or her life (details they have often never shared with anyone else) and then turn their whole life over to this virtual stranger without so much as discussing how much the lawyer charges per hour, the estimated time for completion of the work, the expected disbursements, billing policy or quality of work.

This same individual leaves the lawyer's office, goes home and decides to get the house painted by a couple of university students. What do they do? First they ask all their neighbours about painters they have used and whether they would recommend them. Once they have found their painters, they spend an hour walking around the house, telling them exactly what they want and how they want it done. They demand written contracts, guarantees, a fixed date for completion and references. They want to control the kind of paint that is used and whether these budding painters have liability insurance. Once they have the estimate in hand and the students have jumped through every conceivable hoop, the client wants to "think it over."

The hapless students may make a couple hundred dollars if they get the job, while the lawyer on the other side of town is casually opening a file with what amounts to a blank cheque, having given few, if any, commitments.

How can this contradiction be remedied?

The answer is not to stop asking the painters for a written contract! Start asking your lawyer for one. The lawyer is not going to throw up his or her arms, stamp around the office or sulk as if you have offended them. Lawyers know what retainers are; they use them all the time. Do you think that business people who hire lawyers don't pin them down on the cost? Of course they do, and they insist on answers to a lot of questions. Why should decisions about your life be any different or any less important?

This need not be a painful experience—you are simply asking some-one, supposedly a highly skilled professional, to give you a copy of his or her retainer form. Remember, it does not matter what lawyers call it, it is still a contract. It will describe the parties to the contract (you and the lawyer), the work that is to be done, the fee that will be charged for the work (hourly rate) and other important terms. A basic retainer, which I developed from my time in private practice, is included in Appendix A. You have my permission to photocopy the form (but please not other parts of the book) and present it to the lawyer (if they do not have their own retainer form).

If they balk at the use of a retainer, you don't want them to handle your case. There is absolutely nothing in the retainer provided that is unusual or offensive to an experienced lawyer. Do not hire a lawyer with-out a written retainer.

Ask that a provision be incorporated into the retainer that places a ceiling on the fee that can be charged without further consultation and a further written retainer. Matrimonial proceedings that begin quickly (perhaps in anger) have a way of consuming bundles of money in a very short time. A clause that states simply, "Fees not to exceed $2,000 with-out prior further written authorization" can be a valuable inhibition for those lawyers tempted to litigate first and negotiate later. Ask for a sample retainer to look at.

When describing the service to be rendered, a simple "Obtain divorce" is the equivalent of a blank cheque. (Would you ask the painter to sim-ply "paint house"?) Insist on a specific description of the work and sign a retainer authorizing perhaps only the first few steps (see Chapter 4—Divorce). This again inhibits premature litigation and gives you control of the progress of work. If you are not satisfied with the work that has been done, don't authorize any more until you are.

As I mentioned earlier, lawyers must spend money from time to time. It costs almost $200 to issue a divorce petition. It can cost as much as $300 to have a copy officially delivered to the other spouse (called "service of the petition"). There are dozens of small out-of-pocket items. When lawyers disburse or spend money on these items, they would prefer to do it with the client's money. Consequently, most lawyers ask for an amount up front as a deposit (sometimes also called a retainer). The amount varies depending on the type of case and the degree of complexity, but out-of-pocket expenses rarely exceed $500. In other words, be prepared to provide the lawyer with some money to be applied towards disbursements.

You will note that a paragraph in the retainer refers to client inquiries about fees and disbursements. At no time and under no circumstances should you ever feel inhibited about inquiring about the state of your account, the lawyer's disbursements or fee policy or any other matter related to your file. Being in doubt or unclear in any way is an invitation for disagreement at a later date. If you are not sure, ask! If it's still not clear, ask again! Don't pay for something you do not understand.

I offer you one final caution concerning your relationship with the lawyer during the course of his or her work for you. Lawyers employ junior lawyers, articling students, support staff and secretaries to assist with the work. Without their assistance, little could be done. Do not think that your lawyer is shirking his or her responsibilities by delegating to support staff. On the other hand, you have hired a particular lawyer and you are entitled to meet with that lawyer on a regular basis to discuss your case.

I suggest that you discuss this matter during the initial interview. If you want personal attention, then tell the lawyer at the first interview, not after the trial or settlement.

CONFIDENTIALITY

One of the most important features of the lawyer's relationship with the client is the promise of confidentiality. It is the basis of the client's trust and confidence in a lawyer.

To solve a client's problem, the lawyer must know everything about the client. In order to feel comfortable telling everything, the client must trust the lawyer to keep every word in confidence. Not only is indiscreet chatter about the personal details of clients' problems totally unprofessional and a breach of their trust, it is dangerous. It risks the law firm and lawyer's reputations and may be considered professional misconduct. The Canadian Bar Association's Code of Professional Conduct provides as follows:

> The lawyer has a duty to hold in strict confidence all information acquired in the course of the professional relationship concerning the business and affairs of his/her client, and he/she should not divulge any such information unless he/she is expressly or implicitly authorized by his/her client or required by law to do so.

This rule extends to the whole law firm and staff. Every lawyer is bound by this rule of confidentiality. The confidentiality is known as "solicitor-client privilege." The lawyer cannot be forced to disclose this confidential information even if the court orders it. The lawyer can only reveal the information if it is necessary to advance your case or if you expressly authorize it. In limited situations, such as to prevent a crime or to report child abuse, lawyers are able to breach this privilege.

IF YOU ARE DISSATISFIED WITH YOUR LAWYER

Let's examine this in two parts—first, what is likely to make you unhappy, and second, what to do about your dissatisfaction.

One of the chief complaints law societies receive from clients about lawyers is that they don't return telephone calls or e-mails promptly or, in some cases, at all. Why don't lawyers return telephone calls? The telephone is often the only means by which they can stay in contact with their clients, so why wouldn't they use it?

There are, I think, a variety of reasons. First, most lawyers are too busy to return every telephone call they receive in a working day. Second, in some cases it is just physically impossible. Lawyers are often out of the office, in court, on discoveries, travelling and so on. Third, many lawyers are procrastinators. If they have no good news, only bad news or no news at all, then they are less likely to pick up the telephone.

Experienced family law lawyers will use personalized answering services, e-mail or will have their secretaries return calls. I have heard of lawyers who do not return telephone messages for weeks. This is inexcusable. I recommend a polite but firm warning after the first time it is a problem—"Return my calls promptly or I'll get someone who will."

Another complaint that clients have about lawyers is the lawyer's failure to keep them abreast of developments. An experienced family law lawyer will meet with the client regularly and provide, through periodic letters, reports on the status of the matter (called reporting letters). A good lawyer will not only report on the status of the matter but also summarize what happened, what options were open, which course was recommended, what the client's instructions were and any other considerations.

I place a great deal of emphasis on regular written reporting letters, and for good reason. The goal of this book is to make you an informed consumer of legal services before you enter a lawyer's office. It will have taken some effort on your part to have achieved that status. It will only be maintained if your lawyer takes over the job of informing you about your own case. Reporting letters are no more than a form of continuing education about your own case and the legal system. They provide a record of past decisions and enable you to make intelligent choices about the future. Insist on them.

Lawyers' Accounts

Another frequent area of disagreement is the accounts that are rendered by the lawyer during or at the end of a matter. I have already set out the essential matters that need to be discussed at the time the retainer is signed. Another matter that you may wish to discuss is the method of billing. If an accurate estimate can be given, some clients prefer to be billed in regular monthly instalments rather than letting a huge bill accumulate. Others cannot afford to pay until the case is finished and successful. In either case, make a point of discussing with the lawyer the method by which you would like to be billed.

Generally, lawyers will insist on billing the disbursements to you as they are incurred. For example, if a $200 bill is incurred to serve the documents on your spouse, then often that amount will be invoiced to you immediately. If you have an amount on deposit with the lawyer for the purpose of paying such disbursements, known as a "Disbursements Only" account, you should receive a statement from the lawyer stating that the disbursement was incurred and was paid out of the amount held on deposit. Any account, whether for disbursements only or for services rendered, should also include a specific description of what was done to justify the fee.

Lawyers charge hourly rates, but for obvious reasons lawyers cannot work in blocks of one hour at a time on each file. Sometimes it is a six-minute telephone call with the opposing lawyer, a 45-minute period of preparation for court or 18 minutes of research on a particular issue. To accommodate work of less than an hour, the lawyer divides his work hours into tenths, or units of six minutes. Ten units of six minutes make up each hour. The lawyer will, regardless of how much time was actually spent, never record less than 0.1 of an hour being spent on a matter, because that is the smallest unit of their time.

As the lawyer works through the day, he or she will keep track, either by written docket or computer, of each tenth of each hour. For example, the telephone rings and it's the client making an appointment and the call lasts three minutes. The lawyer will fill out a time docket for 0.1 or six minutes. (Yes, you get billed for phone calls. Time is money.) If the call lasted 12 minutes, the lawyer would fill out a docket for 0.2, two units of six minutes. As each docket is filled out, the lawyer writes down what service was rendered. A typical time docket could look as follows:

Mike C.—Jan. 5, 2006

10:00–10:06

Client—Brown #161

Telephone call re: husband's breach of restraining order 0.1

The lawyer accumulates these dockets usually in the office computer system. When it is time to render an account, a touch of a button yields a full chronological list of all services rendered and a breakdown of time. The account will also total the time and multiply it by the lawyer's hourly rate. Once any disbursements and GST are added, you have a full account.

Insist on full itemized statements of account, whether the account is an interim one or the final account. Under no circumstances should you accept the old chestnut—one sheet of paper with "To Services Rendered—$15,000." You deserve a full statement of services. Be adamant about it.

Let's take a look now at what to do if you think it is better to part company.

FIRING YOUR LAWYER

A client may end the retainer or contract with the lawyer at any time. It may surprise you to learn that the lawyer cannot do likewise. The circumstances under which a lawyer can refuse to continue to act for a client are very, very limited. If a client asks a lawyer to mislead the court or do some other unethical act, the lawyer can refuse to continue representing the client. Similarly, if the client does not pay the lawyer, he or she can refuse to take any further steps. However, if the client provides instructions and pays the lawyer's account, the lawyer cannot refuse to act.

I think most clients are intimidated by the prospect of telling a professional that they are unhappy with the services rendered and intend to seek help from someone else. You will recall my analogy to the hiring of the college students to paint a house. Few people would have trouble putting an end to that work if they thought it was unsatisfactory.

If you hired a contractor to renovate your kitchen at a cost of $15,000 and the work was shoddy, the contractor uncommunicative and your instructions not followed, you would not hesitate to air your grievances. Why do we hesitate to do the same with a lawyer? The answer lies in part with our expectations.

When we hire the kitchen renovator, we probably have a good idea of what we want, when we want it, what it should look like, when it will be finished and how much it will cost. This is not the case when we hire a lawyer. Instead, we have a very vague idea about what we want or need, no idea how quickly work can begin, no idea about what it should look like when it's under way, let alone finished, and no idea about when it will be complete. We only fear how much the case will ultimately cost (perhaps more than the kitchen).

Unlike the kitchen, we have no way of knowing whether the legal work is being done, let alone done well. That makes it very difficult for us to complain.

If you followed the suggestions in the first half of this chapter, you will be in a much better position to evaluate your lawyer's performance. If you have a specific retainer, you will know whether or not your instructions are being carried out within the cost limits established.

Before dismissing your lawyer, take a few minutes to ask yourself what the real reasons are for your unhappiness. It might even be prudent to re-examine where you are emotionally. Reread the checklist at the end of Chapter 1—Taking a Look at Ourselves, and consider the questions concerning motivation. You should also take a few minutes to consider the investment you have already made in this lawyer's handling of the problem. Be aware that when a new lawyer takes over the matter, many of the hours of preparation in familiarizing himself or herself with your case will be a duplication of time and expense.

All lawyers who practise family law are wary of the client who dismisses lawyer after lawyer and is always unhappy with the service. Experienced lawyers can see these clients for what they frequently are—spouses stuck in stage one of the emotional stages described earlier. Like a terminal patient who denies the illness and shops for a second, third or fourth opinion, clients have been known to fire lawyers until they find one who will simply do as they are told. The client may be happy with that lawyer until they move on to the later emotional stages and suddenly look back on a lot of wasteful angry litigation. The lawyer, perhaps out of inexperience or other motivations, will have always done as the client asked, but the client may not have been served well.

Assuming you are comfortable with your decision to fire your lawyer, what do you do next? Do not expect to pull this off without speaking to the lawyer face to face. I still recall clients who would call my secretary and ask that the file be bundled up and left in the reception area. They promised to drop by with a cheque for any balance owing (not always, but most of the time) and swap it for the file. They insisted, "There is no need to see

Mr. Cochrane. Just tell him I'm unhappy and will take my file to another lawyer." Try as they might, they could not pull this off.

Most, if not all, law firms will only end a retainer after a personal interview has taken place to discuss why the problem arose. If you are intent on ending the retainer, schedule an interview with the lawyer, tell him or her what you wish to discuss and attend to the matter with the same resolve you would use to scold the painter or fire the kitchen contractor.

I never argued with the client on such occasions. If they were unhappy, then I considered it their right to have a lawyer with whom they felt comfortable. Tell the lawyer what is on your mind and ask them to turn over the file with a written summary of its status (if you have not received one recently).

You should understand that you will likely receive an account for work done but not yet billed to you at the time the retainer comes to an end. If there are monies being held in trust by the lawyer, they will be applied toward the account and the balance (if any) returned to you.

Once paid, the lawyer has two obligations: First, to return your file to you promptly and second, to render whatever assistance he or she can to your new lawyer. If a new lawyer has been found in advance of ending the retainer, your lawyer may be prepared to simply courier the entire file to the new lawyer.

The file that arrives at your new lawyer's office (or is turned over to you directly) may not be identical to the file you saw sitting in front of your former lawyer at the time the retainer ended. The lawyer does not simply slide the entire file into an envelope (or box in some cases). He or she is entitled to remove certain materials. The following items, however, should be in the file:

- legal documents (pleadings),
- letters written by you to the lawyer (originals),
- letters to the lawyer from the opposing lawyer or others (originals),
- copies of all other letters,
- originals of all evidence and
- any other material needed to advance the case and not available elsewhere.

The lawyer may remove from the file such items as:

- notes and memos to file and
- legal research done to formulate his or her opinions.

Often a lawyer will turn over everything in the file but keep copies for his or her own records. The lawyer may do this if there is any concern that arguments may arise at a later date about the quality of work done.

If the lawyer is owed money for work done, he or she is entitled to be paid before releasing the file. Until paid in full, the lawyer has what is called a "solicitor's lien" on the file and its contents. Many people are familiar with a "construction lien" or "mechanic's lien," whereby a worker or contractor can register on title to a piece of property notice that he is owed money for work done. The property cannot be mortgaged, sold or dealt with until the lien is paid. The same is true of a client's file with a lawyer.

WHAT TO DO WHEN YOU ARE UNHAPPY ABOUT YOUR LAWYER'S BILL

This can be a painful experience. You receive the lawyer's bill for the work done on your behalf. You may even be happy with the outcome, but the cost! It seems like a lot more than you originally estimated or were told it would cost. Can the subject be dealt with in any way other than simply paying and stewing? Yes.

An important beginning would be to discuss the matter with the lawyer directly. Make an appointment to discuss the bill and be prepared to go through it line by line. You should have received an itemized statement of account. Remember, mistakes can be made, misunderstandings occur and they can readily be remedied.

However, if you are still dissatisfied, it is possible to arrange an appointment with a court official for you and the lawyer to have an independent third person assess or "tax" the lawyer's account. To arrange such an appointment, contact the local courthouse and speak to the Taxing Officer. You will be given an appointment and a notice that must be delivered to the lawyer.

Once at the meeting, you should be prepared with notes, your account and your retainer to discuss the agreement you thought you had with the lawyer. The court official will look at the retainer, the number of hours worked, the amount charged, the normal standard for such work, out-of-pocket expenses and so on. He or she has the power to reduce the account—and often does. It is never increased.

It is not an embarrassing hearing for either person. Lawyers' accounts are taxed or assessed all the time. It does not take long and could save you several hundred dollars. There are some notable cases where lawyers' accounts were reduced to zero—that's right, zero. The officer thought the work was worthless and a court subsequently agreed when the decision was appealed by the lawyer.

Hiring a lawyer is a critical point in your handling of your own marriage or common-law relationship breakdown. It should be done from a position of power, which means from a position of being an informed consumer. The checklist set out at the end of this chapter can be consulted during the initial interview to ensure that the lawyer has a clear understanding of your needs as a client. If you have read the entire book and understand your own position emotionally and your legal needs in a reasonably specific way, your lawyer will know from the outset that the necessary standard of work and communication will be a high one.

In addition, if the lawyer is an experienced family law lawyer, he or she should welcome clients who are in touch with their own emotional and legal needs. You will be recognized and respected as a client who provides instructions from a position of informed self-interest and nothing less.

Should you determine that it is necessary to terminate your relationship with your lawyer, you can at least do so with confidence by following the guidelines above. Every client cannot be happy with every lawyer. The individual needs and idiosyncrasies of both are too diverse and personal to have perfect harmony. If you have followed the guidelines, you will have significantly reduced the likelihood of a mismatch. However, if your choice proved unfortunate or circumstances changed (e.g., a new lawyer in the firm took over the file), do not settle for less than you need and deserve. Examine your reasons for wishing to terminate the retainer. If you are confident in your decision, arrange the interview and find someone who can move your case to a conclusion quickly, inexpensively and, with luck, happily.

CHECKLIST

1.　Have you called the provincial Lawyer Referral Service?

2.　Does your province accredit family law specialists?

3. Have you spoken with trusted friends about recommendations?

4. Do you understand the meaning of retainer?

5. Does this lawyer have a sample retainer form to examine? Sample account?

6. Will you need and qualify for legal aid?

7. Does this lawyer accept legally aided clients?

8. What is the lawyer's hourly rate? Estimated cost?

9. What are the billing practices? Interim? Final?

10. Will he/she accept a ceiling on the fee in the retainer?

11. What experience does this lawyer have with this type of case?

12. Does this lawyer have any biases? Hidden agenda?

13. Will this lawyer be doing the work or passing it to someone else? At every stage?

14. What will be the role of paralegals, students and junior lawyers?

15. Does he/she have any potential conflict of interest? For example, has there been a prior dealing with your family business?

16. How would he/she describe the services needed in the retainer?

17. How are disbursements handled? How much is needed in advance?

18. How does the lawyer handle questions about fees that arise while the case is under way?

19. How will he/she stay in touch with you? Telephone calls? Reporting letters? E-mails?

20. Will the accounts have full itemized statements of services rendered?

(Continued)

21. Is this person honest, considerate and professional, with a sense of humour?

22. Do you feel comfortable with this person assisting you with this matter?

23. Do you respect his/her opinion?

24. Does he/she respect yours?

3

TAKING A LOOK
AT THE PROCESS

~

Understanding Family Law and the Legal System

Some general background knowledge about family law is valuable if you are to become an informed consumer. I do not intend to frighten, intimidate or bore you with the constitutional intricacies of which jurisdiction, federal or provincial, has responsibility for laws that affect the family. You may be surprised to know that the easy answer is that they both have responsibility and that they both have enacted laws that complement each other.

Most people understand that the federal government has responsibility for such things as national defence or criminal law. These are areas that affect the entire country and one law is therefore required for everyone, regardless of the province in which they reside. We have a Criminal Code that applies to everyone in Canada. The same is true of the law of divorce.

Our Constitution provides that the federal government has responsibility for passing laws that permit people to divorce. The people of Prince Edward Island use the same Divorce Act that is used by people in British Columbia and Ontario. The procedural rules governing the way in which the divorce is moved through the courts may vary from province to province, but the substantive divorce provisions are the same in every province.

The applicability of the Divorce Act is triggered by one thing and one thing only—a request for a divorce. The Divorce Act only applies if a divorce is sought.

The Act provides guidelines for making orders concerning custody, access, support (for a spouse or a child) and, of course, the divorce itself. The Divorce Act does not say anything about dividing property, the matrimonial home, Marriage Contracts and so on. We all know that those issues can be an important part of family law, so where are they? The answer lies in provincial law.

By virtue of our Constitution, the provinces have responsibility for laws concerning "property," including the way in which property is to be divided when a marriage breaks down. This means that if someone seeks a divorce and wants the court to divide the family's property, then provincial property division laws and federal divorce laws must work together.

If a couple separates and they only want their family property divided (but they do not want a divorce), then the Divorce Act will not apply. We know that provincial law will provide the law for division of their property, but what if they also need to sort out custody of, access to and support of their children? Again, the answer lies in provincial law.

Each province supplies a complete package of alternative law in the event a couple does not seek a divorce, but needs legal assistance with property division, spousal support, child support, custody, access and dozens of other matters.

For example, consider Ontario provincial law. The Family Law Act sets out the law for property division on marriage breakdown. In combination with other provincial laws, it also sets out the means by which spousal and child support are calculated, special rules concerning the matrimonial home and the requirements for domestic contracts (Marriage Contracts, Cohabitation Agreements and Separation Agreements).

The Ontario Children's Law Reform Act sets out the law for determinations of custody and access and applies when a divorce is not sought. We will look at all of these areas in more detail in upcoming chapters, but at this point we only need to see the interconnection between federal divorce law and provincial family law. They are designed to work together so that every combination is covered. Remember that when a divorce is sought, the Divorce Act does everything except divide your property. Provincial law always divides the family property.

There are other federal and provincial laws that are relevant to family law. Many of the provinces now have provincial enforcement agencies to collect support owed by virtue of an order or an agreement. For example, Ontario enacted the Family Responsibility Act, which sets out the structure and power of an agency that will collect support payments ordered under either federal or provincial law. In other words, the agency will enforce a support order, whether or not it was made as part of a divorce. Manitoba was the first province to establish a support enforcement program. Since then, every province has established some form of support enforcement assistance program. The degree of assistance may vary from province to province.

Federally, there is the Federal Orders and Agreements Enforcement Assistance Act, which provides information to those trying to track down support defaulters. It facilitates the work of the provincial enforcement agencies. The support enforcement area is a good example of recent attempts to enact complementary family laws in Canada.

In most cases, when a couple decides to separate and they cannot agree on how to settle their differences, an Application for Divorce is issued, coupled with a request for a division of property under the relevant provincial property law. In Ontario, between the Family Law Act and the Divorce Act, all the necessary court orders can usually be made, whether for custody, access, property division or the divorce itself.

Understand that there is no quick solution in the federal or provincial law. If you and your spouse cannot agree, the law serves as a guide and the judge decides for you. These different laws make up a patchwork designed to help the court sort out the problems experienced when a family splits up.

Why is it organized like this? Why doesn't one level of government make all the laws? Why don't all the provinces get together and agree to have the same laws? Well, the original framers of the British North America Act divided the responsibilities this way and changing the Constitution can be a very difficult thing to do.

There has been talk of transferring jurisdictions between the federal and provincial governments, but very little has come of it or is likely to come of it in the near future. The provinces do try to coordinate their family laws, but there are differences in attitudes and needs that result in different approaches. Some provinces could afford to spend money setting up support enforcement agencies; some could not. Some provinces think property division should not affect a spouse's business assets; others do. So it can be difficult to agree on one law, but we try. (You don't like it? Then turn to Chapter 17—Self-Help Advice and read the section "How to Complain.")

THE LEGAL SYSTEM

There are some other aspects of the legal system that should be understood to place your particular dispute in some context. Proceeding in the absence of some of this general knowledge would be like beginning a board game without even knowing how the board works.

In every province there are two distinct parts of the legal system—civil justice and criminal justice. Most people are familiar with the criminal law because so many news stories concern the justice system's handling of crime. Less well understood, but equally important, is the civil part of the justice system, which encompasses virtually anything not related to criminal justice.

Family law is but one of many areas being handled by our civil justice system. Legal disputes over wills, property, motor vehicle accidents, commercial contracts, defective products and family law are all handled within the system. Each province is the same in this respect. With minor variations, disputes concerning family law enter our civil justice system in much the same way as disputes over motor vehicle accidents or breaches of contract.

The differences between the civil justice system and the criminal justice system cause confusion for many people. In many cases the two systems operate in the same building, use the same judges, lawyers and court staff and, for all intents and purposes, look the same. But they are not.

First, we should understand that civil and criminal justice systems, especially civil justice systems, vary from province to province. Civil justice systems process cases that involve provincial law, which can vary widely from province to province. The criminal justice system tends to be more uniform because it has one national law to apply, the Canadian Criminal Code.

Second, the two systems, civil and criminal, do not reach conclusions in exactly the same way. The differences concern the amount of proof required to get the court to make a decision. This is generally called the "burden of proof." In a criminal case the Crown attorney (not district attorney or DA—that's in the U.S.) must prove "beyond a reasonable doubt" that someone is guilty of a crime. In other words, the judge or jury must be left with no doubts about this person's guilt. There must be no other reasonable explanation for what happened. In the civil justice system (including family law) the burden is different. A person must prove that his or her version is correct "on the balance of probability." This is a lower standard than the criminal system. Here each person tries to tip the scales in their favour with the proof. It doesn't have to be "beyond a doubt;" it just needs to be "probable."

Understanding this subtle but fundamental difference between a family law case and, say, a murder trial may change your approach to solving the problems in your own case. Family law judges are not trying to find out who is "guilty." Rather, they are trying to choose between two possible solutions to the problem. The solution chosen is probably (in their opinion) correct.

FAMILY LAW AND THE COURTS

It is a constant source of amazement to me as a lawyer and to those people who must use the courts for resolving family disputes that there is not simply one court capable of handling all family law problems. The provinces vary in this respect, but many of the provinces have more than one level of court for family law matters. Ontario, until recently, did not have one court for family law disputes, but four.

In Ontario, depending on the specific nature of the dispute, your geographical location, the wishes of the lawyers and the availability of court time, a person's request for help from the court could have ended up in one of two courts. A recent development promises to streamline the court process through the use of unified Family Courts. In a unified court a judge has full authority under all federal and provincial family laws.

THE PERSONNEL OF THE COURTS

Within these different courts you may encounter a variety of people performing the functions that make the justice system operate. These people include:

- judges,
- trial coordinators,
- registrars, clerks and other court staff,
- court reporters and
- lawyers (my friend . . . my learned friend).

We will take a brief look at each person's role to understand the process of family law.

Judges

This job continues to hold great mystique for the Canadian public. It is admittedly a powerful position that gives this handful of men and women control over our property, our children and, in some cases, our liberty.

Judges are appointed to their position by either federal or provincial government. It is a job for life and can pay quite well compared with other jobs ($200,000+), and includes a pension and other benefits. They are free from political interference and cannot be fired or removed from the bench except in the most limited circumstances.

Most judges have been lawyers for at least 10 years and therefore have a certain degree of experience. They are not all political hacks receiving payoffs for service to the political party that appointed them. In fact, by and large, we have good judges in Canada. The quality of Canadian judges continues to grow rather than decline.

Once appointed to the bench, judges are treated differently by their former colleagues and many complain that it can be an isolating experience. It can be difficult to let your hair down publicly when so much decorum and respect is necessary for a judge's work.

The judge's function in the courtroom goes beyond rendering a decision at the end of the case. He or she must listen to the theory of each lawyer's argument, listen to the witnesses, watch their demeanour, take notes, rule on questions of evidence and control the entire courtroom process. It means following each and every question, protecting witnesses in some cases, and prodding them in others. It is a very difficult job and many a judge has sat in frustration as a lawyer did a poor job, knowing full well they could present the client's case better if they themselves jumped down and did it for the lawyer, but they can't. They sit patiently, taking notes of everything said, with observations or questions, and develop their own opinion about how the problem should be solved.

Most judges are called "Your Honour." When in doubt, use "Your Honour" and resist "Your Majesty" (which some poor witness called a judge in a traffic case. The judge was slow to point out the error.) Judges don't expect people to grovel. They only expect lawyers to be clear and concise and witnesses to be direct, honest and easy to hear.

Sometimes a judge will give his or her reasons for judgment or decision at the end of a case; sometimes they do not and "reserve" or promise to give the decision later after they have thought about it.

The judge is the focal point of the courtroom and you should be mindful of that fact should you have the opportunity to appear before one.

Trial Coordinators

In some large cities, traffic is controlled from one computerized control location. The flow and volume of traffic is monitored and when bottlenecks occur it is diverted to an alternative route. This is essentially what a trial coordinator does for a living except he or she manages the litigation flowing through the courts.

A large courthouse may have 10 or more courtrooms hearing motions, trials and even appeals. The trial coordinator ensures that the right judge gets the right case, at the right time, in the right courtroom. This means getting lawyers, clients (and their witnesses), court clerks and a court reporter to the same place as well. Last, and certainly not least, they must ensure that the judge has the court file and appropriate materials in advance of the hearing. Of course, once everything is ready to go, the clients may decide to settle, which means another group of ready, willing and able lawyers and clients must be found. And so it goes. Sometimes a matter scheduled for 30 minutes in Courtroom Number 1 suddenly stretches into a whole day. A bottleneck effect happens, and cases waiting for that judge and courtroom are diverted elsewhere—or simply sent home to wait.

Some courts use a "fixed-date" method, which means that once the lawyers alert the court that they are ready for trial, the trial coordinator assigns them a fixed date for the hearing. This is easier on the lawyers and clients, but can result in downtime for the courts unless some creative over-booking is done to accommodate the inevitable out-of-court settlement.

Registrars, Clerks and Other Court Staff

There is a barely visible world that processes the justice system's paper-work. Tens of thousands of lawsuits are started each year and your case is just one of the many files.

The registrar is the chief administrative officer of a particular judicial district. He or she is responsible for the staff of the courthouse and for ensuring that lawsuits are processed in accordance with the rules of the court. The registrar takes responsibility for opening files, checking documents for rule compliance, taking fees for filing and so on.

Important steps in lawsuits are recorded not only in the file kept at the courthouse but also logged in record books. In this way, orders, judgments and other important matters can be tracked down relatively easily. The registrar's staff does many of these things, but he or she has ultimate responsibility for the local administration of justice.

The court staff also assist the judges and trial coordinator with making sure the right file and materials are available for hearings.

One of the less pleasant aspects of family litigation—any litigation for that matter—is the need to line up to file material at the courthouse. In larger cities the courts are very over-burdened and court staff cannot keep up. It is not unusual to see law students or paralegals or even secretaries lined up at the courthouse waiting to file some important material. It is a stressful environment and a mystery to first-time observers.

Court Reporters

Court reporters are used at trials, appeals and discoveries. In matters such as an important motion, they may also be used. Their sole purpose is to record everything that is said during the proceeding. This includes the opening introduction of the judge by the clerk right through oath swearing, to every question and answer. Theirs is a unique skill that I still do not completely understand—especially when they accurately record every word said when three people are speaking at the same time!

Different methods are used by different court reporters. Some reporters use a steno mask, which is a large plastic device that fits over their mouth and nose. They simply repeat every word said by anyone who speaks whether it is the judge, lawyer, witness or clerk. Other reporters take the proceedings down in shorthand with a pen (this is on the decline) and others use what is known as a silent typewriter. The typewriter is set up at the front of the courtroom and the reporter silently types the proceedings.

Technology is making real-time transcription a possibility. The reporters can produce (overnight if necessary) a transcript of the proceedings. This transcript is used to prove what was said by whom and can be used for example on an appeal. Often it is used to impeach a witness. This means to challenge his or her present statement by showing the person the transcript of what they said on a previous occasion under oath. This type of impeachment often ends with the brilliant question, "Were you lying then, or are you lying now?"

Most witnesses seem to forget about the court reporters as they go about their invisible work.

Lawyers (My Friend . . . My Learned Friend)

Lawyers often refer to the opposing lawyer in the courtroom as their "friend." For example, the lawyer may say, "Your Honour, my friend's point is well taken; however, he neglected to mention that such . . ." Clients are seen shaking their heads as if to say, "Hey, wait a minute, if he is such a good friend, how can he do a good job for me?" They may soon realize that the last thing that these two lawyers are is friends. They may have never met before or may dislike each other intensely. I have yet to hear one lawyer call another "my learned friend" without at least a hint of sarcasm or a smile—or both.

It is simply a courtesy developed to maintain some decorum or civility. Lawyers are reminded that they are merely advocates for clients who come and go, while they are there as adversaries day after day in the courts throughout their careers.

Many courts still require lawyers to wear gowns to court. These include the black cape, black waistcoat, wing-tip-collar shirts and tabs. No one wears a wig to court and no one ever has in Canada—except perhaps a witness or two.

As a final note, if during your own case you see a jury in the court-room, slowly stand up and, as quietly as possible, leave—you're in the wrong courtroom. Family law disputes are never heard by juries.

THE RULES OF COURT

You may recall the first time you played Monopoly and everyone sat patiently (well, nearly everyone) and listened while someone read out the rules. Markers were selected, a little money counted out, the dice were cast and away you went. Well, our court system, in its handling of family law matters, is not unlike that, except you are the marker and the money is real.

If you will bear with me for a minute I will "read the rules," so to speak. Remember, too, that this is a general overview. The court system, lawyers, court personnel and your own case respond to or initiate action by using sets of rules. These rules, which are very specific, actually have the force of law because they are regulations made pursuant to provincial law. Without these detailed rules, no one would know what to do next on a particular case. Everyone would be going off in different directions without any guid-ance or control or, worse yet, everyone would simply sit and do nothing.

Each province has its own set of rules governing procedure in its courts. These rules are known as "The Rules of Practice" and provide for virtually everything that can happen between the institution of proceedings (starting the case in the court system by getting the registrar to authorize commencement of an action) and obtaining a judgment at the end of the case. One published version of the rules and the summaries of cases that interpret them is 1,090 pages in length. The rules also provide for appeals, enforcement of court orders and hundreds of other matters.

The various levels of court within each province have their own sets of rules, as well. A provincial court and a Unified Family Court will each have a different set of rules. So, every level of court for family law has its own set of rules—and you thought this was going to be easy.

By and large, the rules are helpful in keeping everything organized and moving and provide very much the same procedures for the different courts, with some variations. If used properly they can provide a great deal of control over the progress of a case. Some courts now use a system called "case management," whereby the judge takes a more active role in moving the case forward. The lawyers and clients must perform certain steps with-in certain pre-set timelines.

The rules prescribe all of the steps that must be taken to move your case from beginning to end, as well as all of the forms that must be used to make the documents acceptable for filing at the court. A system as over-burdened as ours would not last 15 minutes if everyone filed documents in whatever form they wished, so the rules prescribe everything from the colour and size of the paper to their form and content. The basic steps in any legal proceeding are essentially the same, and include:

1. exchange of letters between lawyers,
2. exchange of legal documents (called pleadings),
3. discovery of each others' cases,
4. motions (mini-trials on matters from time to time),
5. pre-trial/case conference (settlement discussion before a trial),
6. trial and
7. appeal (if necessary).

The following is a brief summary of what happens at each of these steps.

Exchange of Letters

Assuming you have settled upon a lawyer and completed a retainer authorizing the lawyer to act on your behalf, the matter will inevitably begin with your lawyer writing to either your spouse or his or her lawyer if one has already been hired. On the other hand, it may be you who receives a letter and consults a lawyer about what you should do in response. These letters often say the following:

"Without Prejudice"

Dear Mr./Ms. Spouse:

Re: Family Difficulties

We have been consulted by [Client's name] with respect to your family difficulties. [Client's name] has instructed me to explore the possibility of resolving these difficulties through negotiations that would lead to the signing of a separation agreement containing terms acceptable to both of you.

Please have your lawyer contact me within the next few days so that we can amicably resolve the outstanding problems as quickly as possible.

I look forward to hearing from your lawyer.

Yours very truly,

[Lawyer's name]

Sometimes this type of letter contains a deadline, e.g., "If I have not heard from you within 10 days of the date of this letter, I will commence court proceedings." Letters often mention the need to complete financial statements.

These initial letters are important. They set the tone for the negotiations and often list demands and therefore shape the issue. If appropriate, they can open the door to alternatives to the courtroom, such as mediation (see Chapter 11—Alternatives to Court). Given the letter's importance, I suggest that you ask to see the letter your lawyer plans to send. You should also ask about the circumstances under which it will be delivered. For example, it is rarely necessary to have such letters delivered to a person at work, but some lawyers will arrange such a delivery out of thoughtlessness. A person embarrassed at work will not be interested in negotiating anything. Discuss this with your lawyer and make your wishes known. Do not accept standardized letters. Insist on a personal touch.

I have seen entire Separation Agreements (see Chapter 9—Settling Your Differences) negotiated by letters over a several-month period. In other cases it becomes clear early on that a settlement will not be possible without other methods being used. Do not go from this letter-writing stage to the next stage (legal proceedings) without a written opinion from your lawyer about what happened and what is likely to happen if legal proceedings are started. This opinion should also contain an estimate of fees and out-of-pocket expenses that might be incurred.

Exchange of Legal Documents

If the letters have not led to a settlement (which would likely be incorporated into a Separation Agreement), your lawyer may recommend starting legal proceedings. All unresolved issues are submitted to the court, saying in essence, "Judge, these people cannot decide, so decide for them."

The proceedings can be started a number of ways by using documents described in the Rules of Practise. These are court forms printed by legal stationery companies and are available electronically. Most law firms use software in their computers that print the client information right onto the appropriate form.

Family law proceedings can be started by Divorce Application or Statement of Claim and, in some cases, by Notice of Motion. The names of the forms may vary slightly from province to province, but they all have the same effect and seek to achieve the same goal. That goal is to give the court an orderly and uniform summary of what the dispute is all about. The form will describe the people involved, children, if any, where the clients live, what they want, when they are scheduled to appear to present their case and so on. Often evidence is included in an affidavit or financial statement.

Once the appropriate forms have been completed, the lawyer's staff will take the material to the court office to be "issued." This means that the clerks at the courthouse examine the documents to see if they have been completed properly, charge a fee and then sign them to make it all official.

Many provinces require the financial statements to be filed before they will issue the proceedings. Given the amount of detail needed, completion of these statements can delay issuance of the claim for several days. The financial statements should give the court (and the other side) a picture of your current financial circumstances and your plans for the future.

Once issued, the documents must be delivered to the spouse (lawyers call this "serving the papers"). If the other side has a lawyer, it may be possible to facilitate service by the lawyer accepting it on the client's behalf. If this cannot be arranged, then a professional document server (bailiff or process server) may need to be hired. Except in the most unusual cases, the service of documents should be done with sensitivity and not be done to embarrass the other spouse. (Remember, what goes around, comes around. And it's all at your expense.)

Once the other side has received your pile of material (it can swell to a couple of inches of paper very quickly), they must file material in response. If it is a divorce, they must file an Answer or even a Counter Petition, affidavits, and, of course, the financial statements that, more often than not, tell a very different financial story from those issued by your side.

But we are not done yet—you may need to respond to the material you have just received. This can include a Reply, more affidavits and amended financial statements. For historical reasons these all came to be known as "the pleadings," because lawyers used to plead for relief on behalf of their clients. The purpose of responding to the other person's documents has not changed—to narrow the points of controversy until the issues are identified.

At the end of this barrage of material, everyone should have a good idea about where the argument lies. "Everyone" includes you as the client. So do not go to the next step (discovery) unless you have received a written opinion from your lawyer telling you what has happened and what is likely to happen. This again should include a bill for the work done and an estimate of the cost of the next step.

In the next five sections, we will examine the most time-consuming and therefore most expensive aspects of family law litigation: discovery (questioning under oath), motions, pre-trials, trials and appeals.

Discovery/Questioning Under Oath

What you need to know at this point is that discovery includes oral examination of the parties under oath and examination of documentary evidence needed to prove one's case in court. Once the pleadings have been exchanged, each lawyer is permitted to sit down with the other lawyer's client and ask that person questions under oath about the pleadings. The lawyers probe the written version set out in the documents.

Discovery takes place in a small room with a court reporter. Your lawyer is present while the other lawyer asks you questions. Your spouse may even be present while you are questioned. The court reporter takes down all the questions and answers and marks all the exhibits for ease of reference and to be able to make some sense of the transcript later. (For example, the lawyer may ask you to identify a copy of your mortgage and will ask the reporter to mark it as Exhibit number 1). If there are many exhibits, the lawyers may bind photocopies of them into a book for ease of reference. This question-and-answer session may take an entire day or only take a few hours; it depends on the complexity of the case.

It is unusual for your spouse to be present during your discovery and vice versa. However, sometimes the lawyers may ask for the clients to be present if it is necessary to be able to consult with them as the questions and answers evolve. Personally, I think the other spouse should not be present, so that no intimidation occurs and to ease the anxiety for everyone.

In advance of this oral discovery, the lawyers should have completed their documentary discovery. This means that if the client intends to rely on a particular document at trial, then they must produce a copy of it in advance of the oral discovery. "Documents" can include tapes, letters, photographs, drawings, computer files and so on.

Discovery, oral and documentary, is designed to further narrow the issues and prevent surprises at trial. Nobody wants to go all the way to the court to suddenly see a document that proves the other side was right all along. In fact, the court can penalize with legal costs a person who withholds evidence and springs a surprise at trial.

After the discovery, the lawyers will ask the court reporters to prepare a transcript of the questions and answers. Once the transcript arrives, two or three weeks later, the lawyers review it to evaluate the likelihood of success. They also look to see if there were any questions that the client was unable to answer. In such cases, the lawyer and client sometimes "undertake" or promise to get the information and send it along later. These promises are called "undertakings" and must be kept or you risk being penalized.

The lawyer should now prepare a written opinion setting out what has happened and what is likely to happen at the next step. This opinion should include the lawyer's opinion on the likelihood of success. It should speak in terms of "if this matter went to court I think the court would…"

You are paying the lawyer for his or her opinion on what will happen, so make sure you get it in writing. Do not do anything until you have this opinion in hand. Be prepared to sit down and discuss it with the lawyer, not the student, the paralegal, the secretary or anybody else. You will also want to discuss the expected cost of going to the next step—trial.

Motions

A motion is an application to the court for an order on a particular issue. Motions can occur at any time after the proceeding has been issued at the courthouse right up until the time of trial. Lawyers will use motions to sort out interim problems and procedural matters. It amounts to asking the court to settle an issue (like custody) until the final trial.

The motion is held in front of a judge and usually involves the clients. Two documents are needed for a motion, the motion itself and an affidavit. The motion itself, which is a document that can be two or three pages long, identifies the people involved, describes what they want from the court and sets out a time and date for a presentation to the judge. Motions are scheduled, since the date and time must be coordinated with the court office and available judge time.

The motion is supported by an affidavit sworn by the client. This affidavit is the evidence and takes the place of the client appearing and giving testimony orally. There is nothing to prevent you as the client from attending a motion. I have always found it interesting to watch other lawyers at work when their clients are present. It is a real insight. (Be forewarned, though, there can be a lot of waiting.)

The motion may be adjourned, indefinitely or to a specific day, to allow the lawyers to cross-examine the clients on the contents of any affidavit filed. In such a case, the discovery process is repeated but only with respect to the affidavit. A transcript of the question-and-answer session may be requested by the lawyer and used as evidence on the motion.

Once the motion is again before the judge, the matter is discussed and the judge makes an order. The motion may be dismissed (rejected), the order sought may be granted, or some other order may be made somewhere in between what the lawyers were asking the court to do. For example, a wife may ask for an order that she have exclusive possession of the home until trial (approximately one year away). The husband may ask the court to order that the house be sold immediately and the proceeds of sale be divided equally. The judge could order that the wife have exclusive possession until the house is sold and fix the terms of sale to include a stipulation that the deal not close for at least six months.

If an order is made, the judge will usually just scribble his or her endorsement on the back of the papers in the file. The lawyer's staff will obtain a photocopy and have it typed into a formal order, which is then approved by both sides as accurate and filed with the court clerks. The order is issued by the court staff and becomes an official order of the court.

Motions may cost thousands of dollars each, not including the cost of disbursements, such as the court reporter's transcript of a cross-examination (perhaps around $1,000). Your lawyer should not bring motions without your express consent and then only if there is no other alternative way of solving the problem.

Pre-trials/Case Conference

Every province has some method of screening family law cases before they go to trial. In many cases this is known as a pre-trial; in others, a settlement or case conference. A pre-trial takes place once the people involved have indicated that they are unable to resolve the matter and are ready for trial.

An experienced person, often a family-court judge or senior lawyer, examines the pleadings and meets with the lawyers and their clients. In all but the most unusual cases, the clients should be available for, and participate in, the pre-trial conference. Once again, the goal of this exercise is to help the people settle part, if not all, of the case. The issues may become narrowed even further or part of the case may be settled simply by having a four-way discussion.

The pre-trial also allows the lawyers and clients to get a second opinion about their positions. The judge who conducts the pre-trial will not hear the trial, so he or she is free to state frankly how he or she would rule, which can have a powerful effect on a difficult lawyer or client. In most systems, this type of conference is a pre-condition to being given a trial date.

Again, do not go to the next step (trial) unless you have the written opinion from your lawyer about what happened and what is likely to happen next.

The Trial

Settlement discussions have produced nothing, pleadings and discoveries are finished, motions have been exhausted and a pre-trial has not resolved the matter. It may have taken years, but you now stand near the end of the trail—the trial.

Assuming you have actually got a judge, a courtroom, all the witnesses, an opponent and are ready to go, most trials take more than one day. The approximate cost is at least $2,500 per day per client and it is therefore not unusual to see a three-day trial run $7,000 to $8,000 for each party.

You should understand that everything you have written in affidavits, explained at discovery or achieved on motions must now be recounted for the court orally. We will go into more detail in later chapters. From the most obvious questions (What is your name?) through to the most complex (Can you explain the differences between your financial statements for 2005 and 2007?), they will all be traced in public in the courtroom with the goal of persuading the judge that you, after all, are correct and have been since the proceedings were commenced a year and a half ago.

After the evidence has been reviewed by the judge, he or she will render a judgment on the issues placed before the court—custody of your children, access rights, property division, and the divorce itself. The judge will also order who must pay the costs of the lawyers and how much, depending on how the case was conducted.

The Appeal

Almost any order or judgment can be appealed to a higher court, although some orders are considered to be of such a minor nature that they cannot be appealed.

Appeal judgments must contain some serious error in fact or law to be successful. If an appeal is undertaken, a further six months to one year may be required. A transcript of the entire trial must be ordered, at a cost of thousands of dollars, just to be able to determine whether an appeal is feasible.

I have set out the stages above for one reason: You must appreciate that when a case is not resolved and it goes to court, it must then wind its way through all these procedures. And remember, I have set out a *brief* version of events.

Lawyers who promise quick results in court are either misleading you or haven't been there enough to know better. In either case, think twice about anyone who promises fast results.

You now know as much or more about the legal system and family law than do most law students. It should be clear why starting proceedings in court is like playing Monopoly: everyone gets a turn, the game often takes a good deal of time and ends only when one person has all the money.

Remember that you will be paying for this with your own money at rates in excess of $300 an hour and more. It can be an expensive exercise.

This is not to say that you should never go to court; sometimes it is simply unavoidable. But if you must use the wheels of justice, remember: they turn slowly using up time, energy and money.

CHECKLIST

1. Do you understand how federal and provincial laws work together on family law cases?

2. Remember that family law is a part of the civil system, not the criminal system.

3. Do you understand why lawyers treat each other with courtesy and refer to each other as "friends?"

4. Remember the seven stages through which a case may proceed, beginning with the writing of letters through to the possibility of an appeal.

5. Do you have a clear understanding of how the wheels of justice turn slowly and how they use up time, energy and money?

6. If you're proceeding from one stage to the next, have you received a written opinion from your lawyer?

7. Do you understand your chances of success?

8. Do you have a written estimate for the next stage?

4

DIVORCE

Dissolving the Marriage Vows

I thought we should start our discussion of the proceedings with something easy—the divorce itself. Lawyers and clients sometimes forget during the intensity of a family law dispute that the goal is to actually end the marriage, to dissolve it. This is because the granting of the divorce itself in many cases is the least contentious issue. This wasn't always the case. Before 1985 when significant changes were made to the Divorce Act, couples had a list of reasons for divorce that included such things as adultery, homosexual activity, bestiality, prison sentences, rape and so on. Little wonder that people felt they had to defend themselves in a divorce proceeding when such horrible allegations could be made.

The Divorce Act amendments ended many of those disputes by going to an almost completely no-fault system of divorce in Canada. The amendments themselves came into force on June 1, 1986, and apply to all divorces subsequent to that date. We will examine these "grounds for divorce" shortly, but let's consider some background information to put this chapter in perspective.

You will recall that the Divorce Act is federal legislation and applies only to people who are legally married. If a divorce is sought, the Act provides the court with the authority to make custody orders, access orders, spousal support and child support orders, as well as other miscellaneous orders. In this chapter we will only consider the divorce itself, the order that dissolves the marriage and some related issues.

This is as good a time as any to remind you that Canada now recognizes marriages between same-sex couples. Once married, a same-sex couple is entitled to all of the rights and obligations of our divorce laws and our family laws. This has meant some modification in our approach to certain issues. Later in this chapter, I mention some of the concerns that same-sex couples may have as they consider a divorce.

Tens of thousands of Canadians go through a divorce each year. There have been debates about the level of divorce, but it would seem that about 30 per cent to 40 per cent of Canadian marriages end this way. We often hear American statistics stating that one in every two marriages fails, but I do not think that the Canadian level of divorce has yet reached that level. Remember, as well, that many Canadians are now living in common-law relationships, which appear to be much more volatile than legal marriages. We will consider common-law couples in Chapter 8. Common-law spouses do have rights, too.

I think that many Canadians will likely someday prefer to have the South Korean system of divorce, whereby the couple often arrives at the courthouse on a Monday morning, angrily completes some forms—with the help of clerks—and for a few mere dollars obtains an immediate divorce the moment the papers are signed by a judge. This easy divorce procedure unfortunately led to the South Korean divorce rate more than doubling between 1995 and 2005. Canada, sadly, is at the other end of the spectrum, where divorce is often long, drawn out and expensive.

GROUNDS FOR DIVORCE

There is only one ground for divorce in Canada: "marriage breakdown." The Divorce Act sets out three circumstances in which the marriage will be considered to have broken down:

1. The spouses have lived separate and apart for at least one year immediately preceding the determination of the divorce proceeding.

2. One of the spouses has committed adultery.

3. One of the spouses has subjected the other to intolerable physical or mental cruelty of such a kind as to render intolerable their continued cohabitation.

When one considers that the previous Divorce Act required people to be separated for three years, you can appreciate how these amendments have made access to the divorce procedure itself easier. A recent survey of Canadian lawyers found that 83 per cent of people filing for divorce seek the divorce on the basis of the one-year separation.

For a one-year separation to be used as a reason for the divorce, the separation must have occurred because there were difficulties in the marriage. A man could not file for divorce because his wife went to study at a university in another city for a year or because one spouse went to work in Saudi Arabia on a short-term contract. At least one of the spouses must intend to live separate and apart because the marriage was having problems.

If this circumstance of marriage breakdown has occurred, there is no need to describe the problems or lay the blame with anyone for the marriage's difficulties—the separation itself is the proof of the marriage breakdown.

Separation need not mean separate houses, although that is certainly the case in most situations. The courts have considered cases in which the husband and wife lived separate and apart but under the same roof. For example, if a husband and wife had marital problems but could not afford separate accommodations, then they could agree to share their home but live separate from each other in it. This would mean no sexual contact with each other, separate sleeping arrangements, separate meals, separate lives, minimal communication and the leaving of each other to fend for themselves with respect to cleaning and other domestic work.

In most cases, however, the couple separates into their own new lives and it is not difficult to see that they are intentionally living separate and apart from each other. If we were looking for some criteria to guide us in determining whether a couple has actually separated, the court considers the following:

1. Whether there has been an actual physical separation. The separation, as I stated above, can be under the same roof.

2. Whether there has been a withdrawal by one or both of the spouses from their obligations in the marriage. This withdrawal must be intended to destroy their partnership or repudiate their relationship.

3. Whether there is an absence of sexual relations, but this in itself is not conclusive.

4. Whether the couple continues to discuss and try to work out family problems and communicate. In this respect I sometimes ask couples

what their neighbours would think looking from the outside in at their marriage. In other words, do your neighbours think that you're still married? If you've fooled them, then you may not be able to convince a court that you were separated.

5. Whether there is an ongoing performance of household tasks and duties. In other words, is the couple still carrying on as if the marriage was under way?

6. What the true intent of the individuals involved is. In other words, do they consider themselves married or are they simply filing income tax returns as "married" or "separated"?

We have all heard the old melodramatic line in the movies, "She won't give him a divorce!" You may be relieved to know that a spouse cannot deny a divorce. Once the separation has occurred, either the husband or the wife can file for divorce. When I say that the separation has occurred, I do not mean that the full year of separation is complete, but rather that the day after the separation has occurred either may file for divorce. The court, however, will not make the divorce order until the year of separation has expired. If the ground of marriage breakdown is met, the court will grant the divorce no matter what the other spouse says or wishes. Therefore, there can be no withholding of consent to the granting of a divorce.

Adultery has always been one of the more lurid allegations hurled by one spouse at the other. It is, if proved, considered proof of marriage breakdown and will result in an immediate divorce order. This method of establishing marriage breakdown is being used less and less because of the availability of the one-year separation method.

The spouse who committed adultery cannot start the divorce; only the other spouse may do so. This prevents spouses from going out and committing adultery simply to entitle themselves to an immediate divorce. The only restriction on a divorce based on adultery is that the court is careful to ensure that the spouse who is seeking the divorce did not "forgive" the adultery. Forgiveness will excuse the conduct and prevent the divorce from being granted.

Not surprisingly, there are fewer and fewer cases in the courts dealing with adultery. It is used less and less as grounds for divorce. Interestingly, many years ago in 1921, the court dealt with a situation in which a wife allowed herself to be artificially inseminated without her husband's knowledge. This resulted in the conception and birth of a child. The court considered it to be adultery and granted a divorce on that basis.

Until very recently, homosexual conduct would not entitle a spouse to divorce on the grounds of adultery. Adultery could only be committed with a member of the opposite sex. If a spouse was engaging in homosexual activity that the other spouse found objectionable, it may have constituted mental cruelty but it was not adultery.

This changed as a result of recent court decisions where judges have simply said that homosexual activity is adultery. This is a little strange from a lawyer's point of view, because adultery has a specific legal definition that includes intercourse between a man and a woman. This little bit of "judge-made law" became necessary because if same-sex couples were to have access to the same grounds of divorce as heterosexual couples, then the definition of adultery would need to be tweaked.

One spouse's physical or mental cruelty towards the other spouse is the third method of proving that the marriage has broken down. The result of the abuse must be that it makes the possibility of living together intolerable. Again, the spouse responsible for the abuse cannot seek the divorce. It must be the abused spouse, and he or she may seek it any time the abuse becomes intolerable.

The law books are filled with cases in which the court has been asked to decide whether or not the physical or mental cruelty is sufficient to render intolerable the continued cohabitation of the partners.

In a nutshell, you may be entitled to a divorce if you separate for at least a year, if your spouse has committed adultery or if your spouse has been physically or mentally cruel to the extent that you cannot tolerate living together. These rules apply to any marriage, regardless of where it took place in the world. Whether you were married in the United States, Europe, India or elsewhere, as long as you have lived in Canada for at least a year prior to the application for divorce, you may use the Divorce Act.

An interesting issue for same-sex couples arises when the couple has come to Canada to marry and then returns to their regular home elsewhere in the world. Imagine, for example, a couple coming to Ontario from South Carolina. The same-sex couple obtain a marriage licence in Toronto, marry, honeymoon in Canada and then return to South Carolina. That jurisdiction does not recognize a same-sex marriage. If the relationship breaks down, the couple will be unable to divorce in South Carolina, the jurisdiction in which they are ordinarily resident. If the couple returns to Ontario, they will not be able to apply for divorce in this jurisdiction because they are not ordinarily resident in Ontario. They effectively will be unable to divorce, which means that they will be unable to remarry.

Note, however, that some of the more unusual forms of marriage may require a second look by a lawyer. There are a few types of marriage (e.g., polygamous) that we do not recognize for "reasons of public policy." If in doubt, have a lawyer check out the circumstances of your marriage to determine whether it is recognized as a marriage for the purpose of divorce in Canada.

RECONCILIATION

Reconciliation (getting back together) is always a possibility. I remember cases of couples reconciling shortly before the court was going to deal with their divorce. They were less than 24 hours from what they thought would be freedom and they decided to give the marriage at least one more try. In one case, a divorce judgment had to be stayed (or "frozen") when the parties reconciled after the divorce judgment was granted, but before the divorce judgment could take effect.

Some couples try reconciling more than once and this is fine, since no one wishes to discourage people attempting to work things out. However, we need to keep in mind the effect this will have on the one-year period of separation—either the spouses are separated or they aren't.

The Divorce Act sets a total limit of 90 days of living together, and if you go over the 90-day limit, the one-year period of separation is interrupted and you must start over again. The 90 days total can be made up of more than one attempt. So, for example, a husband and wife could try for a week in the summer, then a month in the fall and even another month at Christmas and still be entitled to a divorce on the basis that they have been separated for a full year.

Regardless of the number of attempts and failures, reconciliation is only possible if both parties agree. It doesn't matter if one really, really, really wants to reconcile; if the other spouse does not, there is no reconciliation.

Incidentally, reconciliation attempts are not considered forgiveness of cruelty or adultery, so couples are given some flexibility in working things out.

A survey of lawyers found that the 90-day re-cohabitation provision was not used much. About one-third of divorcing couples report that they separated but tried reconciling before they gave up and actually went ahead with their divorce.

The Divorce Act has provisions in it that encourage couples to reconcile if at all possible. Lawyers even have a legal obligation under the Divorce Act to canvas the possibility of reconciliation with every client who comes to their office seeking a divorce. Lawyers have an obligation to inform the spouses of the availability of marriage counselling or guidance facilities that might be available in the community to help them. We often get some funny looks from clients when we ask the question: "Are you sure there's no chance you two can work it out and get back together?"

THE PROCEDURE FOR A DIVORCE

Most lawyers will tell you that there are only two kinds of divorce—contested and uncontested. It can actually be a little more involved than that, but the dynamic of the divorce does depend very much on whether the couple agree to settle matters or not. We will examine in upcoming chapters the consequences of settling or not settling and at this stage will instead focus on what it means procedurally to seek a divorce from the court. Remember, we are thinking now only about the divorce itself, not the custody or access or property division orders.

Since the Divorce Act is federal, only federally appointed judges may make orders for divorce. These judges sit on what are called "superior courts" and they have different names depending on the province in question. In Manitoba, Alberta, Saskatchewan and New Brunswick, they are called the "Court of Queen's Bench." In other provinces they are called simply the "Supreme Court." In Ontario it is now known as the "Superior Court of Justice." Regardless of the name of the court in the different provinces, it is these courts that grant divorces.

Whether you use the court in one province or another is dictated by whether one or both of you has been ordinarily resident within the province for at least the previous year. "Ordinarily resident" does not mean the province where your cottage is located or where you took a summer university course. It means the place where you normally have your home. In one case, a young woman moved from Ontario to British Columbia following her husband to attempt a reconciliation. After two months, they realized the marriage would not work and she wished to file for divorce in British Columbia. She was not considered to have been ordinarily resident in B.C. (nor was he) and they could not complete the Application for Divorce. In order to complete that Application, at least one of the spouses must have been ordinarily resident for at least a year in the jurisdiction in which the divorce is sought.

As a rule of thumb, the court will consider somebody ordinarily resident in a certain place if that person regularly, normally or customarily lives there in a settled routine. The key that the court is looking for is some element of permanence in their lifestyle. This question of ordinary residence is considered to be a question of fact by the court. It is not dependent on citizenship. It is not dependent on immigration status. A person can be ordinarily resident in Canada even if they do not have status as a legal immigrant or other status. With the increased mobility of Canadians, not just from province to province but to and from Canada and other countries, "residency," for the purposes of divorce, will continue to be a difficult point for some couples at the time of separation and divorce.

A Central Divorce Registry in Ottawa collects statistics on divorces filed across Canada and is a critical part of this rule's enforcement. The Registry ensures that where two spouses residing in different parts of the country file for divorce without knowing of the other person's filing, the one who filed first is permitted to continue with the divorce action and the other divorce action is discontinued.

Not only will the residence of the adults affect the location of the divorce; the child's residence is important, too. If a child is affected by the divorce, the court reserves the right to transfer the entire matter to the province that is most convenient for the child. So, for example, where a child is resident in Ontario with his mother and attending school but the father seeks the divorce in Newfoundland, along with a particular custody or access order affecting that child, the Newfoundland Supreme Court could transfer the matter to Ontario. Those best able to comment on the child's life would then be available for the court's consideration.

UNCONTESTED DIVORCES

In many cases there are no outstanding issues to be resolved, since any problems concerning custody, access or property division may have been solved by a Separation Agreement. (See Chapter 9—Settling Your Differences.) The parties are then able to ask the court to simply dissolve the marriage and in some cases incorporate the terms of the Separation Agreement into the court's order at the same time.

Years ago, even when the divorce was uncontested, it was necessary to attend court for a hearing. This was considered by many people to be a waste of time and money for the court and people involved. So when the Divorce Act changes came into force on June 1, 1986, the provinces were given the power to create a procedure for granting divorces without the necessity of the people attending a court hearing. Every province has created such a procedure and in some provinces as many as 98 per cent of the divorces are granted in this way. In Quebec, the availability of the procedure is limited to cases that do not involve children. Nationally, about 68 per cent of divorcing couples use the no-hearing method.

In this procedure, the couple simply fills out the appropriate divorce forms and supporting documents and files them with the court. It was expected that this system would lower legal fees for the couple involved. Unfortunately, this has not been the case and the procedure has not reduced costs significantly.

One positive development with this procedure is the increase in speed with which the uncontested divorce can be processed. On average, it now takes about 17 weeks when no hearing is needed. In addition, clients rarely like attending court so the procedure makes it less of a strain for the people involved. It also tends to steer them away from the courtroom generally in resolving family law disputes.

JOINT APPLICATION FOR DIVORCE

An interesting innovation introduced in the Divorce Act reforms was the Joint Application for Divorce. If the couple can agree on the ground for the divorce and no other matter is in dispute, they are able to jointly issue an Application for Divorce. However, only a small percentage of divorcing couples in Canada have made use of this procedure.

The research available on the use of Joint Applications suggests that those who use it tend to pay considerably less in legal fees, have their divorce finalized more quickly, are more likely to use joint custody and are slightly more generous with the amount of support paid.

CONTESTED DIVORCES

A contested divorce is one in which the parties cannot agree on an issue, forcing them to exchange the "special divorce documents" (see Chapter 3—Taking a Look at the Process) for a divorce action. An Application for Divorce must always be issued to start a divorce action. However, what makes the case contested is the need for the respondent to deliver an Answer. In the Answer, the Respondent replies to all of the allegations made by the Applicant. They also have an opportunity to make a counterclaim in the divorce action.

It is difficult to predict how long it will take to resolve a case once it is contested. Many contested divorces go on for years, particularly, research indicates, if the dispute concerns property. Where custody is an issue and assessments are needed or trials occur, it takes much longer to finalize than an uncontested divorce does.

Regardless of the contested or uncontested nature of the divorce, once the court actually deals with the dissolution of the marriage, it becomes effective 30 days after the judge has made the divorce order. The marriage is over and dissolved on the 31st day. This 30-day period is designed to give either of the people involved an opportunity to appeal. If one of them appeals, the divorce cannot be effective until the appeal is resolved once and for all. Once launched, it can be several months before the appeal is heard.

In some cases, the husband or wife needs the divorce order to be effective before the 31st day; they may, for example, be remarrying. A remarriage cannot take place until the divorce order is final and effective. All jurisdictions therefore allow the couple to have the order made effective sooner if they both undertake in writing not to appeal and if special circumstances require the earlier effective date. Most family law lawyers have witnessed the look of panic on the faces of those who wish to remarry within that 30-day period because the bride-to-be is expecting and the couple wants the child to be born in wedlock. In such a circumstance, the court would abridge the 30-day period and grant the divorce immediately.

What do you get for all this work? A Certificate of Divorce! It is available at the court office and provides an official record of the marriage's dissolution and the effective date of dissolution. The Certificate may come in handy if you plan to remarry at a later date. With it, you can prove that your previous marriage is over. You will need it when you apply for your next marriage licence.

BARS TO DIVORCE

Even though there are thousands of divorces going through Canadian courts, the court does not always simply rubber-stamp every pile of papers filed with the correct fee. In divorce proceedings, the court has a duty to satisfy itself that there have been no "deals" to facilitate the granting of a divorce that wouldn't otherwise get the approval of the court. So, for example, the court does not want to see that there has been some form of collusion between the Applicant and the Respondent in order to get the divorce on grounds that don't exist, or sooner than is otherwise legal. More than one individual has arrived at a lawyer's office asking if they can simply agree that they have been separated for a year when they have only really been separated for a month.

The court also tries to satisfy itself that reasonable arrangements have been made for the support of any children of the marriage. The divorce papers require that children be identified, along with their birth dates, schooling arrangements and child support arrangements. If the court doesn't like what it sees, it has the power to stop the divorce from going forward.

The court also has the power to block a divorce where there have been suspicious circumstances. So, for example, a court would probably not grant a divorce if it discovered that one spouse had suggested to the other spouse that they commit adultery to allow a speedy divorce. This would be considered connivance.

MARRIAGES OF CONVENIENCE

This is as good a time as any to deal with a growing problem in Canada, that of "marriages of convenience." While no statistics are kept, all lawyers hear frequently about these so-called marriages of convenience. These are marriages in which a Canadian citizen offers to marry someone in order to facilitate their immigration into Canada. Usually the story involves a couple agreeing to marry and then, after an appropriate period, obtaining an uncontested divorce or annulment.

Anyone who is contemplating such an undertaking must be aware of two things: First and foremost, you will be required to go through a form of divorce the same as everyone else and secondly, sponsorship of the immigrant should not be taken lightly. There are cases in Canada where a husband sponsored a wife's immigration to Canada and agreed to be financially responsible for her for a period of time. The parties eventually separated before the husband could fulfill the entire sponsorship under-taking. At the time of the divorce, the husband was ordered to pay a lump sum to the wife in order to facilitate her training in the area of computers and he was also ordered to pay a periodic sum on a monthly basis.

Entering into marriage, whether for "convenience" or not, entails all of the rights and responsibilities, including a requirement for a divorce, the possibility of spousal support and even the division of matrimonial prop-erty acquired between the date of marriage and the date of separation.

If you don't believe me, there are recent cases where a divorce was denied when it was discovered that the wife had married the husband sole-ly to allow him to immigrate to Canada. The parties had separated virtually on the day of the marriage. In one case, the wife sought the divorce from her husband in order to marry a man who was in Canada illegally because his visa had expired. The wife wished to marry the illegal immigrant to allow him to stay in Canada. The divorce was not granted. In another case, a marriage entered into simply to facilitate immigration status was not dissolved by the court and the couple was forced to stay married.

This problem of marriages of convenience is growing. I have had discus-sions with judges who are aware of the situation and do not feel comfortable speaking publicly about it. I have met individuals who have paid large sums of money in order to marry Canadian citizens and to gain access to Canada. I have been told of criminals in various communities facilitating these mar-riages for colossal sums of money. In one case in Toronto, a young girl was kidnapped and killed in an attempt to extort money that would then be used to facilitate any illegal marriage, simply to allow a young man to remain in Canada as his visa had expired.

I have personally seen cases within the last five years where young women in certain ethnic communities have been cruelly exploited by their families. They are taken from Canada to their country of origin, married to strangers, sometimes in exchange for that individual's family agreeing to marry someone else who will be sponsored to Canada. These women then sponsor these individuals into Canada. Children are born in the marriage and the family is then abandoned. The woman, with the assistance of her family, seeks a divorce, and once it is granted, she is promptly returned to the country of origin to marry again.

This exploitation of women, of immigrants and of our justice system is a disgrace, yet no one acts on it. Perhaps judges will be forced to refuse these divorces. Perhaps lawyers will need to have new duties imposed on them to weed out such abuses. Perhaps rules with respect to immigration, immigrant sponsorship and separation and divorce will need to be altered to prevent these abuses. Reform is needed immediately.

LEGAL FEES FOR DIVORCE

When I wrote the third edition of this book, I was able to say with some confidence that most people are represented in their divorce proceedings by lawyers. At one time, studies suggested that women were four times more likely than men to have legal aid lawyers acting on their behalf.

The truth of the matter is that more and more people are forced by financial issues to represent themselves in their divorces. It is impossible to say with any certainty the actual average cost of a divorce. Most lawyers who see the published numbers know that the numbers are not realistic. In some cases, we see posters advertising Uncontested Divorces for as little as $300. Paralegals are often more than happy to complete those kinds of divorces. The fees alone for filing a divorce can exceed $200. This means that someone is processing simple paperwork for a fee of between $50 and $100. A divorce involving division of property, custody of children or support cannot possibly be done in such circumstances.

I am aware of one particularly sad case in which a woman was desperate for a divorce. She approached a paralegal who completed the paperwork pursuant to her instructions. She sought only a divorce in the hope that she could free herself from a painful situation. The divorce was served on the husband, he gratefully cooperated and a divorce was granted. They had not dealt with their property, however, and since she was no longer married to her husband, their home no longer had the special status of a "matrimonial home" for the Family Law Act of Ontario. This meant that any right to claim possession of that home was lost the minute the divorce was granted. This was a terrible tactical mistake by the woman and her paralegal and it could not be rectified.

Costs are always a concern in divorce and my own view is that the best way to manage cost is to become an informed consumer. There are many free legal resources available online and otherwise, and there is simply no reason in this day and age to make hasty decisions with respect to the important matters of ending your marriage, arriving at a property settlement, dealing with custody of your children or support issues. You may want to review the advice that I give in Chapter 2—Taking a Look at Lawyers. There are many ways to manage the costs, even in difficult cases.

CONCLUSION

While divorce is in fact the easiest issue for determination by a court, it is linked to many other aspects of the marriage breakdown. I often recommend to clients that they consider getting the divorce last. In other words, deal with all other issues first and then get the divorce. Only if there is some urgent need for the divorce, such as a remarriage or a child on the way, should it be made a priority.

CHECKLIST

1. What is the basis of your claim for marriage breakdown? One-year separation? Adultery? Mental cruelty? Physical cruelty?

2. Will your divorce be contested or uncontested?

3. If it is uncontested, is a Joint Application possible?

4. If the marriage breakdown is to be evidenced by adultery or cruelty, is it likely that a one-year separation may apply by the time such a hearing could be arranged?

5. Is there any chance of reconciliation?

6. Do you understand the 90-day total attempt at reconciliation?

(Continued)

7. If cruelty or adultery is the evidence of marriage breakdown, has there been any forgiveness of this conduct?

8. Will a child be affected by the divorce? If so, will this affect the jurisdiction most suited to hearing the divorce?

9. If a divorce is granted, will you require it to be effective within the 30-day period after the order is made?

10. Is remarriage or the birth of a child a consideration?

11. Have you been a resident of Canada for at least one year?

5

DIVIDING THE FAMILY'S PROPERTY

~

Get Your Fair Share from the Marriage Partnership

The bottom line is that marriage now has a bottom line. Certainly entering into marriage means entering into an emotional partnership, but let there be no doubt that marriage creates a financial partnership as well. This partnership begins the day of the marriage and ends the day of separation. Any and all assets acquired by the marriage partnership are on the table for division if the partnership fails and its assets and liabilities must be divided.

Most Canadians own homes and cars, and have RRSPs and other forms of savings. In some cases they are lucky enough to have cottages, cabins or recreational property and other interesting assets. A fair division of the assets of the marriage partnership is absolutely critical if both spouses wish to be able to move on to new, independent and financially secure lives. They will be taking away from the marriage this "nest egg," which they must use wisely as they start over.

In this chapter, we will examine what this marriage partnership acquires in the way of property and debt, and how that property is valued and divided along with the family debt. As well, we will consider some of the special circumstances that may arise in some marriage breakdowns.

Property division in a marriage breakdown situation is governed entirely by provincial law and therefore varies from province to province.

It was because each province has its own property division scheme that this chapter was one of the most challenging to assemble. The number of generalizations that we can make about property division law in Canada is, as a result, limited. So, in this chapter I will attempt to provide a sense of the common goals of property division and examine some of the more practical aspects of this area.

It is safe to say that the goal of property division schemes in all of the provinces and territories is to divide fairly, if not equally, the value of all assets acquired by the couple between the date of the marriage and the date of their separation or divorce. The marriage partnership, like any business, sees each partner bring a contribution to it. Assets and liabilities are acquired over the life of the partnership and at its conclusion they are divided fairly between the partners.

This "partnership" arises upon becoming legally married in Canada. (In Chapter 8—Common-Law Spouses Have Rights, Too, we examine the very serious limitations on the entitlement of common-law spouses to share property at the end of a relationship.) The rules and guidelines we are discussing in this chapter *only concern legally married spouses*, including same-sex marriages, which now benefit from the marital property division laws in all of the provinces.

While it is difficult to say whether or not married couples are any better off materially now than twenty or thirty years ago, it is safe to say that today's couples are subject to a much more complex scheme of provincial property division and that they are acquiring assets that have a much more complex nature and value. The typical Canadian family may own (or rent) a home, car, furniture and other miscellaneous personal items, and have an interest in a pension plan. Others may own or lease more than one vehicle, a cottage, recreational vehicles, stocks and bonds, RRSPs, Guaranteed Investment Certificates and so on. Court cases have considered hundreds of different types of property that spouses have acquired in marriages, but have been unable to agree upon an appropriate method of dividing them at the time of divorce. Assets argued over have included oil paintings, coin collections, books, heirlooms, just about every conceivable personal effect and, yes, even pets.

The complexity of the rules of property division and the types of property that couples own demands the involvement of lawyers and in many cases chartered accountants and valuators. Thus, we begin this chapter with a caution that in this area you may need to rely heavily on legal advice and that you will be bearing a great deal of the responsibility yourself for locating, describing and valuing your marriage's assets.

Property division is one of the issues the court prefers to settle first. Once the family's property has been divided, the court can then turn its attention to questions of custody of the children, access to them, child support and, depending on the amount of property received, spousal support. This is particularly so in determining who will have the matrimonial home.

Time Limitations

As with any claim that can be made in a court, you will face certain time limitations. Each province provides its own cut-off date for claiming things such as property division and spousal support. For example, in Ontario an application to the court to equalize net family properties based on marriage breakdown shall not be brought after the earliest of (1) two years from the divorce or a decree that the marriage was *a nullity*, (2) six years from separation or (3) six months after the other spouse has died. If you have separated from your spouse, one of the best reasons to consult with a lawyer as soon as possible is to ensure that you know the time frame within which you must make a claim for property or support.

WHAT IS "PROPERTY?"

The definition of property varies a little from province to province. For the most part, property includes all real and personal property and all interests in property.

While there are some subtle differences in the approach to property division in each of the provinces, the net result tends to be the same: with an equitable division of the value of property acquired between the date of marriage and the date of separation.

The safest approach to division of property and to understanding what can be captured by that word is to simply include everything that was acquired by either of you between the date of your marriage and the date that you separated. This would include the acquisition of property worldwide. Consider the following property that has been included in property division in actual Canadian cases: household contents, vehicles, art collections, pensions, cottages, cabins, time-shares, severance payments, a milk quota, disability pensions, airline points, stock options, shares in companies and on and on.

So, for example, if you acquired a time-share in Florida, it should be included in the definition of property. If you acquired airline points because one or both of you travel a great deal, then that must be included in property. Any assets or personal property, such as coin collections, art or investments, should all be included in the definition of property.

An advantage of using the over-inclusive approach is that no one will ever accuse a spouse of hiding an asset. The last thing either person wants is to be accused of hiding an asset and having a settlement overturned because there should have been more on the table than was actually disclosed. Even if it were an honest mistake, the settlement could be set aside if the asset's value was significant and the outcome would have been different had it been disclosed.

WHAT IS DIVIDED?

The various provincial schemes for division of property focus not on the physical division of the assets themselves but rather the values of the assets. This means that property that is in the name of either the husband or the wife is valued to determine who has the greater total property values. Once the total values are known, an adjustment is made so that one spouse pays to the other spouse an amount of money (or transfers certain pieces of property) to ensure that each spouse leaves the marriage with approximately the same *value* in assets.

It is the net value of all property owned by either spouse, subject to some very limited exceptions, that is divided between the spouses at marriage breakdown. The values that are divided are net values. This means using the value of an asset *after* deducting any liabilities connected with a particular asset.

So, if a couple owns a cottage that is worth $200,000 but it is subject to a $100,000 mortgage, its net value is $100,000 and it is that net value that is divided between the couple if and when their marriage breaks down. The same is true for a car that is subject to a bank loan, a home that is subject to a mortgage and even stocks that are purchased on a line of credit provided by a bank. The debts must be repaid first and any remaining value is divided.

WHAT IS NOT DIVIDED? EXEMPT PROPERTY

Each province provides a list of exceptions—assets that will not be divided upon marriage breakdown. For example, every province allows a couple to exempt property from division by use of a marriage contract. If a couple, at the time they were married, agreed in a marriage contract that a particular piece of property, for example, a family cottage or a family business, would not be shared if the marriage broke down, the property would be exempt.

The following types of property are typical of exemption (double-check with your lawyer to see which exemptions are available in your province):

- any property owned in advance of the marriage and brought into the marriage,
- a gift or inheritance received during the course of the marriage,
- a court award or a settlement giving a spouse damages for personal injuries they suffered, for example, in a car accident,
- personal items, such as clothing, basic jewellery and sports equipment,
- family heirlooms and antiques,
- proceeds from a policy of life insurance (e.g., the amount of money received if a husband's mother died and left an insurance policy payable to him),
- gifts from one spouse to the other,
- traceable property (this means property that started out in one exempt category but may have ended up in some other form; for example, if a person took their damage award for injuries suffered in an automobile accident and purchased Guaranteed Investment Certificates, the Certificates are still exempt because they can be traced back to the original exempt category),
- property exempted by virtue of a marriage contract and
- property that is acquired after the date of separation

It is possible for someone to lose the ability to characterize a piece of property as exempt. If, for example, someone received an inheritance that was exempt but they blended that money into the couple's joint accounts, bought furniture for the house and generally mixed it in with the assets of the family, it will be almost impossible to claim an exemption for it. This is bad, since having exempt property can be very valuable at the time of separation and divorce.

HOW IS VALUE DETERMINED?

Since it is not necessarily the asset itself that is being divided but rather its value, one of the arguments that can arise in the area of property division is over the value that should be attached to a particular asset.

The following example is a good illustration of how different valuations can be. A man and woman had been married for approximately 30 years and operated a dairy farm. Over the years, the dairy operation was gradually surrounded by housing subdivisions from a nearby city. The dairy operation was successful and the father and mother intended, throughout most of the marriage, to pass on the farm to their children. However, the marriage had difficulties, the couple separated and the value of the dairy farm came into question. The husband pointed out that the dairy operation had a particular "book value" of approximately $700,000 and that he was prepared to divide that value with his wife and later pass on the farm to the children as agreed. The wife, on the other hand, obtained a valuation of the property which concluded that the farm should be valued at $3,500,000.

Why the discrepancy? The wife's valuation was based upon ending the dairy farm operation and selling the land to developers for a new subdivision of homes. Which valuation is correct? Both. Which is the best solution in this particular case? None of the alternatives satisfied all of the people involved, particularly the children who were expecting to inherit the property.

The point of the above example is to illustrate that valuations can be quite different and you will need to explore your alternatives with your lawyer. Some provinces specify that the value to be used is the "fair market value." Other provinces do not specify the basis of valuation and allow each case to be decided on its own facts. This means that in cases involving difficult or unusual assets various approaches will be used, including "current market value," "fair market value," "cost," "book value" and "liquidation value."

Another twist that can be applied to the valuation issue is whether or not tax obligations and other costs of disposition should be taken into consideration when arriving at a value for an asset. For example, if a party would incur tax consequences for a particular disposition, should those tax consequences be factored in to reduce the value of the asset as divided? (See the tax tips that I have included at the end of this chapter.)

Similarly, if costs would be incurred to dispose of a piece of property, a question arises as to whether or not those costs of disposition should be deducted from the value as divided. So, for example, where a couple own a home and its value is to be divided, but one party does not wish to have the property sold and will, therefore, buy out the other person's interest, a question arises: Should the value be the fair market value of the home after the deduction of an amount for real estate commission? If the property was sold on the open market, a commission would likely be paid, so should the commission be taken into account in reducing the amount that must be shared with the other spouse? For the most part, the answer is yes. When assets are transferred between spouses or when assets must be sold, the courts usually include a reduction to account for the costs of disposition, such as real estate commission. In the case of RRSPs, there is a discount for the future tax consequences of redemption. Discuss with your lawyer the appropriate and fair costs of disposition of particular assets to ensure that the right values are being divided. These are all questions that must be answered in the effort to arrive at an equitable division of the family's property. Remember that valuation methods vary from asset to asset.

Each year, there is some new and interesting challenge for lawyers and courts in trying to establish a value for a particular type of property. For example, valuing airline frequent flyer points can be difficult. Some courts have simply ordered that the points themselves be divided rather than attributing a value to them. Leasing vehicles has become more popular. In some cases, it has been necessary to determine if a vehicle has any equity in it. Stock options have presented some challenges to the courts. In some cases, the stock options are certainly property, but in other cases they are also a form of compensation. Small businesses have also presented challenges. Commercial goodwill, personal goodwill, family farming operations and businesses that have no realistic comparable value have all been considered by the court. Dozens of cases have considered various methods of valuing pensions and even the Supreme Court of Canada has commented that there is no one valuation method that is appropriate and must be used for all cases.

A veritable cottage industry of valuation experts has built up around the family law practice. Experts on pension valuations, stock options, art appraisers, real estate appraisers and so on are all available to assist—for a fee. Valuations can be considerably expensive and it is not uncommon now for one spouse to insist that a forensic accountant/valuator become involved to provide guidance on more complicated asset situations. Determining the value of property can be an expensive proposition.

Jointly Held Property

The formulas used by the various provincial property division schemes rely on each spouse setting out the property and the value of the property that is in his or her name, but sometimes the property is held jointly. This means that the property will appear in both parties' property summaries and it will also mean that the value of the property may fluctuate. So, if a couple owned a property jointly at the time they married and jointly at the time they separated, and the separation took two years for them to sort out, there may in fact be three values for the property. It is not unusual in protracted family law cases for property to be valued over and over again to ensure that the court has the most recent and most accurate valuation.

DATE OF VALUATION

As I mentioned earlier, the provinces each have their own methods for dividing property at the time of marriage breakdown. Every provincial property scheme needs to know the value of property that was owned on the date of marriage and each property division scheme needs to know the value of the property at the date the relationship ended. Generally, that valuation date is one of three events: (1) the date the parties separated and there was no reasonable prospect that they would resume cohabitation, (2) the date of the divorce or a *nullity* judgment or (3) the date before the spouse died, where the marriage ends by virtue of one spouse's death.

Figuring out the date of a marriage is easy. Sometimes determining the date of separation is difficult, particularly if the relationship unravelled over an extended period of time. One person may consider the marriage to be absolutely over, while the other is operating under the assumption that they are working at saving the marriage. Reconcilitations, trial separations and participation in marriage counselling can blur the line of a date of separation. This means that it can be difficult to pick the date for the valuation of assets.

The same is true if the couple lived together in the same home but were separate and apart.

UNEQUAL DIVISION OF PROPERTY VALUES

Every province provides an exception, a method for the court to divide the net value in a way that is *not equal*. Every provincial legislature recognized that there may be circumstances in which it would not be fair to divide the family assets equally between the two spouses. They did, however, take a different approach in describing the circumstances in which the court can exercise that discretion.

Some provinces, such as Ontario, Manitoba, Newfoundland and Nova Scotia, have provided in their laws that assets should only be divided unequally where to divide them equally would be *grossly unfair or unconscionable*. This is a very high standard. It means that the court would need to find that it was almost shocked by the effect of an equal division for it to depart from that general rule. Other provinces, on the other hand, give the court the discretion to depart from an equal division of the value of the asset where to divide equally would be merely unfair.

I should provide a little reminder at this stage that when the court is considering a division that is not equal, it is not interested in either spouse's complaints about the other spouse's conduct. For example, the fact that a spouse committed adultery is not a reason for the unequal division of property. The fact that a spouse was engaged in conduct that might even be considered mental or physical cruelty is not a reason to divide the property unequally.

What the court is looking for in these cases of unequal division is evidence that if the property was divided equally it would shock the court's sense of fairness. For example, if a wealthy man married a woman and the marriage only lasted six months, the court's sense of justice might be offended if all of that man's property was to be divided equally. In one case, a spouse engaged in reckless conduct (gambling) that basically resulted in him losing all of his property. In addition to losing property, he ran up debts that had to be repaid by both spouses. In a case like that, the court's sense of justice might be offended if what was left over still had to be divided equally. The court will examine the conduct related to the property and how it was acquired, maintained or managed during the relationship.

Because of the existence of this provision in the laws of some provinces, discuss with your lawyer the circumstances under which your provincial legislation will allow the court to depart from an equal division of the property. You should be aware when discussing this issue, of course, that unequal division of assets can be a double-edged sword.

THE MATRIMONIAL HOME

The matrimonial home is a special asset that requires separate consideration. All provinces provide for a restriction on one spouse's ability to dispose of or encumber the matrimonial home without the other spouse's consent. Therefore, one spouse cannot sell the matrimonial home without the other spouse's consent nor place a mortgage on the property without the other spouse's consent. This protects the value of the property for sharing at marriage breakdown.

Most couples starting out acquire their home after marriage. It is usually placed in their names jointly so that one would inherit automatically if the other one died. The house becomes the main asset of the family and is usually divided equally unless there is some very unusual circumstance.

More and more often lawyers are seeing couples in which one has acquired a home in advance of the marriage. If the couple decides to use it as their matrimonial home, then its value may be divided equally. If a spouse brings a home into the marriage, special protection, perhaps through a marriage contract, is something that must be considered.

Another consideration is possession of the matrimonial home at the time the marriage breaks down. Possession does not necessarily relate to ownership of the matrimonial home. For example, Manitoba, New Brunswick, Newfoundland, Nova Scotia, Ontario, Prince Edward Island and

Saskatchewan all provide an automatic equal right to possession of the matrimonial home at the time of marriage breakdown regardless of ownership of the home. This means that if the couple separates, either or both spouses can apply to the court for an order giving one of them exclusive possession of the matrimonial home. In cases of family violence or where there is a need to keep children in a particular neighbourhood for reasons of continuity, an order for exclusive possession can be a valuable tool. Discuss with your lawyer the availability of orders for exclusive possession in your particular jurisdiction. For further discussion of exclusive possession and its enforcement, see Chapter 12—Enforcing Family Law Orders.

Be aware at this stage that you can also obtain an order from the court prohibiting your spouse from dealing with any of his or her property until further order of the court. This allows the court to preserve the assets until the end of trial, if necessary, so that there will be property available to divide and to pay for satisfaction of the judgment.

PENSIONS

Another special asset is a pension. It is quite common for one or both spouses to have private pension plans. If the particular province considers the pension to be a family asset, then it must be valued and divided like any other asset owned by the family. Valuing pensions is an intriguing experience, with values varying from pension to pension and pensionholder to pensionholder. Since the amount of the pension to be divided may be only the amount of pension accumulated during the marriage, the entire value of the pension may not need to be calculated.

Different methods used by valuators and accountants include the "termination method" or the "retirement method." In examining the value, the person doing the valuation will also consider mortality tables, the role of interest, early retirement provisions, death benefits that may be available after retirement and the tax consequences of the benefits upon receipt.

Indexed pensions are a separate matter. The issue of pension division and valuation continues to vex the courts. In some cases, spouses have requested an "if and when" division, whereby a pension is shared if and when it is received by the other spouse. This allows both spouses to share in the actual benefit when the employee receives it under his or her pension plan. This type of division was not really contemplated by provincial laws related to pension division and the courts have struggled to find a way to make such orders. In most cases, they have stressed to the parties that they can consent to such a division, in the process perhaps saving themselves the expense of a valuation.

In the case of Best v. Best, the Supreme Court of Canada tried to offer separating couples and lawyers some guidance on pension division. The court suggested that "if and when" division of pensions may be limited to exceptional cases, for example, where most of the equalization entitlement at the end of the marriage is in a pension and where retirement is imminent, forcing someone to make an equalization payment would be a hardship.

The Canadian Institute of Actuaries has developed a system called the Deferred Settlement Method. This method is designed to assist spouses in dividing one pension into two pensions after a marriage breakdown. It requires some cooperation from pension administrators and the consent of the parties, but it may offer some hope to separating families who are dividing pension assets.

You should be aware that those who do pension valuations or valuations of any assets for that matter do not work for free. Their bills for valuations can represent a significant disbursement on your lawyer's account, a disbursement that is eventually passed on to you. You should receive an estimate from your lawyer in advance before authorizing the valuation of an asset as significant as a pension.

It is not uncommon to hear a spouse state that if all the property is going to be divided, then they will simply retire and start living off their pension. This does not change the fact that the pension existed as an asset on the date of separation. If a spouse indicates that he or she intends to retire immediately, this has an effect on the value that will be attributed to the pension at the date of separation. The later a person retires, the lower the actual value of a pension at the date of separation. It is not recommended that frustrated spouses cash in their chips and retire or threaten to retire. It is counter-productive for the calculations of a pension value.

In the area of pensions, the Supreme Court of Canada gave an interesting decision recently in the case of Boston v. Boston. This case dealt with the troubling issue of what is known as "double-dipping." Mr. Boston and his wife had divided the value of his teacher's pension at the time they separated. Mr. Boston was ordered to pay spousal support to his wife. They both went their separate ways and several years later Mr. Boston decided to retire. He then began to draw on his teacher's pension and, because he was earning less, asked the court to reduce the amount that he would pay for spousal support. The issue arose as to whether Mrs. Boston could look to his teacher's pension again for the purposes of spousal support. After all, it had been divided at the date of separation. To allow it to be used again for payment of spousal support would in effect be "double-dipping." The Supreme Court of Canada considered the problem and concluded that double-dipping should be avoided and that in the case of Mr. Boston only that portion of his pension that accrued after the date of separation should be used for the payment of support. Accordingly, the amount that he was paying on a monthly basis was reduced.

This case is also important in that it refers to the obligations of the spouses to use the property settlement wisely after the separation and to invest it in a way that contributes to their self-sufficiency. This is an important message to spouses at the time of separation. The Supreme Court of Canada has said essentially that each spouse must take the nest egg and invest it in a way that contributes to their financial independence. The Supreme Court of Canada even went so far as to suggest that the nest egg should be invested in a capital-depleting, income-generating fund, essentially creating a pension for each spouse. Your lawyer will explain the way in which the Boston ruling may apply to your case.

One pension area of special interest is the Canada Pension Plan credit-sharing scheme. The Canada Pension Plan was amended in 1978 to provide for the sharing of the pension credits accumulated by one or both spouses during the years of their cohabitation. This sharing of credits takes effect upon the dissolution of the marriage. It was designed to ensure that low- or non–income-earning homemakers whose marriages had ended were provided with some pension coverage.

People who can claim a division of pension credits include married spouses who have been separated for at least one year, as well as common-law spouses whose relationship has ended with the death of one of the parties or a separation lasting at least one year. The general rule applied is that upon the dissolution of the marriage or the ending of the common-law relationship, all unadjusted pensionable earnings of either spouse during the eligible years of cohabitation are added together, and one-half of the total is credited to each spouse's Canada Pension Plan or provincial pension plan account.

The method by which the credits are divided is related to the contributions made by the respective spouses to the Canada Pension Plan. A wife who never worked and was therefore never eligible to contribute to the Canada Pension Plan but whose husband always made the maximum allowable contribution would benefit to a large degree from the division scheme. If, however, the spouses had incomes throughout the marriage that were relatively equal, their pension credits would remain relatively unchanged.

Your precise entitlement to a sharing of Canada Pension Plan credits can vary and you should therefore consult your lawyer during the discussion of property division to determine whether or not you are entitled to a credit and, if so, to what form of credit.

FINANCIAL STATEMENTS

Returning to some of the more practical considerations of property division, we should think about the all-important Financial Statement for a moment. If spousal support, child support or property division are claimed by either party, Financial Statements must be filed. Only in very limited circumstances of uncontested divorces where all financial matters have been resolved will Financial Statements be dispensed with. Each province has its own particular form of Financial Statement.

It is very likely that the first document a lawyer will present you with, after a family law Client History form, is the particular province's Financial Statement. You will be sent home to complete the form to the best of your ability and return it to the office. So much depends upon the accuracy of this statement that it must be a full statement, complete, up to date and meaningful. There is no point in trying to avoid a description of an asset, artificially undervaluing an asset or describing it in such vague terms that it cannot be understood. The content of the Financial Statement will be scrutinized by the lawyer for your spouse and, ultimately, by the court.

While it is your job to locate the information and supporting documentation for the Financial Statement, it should be prepared under close supervision by your lawyer. Remember, the form is designed to save time and money by ensuring complete financial disclosure as early as possible in the legal proceedings.

Your all-important credibility in a legal proceeding is at risk if the Financial Statement is not prepared accurately. The courts look with disfavour upon a party who has neglected to give full and complete disclosure. You should remember that these statements are sworn affidavits. Any attempt to mislead the court can draw a negative inference from the judge.

Your credibility is also at risk if the form is not honestly completed and honestly kept up to date throughout the proceedings. It may be necessary, from time to time, to file amended statements showing updates and corrections. I have seen a client's case improved immeasurably at trial when they have withstood a probing cross-examination of the Financial Statement and can demonstrate to the judge and the opposing counsel their total honesty and accuracy in completing the statement.

In some cases, clients worry about the disclosure of confidential financial information in a public proceeding. Many provinces have now incorporated provisions into their rules of procedure that allow the Financial Statement to be shielded. If this is a concern, you should immediately consult with your lawyer so that you receive that type of protection if appropriate.

PAYING THE JUDGMENT

Payment of the judgment can be an interesting exercise. The goal of the formula provided by provincial family law is to calculate a sum of money that is owed by one spouse to the other. The judgment can therefore be paid simply by a cash payment from one spouse to another or can be paid by the transfer of particular pieces of property. If, for example, the court finds that the wife is entitled to $100,000 for her interest in the family property and finds that the matrimonial home has an equity of $100,000, the court could simply order that the matrimonial home be placed in the wife's name alone in satisfaction of her interest in the family property.

SOME TAX CONSIDERATIONS

One of the issues that will arise during your discussions of the way in which property will be treated in your case is income tax considerations. In this section, I have set out some considerations that may arise concerning income tax.

Canadian income tax law is affected by changes on an almost annual basis, so it is important for you and your lawyer to check with the income tax law specialists prior to entering into any Final Agreement. The income tax consequences of property settlements, support payments, investments, RRSPs and even legal fees can have a significant impact on the net value of the settlement. In the following list, I have set out some of the more common tax considerations. Keep them in mind as you consider your options.

1. Sometimes a settlement of the property and support issues in a separation and divorce will involve the transfer of property from one spouse to the other. The income tax laws generally do not affect such transfers, as they might impede fair settlements of family property claims, but rather work in a way to encourage settlements. However, transfers of capital property between spouses are deemed to take place at the transferor's adjusted cost base. For tax purposes, spouses are able to "roll over" capital property. Any tax status of the particular piece of property rolls over from the transferor to the transferee. Whenever property is being transferred from one spouse to the other as a part of a settlement, extra

caution must be exercised to ensure that undesirable tax consequences do not flow from the transaction.

2. When dealing with the matrimonial home, it is important to know that each family is only entitled to have one principal residence. A principal residence can be sold and any gain is tax free. If a family has more than one property, then only one property can be designated the principal residence to avoid income tax on possible capital gains. Professional advice is needed where there are two or more possible principal residences. This advice is needed prior to settling the case; after, it will be too late.

3. All or any part of a spouse's RRSP can be transferred to the other spouse's RRSP without any income tax consequences. Again, Canada Customs and Revenue Agency has set specific conditions that must be met. Review these conditions with your lawyer and financial planner prior to concluding the settlement.

4. The Income Tax Act also contains a number of rules concerning income attribution. This means that even if one spouse owns a particular property, income from that property (or gain in its value when sold) might be attributed to the other spouse for income tax purposes. Therefore, an unsuspecting spouse may end up with an unpleasant tax burden. Prior to settling your case, review with your lawyer or financial planner the income attribution rules that govern these transactions.

5. This will come as a shock to many people, but married persons may be held responsible for their spouse's unpaid tax liabilities in certain limited circumstances. For example, if one spouse transfers property to the other spouse by way of a gift or sale, there may be joint and several liability for a spouse's unpaid tax to the extent that the actual fair market value of the property exceeded the amount paid. Again, review these rules prior to settling. Once an agreement has been signed, a spouse who finds himself or herself suddenly saddled with an unwanted tax burden may have little recourse.

6. In some circumstances, legal fees paid may be deductible. Ask your lawyer to identify in his or her bill those fees that are directly attributable to enforcement of child support or spousal support. This area has recently been open to interpretation and there have been several court cases, so speak with your lawyer to make sure that you receive the maximum benefit.

7. A spouse's release of marital and support rights in return for a property settlement will not give rise to a taxable disposition of property.

8. As of January 1, 2001, for all purposes of the Income Tax Act, same-sex common-law couples are treated the same as other couples. This means that they are eligible for the same tax benefits. It also means they are subject to the same obligations as married couples and opposite-sex common-law couples.

Every Budget brings changes to the income tax laws. The above points that I have provided in an overview form are designed to alert you to some of the more common income tax considerations at the time of separation and divorce. These points are up to date as of the date of this publication. However, because the income tax laws inevitably will change, I defer to your financial planner and family law lawyer. They will provide you with the most current information and will know how to apply for the maximum benefit in your case.

SOME STRATEGIC CONSIDERATIONS

I would like to offer some tips and strategic considerations with respect to property. Every year, I make several presentations to hundreds of financial planners. The purpose of these sessions is to provide these planners with an overview of family law so that they can be in a better position to advise those of their clients who are in troubled marriages or are experiencing separation and divorce. In some cases, these financial planners are providing advice to individuals who are considering common-law cohabitation, first and even second or subsequent marriages and so on. When I set out a few of the strategic considerations, some of the financial planners are shocked at the cynicism and mercenary attitudes taken by couples at the time of separation and divorce. I describe real-life instances, cynical perhaps, but they were very real. Consider the following as you go forward with your property discussions:

1. I recommend that you consult with a financial planner as you go forward with any separation and divorce. Financial planners can provide a great deal of advice that is generally not available from lawyers. Lawyers are trained to deal with legal problems and we, like others, must rely on other professionals to give guidance on tax issues, investment options and financial strategies.

2. Occupation of a matrimonial home can be a key consideration in the way in which a case unfolds. If a spouse maintains possession of a home and there are children involved, it is more likely that the spouse will have custody of the children. The reverse is true as well, that is, the spouse who obtains custody has a very good argument to

be left in possession of the matrimonial home because that would likely be in the children's interests. Either way, possession of the home is a critical consideration. I have met both men and women who tell me that they cannot continue to reside under the same roof as their spouse. Their bags are packed; they're ready to go. Good lawyers advise them, however, that remaining in the home until custody and property division are resolved is a very wise strategic move. Moving out leaves the other spouse not only in control of the home but with a leg on in a custody claim.

3. Following on the previous point, the spouse who has custody will automatically receive child support in accordance with the Child Support Guidelines. These Guidelines are driven by the gross annual income of the spouse who is paying child support. You can see how the dominoes begin to fall when a spouse obtains possession of the home and then custody of the children and then child support in accordance with the Child Support Guidelines.

4. If a spouse is left in possession of the home on even an interim basis, the other spouse, who is no longer in possession, can fairly be asked to contribute to the costs of operating that home pending its sale or the trial. You can see how quickly one spouse can lose all leverage and negotiation power simply by moving out and giving up possession of the home. I have met with many spouses, both men and women, who moved out of a matrimonial home and soon found themselves not only out of that home but with limited contact with their children, a child support obligation and a financial obligation to continue to maintain the home itself. In addition, they had to rent their own accommodation and look after themselves financially.

5. Let me start this point with a short story. I met a young man who was very successful financially. His marriage, however, was in trouble, and he came to consult me about what would happen if he separated from his wife. We discussed his interest in maintaining a relationship with his three children. We looked at his stock portfolio, the home, their cottage and various investments. We also discussed the fact that his wife had stayed home to look after the children and had been out of the workforce for some time. After reviewing all of the factors, I provided him with an opinion about what would happen if he separated in the immediate future. I told him that he would not be a candidate for custody of his children because due to work obligations, he had a limited involvement in their upbringing. I explained that he would likely pay spousal support for an indefinite

period of time and at least until his wife had retrained and re-entered the workforce. I calculated for him the exact amount of child support and the likely amount of spousal support that he would pay. I also explained how his assets and the assets of the family would be divided roughly equally. He was in shock to say the least. I asked him if he intended to go forward with the separation. His answer was that he was going to "think about it." He went back to his marriage and became very involved in the upbringing of the children. He also pressured his wife into returning to school and getting back into the workforce. He began to manage his finances in a different way. For example, he stopped his rapid paying off of the mortgage on the family home. In particular, he stopped using inherited money to pay family expenses. A few years later, he returned to my office ready to separate. The outcome would now be very different. The message in this short story is that spouses need to be aware of the benefits of strategic planning, but also the possibility that their spouse has done some strategic planning. I have met many people who are patiently tolerating intolerable marriages in order to strategically advance their case for the day that they, ultimately, decide to separate.

6. On a similar note, I recall a case where a woman consulted me about needing to separate and divorce. Her main complaint was her husband's lack of involvement with the children. He was a workaholic and she did not see much of a future in their relationship. I gave her a full opinion about what would happen if she separated and she went home to think about it. About six months later, she contacted me just for follow-up and told me that she had decided to stay in the marriage because, miraculously, her husband was now very involved in the upbringing of the children. They had come close to separating, but he had "seen the light" and was now a reformed father. He was also working less, had taken over management of the family finances, was even encouraging her to return to school and get a job . . . I asked her whether he had "seen the light" or seen a lawyer. I explained to her that he might simply be positioning himself for a more strategically advantageous separation in a few years. Sadly, I was right.

7. Bottom line? Be aware. Know your options. Work strategically with your lawyer. Choices are interconnected.

CONCLUSION

Marriage is a financial partnership. The assets and liabilities of the partnership are going to be divided equitably at the time of separation. As we have seen, property has a very broad definition; the valuations of property can vary, and there are special rules governing exemptions for particular pieces of property and even the possibility of unequal division in limited circumstances. Your lawyer should review with you the various choices and options available to you in seeking to divide your property.

Both you and your lawyer have a special role in the preparation of the information that will guide the court in its effort to divide your family property. Your primary goal is to ensure that your lawyer prepares, on your behalf, the most complete, honest and accurate financial statement possible. It is your job to ensure that the statement retains that status from the beginning of the proceeding through to the trial, if necessary.

CHECKLIST

1. Have you prepared a comprehensive list of all property that both you and your spouse acquired between the date of marriage and the date of separation?

2. Have you developed a comprehensive list of the assets and liabilities at the time you got married?

3. Do you understand your provincial formula for division of property?

4. Have you remembered to include debts and liabilities? The net value is divided after deduction of debts and liabilities.

5. Have you consulted a financial planner?

6. Have you considered obtaining professional valuations of your property?

7. Have you discussed with your lawyer, accountant or financial planner the possible tax consequences of the options?

8. Do you understand the categories of exempt property for your province such as inheritances, gifts and traceable property?

9. Have you considered the way in which the property was acquired, maintained or managed?

10. Do you understand the calculation for unequal division?

(Continued)

11. Do you understand the special status of the matrimonial home and its importance strategically in a separation and divorce?

12. Do you understand the special rules with respect to possession of a matrimonial home at separation?

13. Do you understand that it is the value of assets, not the assets themselves, that is divided?

14. Are there pensions involved? Have they been valued properly? Is there a danger of double-dipping in your situation, where the value of the pension as an asset is divided and then it is also used to pay support?

15. Have you received a Financial Statement from your lawyer and completed it honestly and with reference to every possible asset and liability?

16. Have you read the list of strategic tips at the conclusion of this chapter? Keep your guard up.

6

THE CHILDREN

~

Every Parent's Top Priority

It is safe to say that custody of children can be *the* issue in a family dispute. No other issue dredges up such strong emotions or such total commitment by a parent to the achievement of a particular result. It is not uncommon to hear one parent threaten the other with a "scorched earth" policy in the approach to custody of children.

In this chapter we will examine the meaning of custody and access, the considerations used by the court in ordering it and some of the more important features of custody and access orders. We will also examine the methods for dispute resolution in custody, as well as their costs and some of the tactical considerations. At the end of this chapter, I have included a new section entitled "What Will We Tell the Children?" Read it.

Even though I have been at this work now for over 25 years, I am still shocked at what parents will put their children through at the time of divorce. Perhaps the most incredible aspect of the pain they inflict on their children during divorce is the lengths to which a parent will go in justifying their behaviour. Somehow, everything a parent does is designed to "advance the best interests of the children." Under that banner, I have seen parents deny their children vacations to Florida, block summer vacations at favourite camps, force the sale of homes close to a child's favourite school, prevent Christmases with both sides of the family and on and on, all in the name of protecting their child's best interests.

To me, the cause of pain to children at the time of separation and divorce is rooted in one thing and one thing only: conflict between their parents. Certainly, children are heartbroken about their parents separating, but most children can, over time, adjust to separation and divorce. What they cannot adjust to is standing in a no man's land between two fighting parents, both of whom profess to have their best interests at heart.

Canadian family law states that neither parent has a head start in obtaining custody of a child. If the parents cannot agree, then the court will decide for them. The court will look to see who can best care for this child and will make the appropriate order. Unfortunately, this has created a foot race between parents to run each other down in the eyes of the court in order to prove that they should have custody. In many cases, it has become a direct incentive for conflict. We will see how that perverse result arose when we consider the concept of joint custody later in this chapter.

My own views have evolved considerably over the last few years and I am now a firm believer that our laws should provide that each parent is equally entitled to time with the children and to have a role in decision-making about their children, unless a court orders otherwise. In other words, our courts should be starting with a presumption of joint custody of children and only moving to a custody-access arrangement if one parent is clearly not up to the job of being a full joint custodial parent. I honestly believe that this would contribute to a decline in hostilities in Canadian families at the time of separation and divorce.

There has been talk over the last few years about amending our Divorce Act, to move away from the concepts of custody and access to concepts such as shared parenting, presumptions of joint custody or co-parenting. These amendments would have been of huge benefit to Canadian families, but, alas, these changes have fallen by the wayside and will likely not be revisited any time soon. This means that we have to work with the system that we have, as broken as it is with respect to custody and access. Let's consider some of the concepts.

CUSTODY AND ACCESS

Both federal and provincial family laws contain provisions with respect to custody of and access to children. The Divorce Act provides the court with the power to make an order with respect to custody of or access to a child at the time it grants the divorce judgment and on an interim basis (meaning until a final order can be made). Virtually all provincial and territorial family laws contain similar provisions and, as described earlier, the choice of a provincial, territorial or federal law is dictated entirely by whether there is a request for a divorce for legally married spouses. This is another type of "corollary relief" under the Divorce Act. It is an extra, related order made at the time the court grants the divorce.

The Divorce Act states that an order for custody of a child or access to a child can be made in favour of one or more persons. It is this language that enables the court to make a sole custody award in favour of one parent or to divide custody between two parents by means of a joint custody order. Both the federal Divorce Act and provincial and territorial family laws contemplate custody being with more than one parent or, in some circumstances, with a non-parent (see Chapter 13—Grandparents and Other Interested Persons). We'll examine these terms in more detail in a moment, but it is important to first understand that the court has a wide discretion in deciding who shall have custody of and access to children.

WHO IS A CHILD?

The Divorce Act defines a child of the marriage as a child who is under the age of majority and still in the care of one or both parents, or a child who is of the age of majority or over but is still being cared for by the parents by reason of illness, disability or other reason and is therefore unable to withdraw from their care or obtain the necessaries of life on their own. In this latter case, this usually means children who are suffering from some mental or physical disability and must stay with the parents.

When clients discuss with lawyers their rights and responsibilities with respect to their children in the context of separation and divorce, we usually explain to parents that responsibility for a child continues until about the age of 23 if the child goes on to university. This means that parental responsibility extends from birth to adulthood. The court can make a custody order with respect to children whether they are one month old or 23 years of age—or more!

The main reason the responsibility continues is financial. Child support orders typically continue until a child has left school.

This can include the completion of their first degree at university, which is approximately at the age of 22 or 23. Having said that, a lot depends on the child involved. Some children need an extra period of time at the end of high school to prepare for university. Some children take a year off in order to work and save money to assist with their university expenses. Some children attend school part-time or require remedial work. All of these matters are taken into consideration.

In addition, there have been some cases in Canada where courts have considered that, for this particular child, one undergraduate degree is not adequate to allow that child to truly complete their education. Parents have been required to contribute to post-graduate studies for some children. We will discuss this more in the section dealing with support (see Chapter 7—Support). My point here is that issues of custody and access of children may continue for a very long time.

This may be more of a financial consideration than a custodial one. Courts are reluctant to make custody orders in relation to children who are in their teens and beyond. These young people will live where they wish, but for the purposes of such things as child support, they will certainly be considered a child of the marriage.

In order for the court to have jurisdiction to make a custody order, the child must be in the jurisdiction of that particular court. For example, for a Saskatchewan judge to order custody of a child to one party, that child must reside in Saskatchewan.

THE CHILD'S BEST INTERESTS

The expression "the child's best interests" is an important one in custody and access matters. The determination of what is best for a particular child is the overriding consideration in all applications to the court concerning children. Provincial family laws have made an effort to set out considerations that the court should follow when attempting to determine the best interests of a particular child. Ontario's Children's Law Reform Act, for example, provides a list of examples of the needs and circumstances of a child that should be considered:

- the love, affection and emotional ties between the child and (i) each person entitled to or claiming custody of or access to the child, (ii) other members of the child's family who reside with the child, and (iii) persons involved in the care and upbringing of the child,
- the views and preferences of the child, where such views and preferences can reasonably be ascertained,
- the length of time the child has lived in a stable home environment,
- the ability and willingness of each person applying for custody of the child to provide the child with guidance and education, the necessities of life and any special needs of the child,
- any plans proposed for the care and upbringing of the child,
- the permanence and stability of the family unit with which it is proposed that the child will live and

- the relationship by blood or through an adoption order between the child and each person who is a party to the application.

The above list is not intended to be exhaustive, but does provide a very broad guide for assessing a child's best interests.

Nationally, the following general considerations have emerged as guides for the court in making custody and access determinations:

- the physical well-being of the child,
- the emotional well-being of the child and security of the child,
- the plans for the education and maintenance of the child as described by those requesting custody or access,
- the financial position of the parents, so as to be able to apportion responsibility for support,
- the religious or ethical needs of the child,
- the moral and ethical standards of the person seeking custody or access according to local community standards and
- the sensitivity of the person seeking custody or access as a parent and, in particular, that person's understanding of this particular child's needs.

OTHER CONSIDERATIONS

In addition to the above statutory items, the courts will be interested in other important considerations.

The Psychological Parent

Some experts describe the assessment process as a search for the "psychological parent." It is not uncommon, particularly for younger children, to have a greater bond with one parent than the other. This may be related in some ways to the child's stage of development and the sex of the parent. Nonetheless, the person doing the assessment and the court are searching for the person who is best able to meet the child's needs. If the psychological parent has certain shortcomings, such as inadequate resources, the court can address that through financial support from the other parent. This search for the psychological parent can present quite a dilemma when that parent is not the biological parent of the child. In some cases the psychological parent may be a grandparent or other family member and could even be a daycare worker or babysitter.

Behaviour of the Parents

Another consideration is the behaviour of the parents. The court is not supposed to consider a person's past conduct when making custody or access orders unless the conduct is relevant to the ability of that person to act as a parent. The Divorce Act is also explicit in its direction to the courts and divorcing couples to consider which parent is most likely to facilitate the maximum contact for the child with both parents.

In other words, a factor in determining what is best for the child is which parent is most likely to facilitate an ongoing relationship with both parents. If a parent seems obstructive or appears to be reluctant to allow another parent's contact with the child, that person runs the risk of not being the custodial parent.

This type of provision has come to be known as a "friendly parent" rule. It has the effect of each parent trying to present himself or herself to the court as "friendly" to the other, so as not to jeopardize a claim for custody.

The court will concern itself with conduct by a parent that may adversely affect the emotional, psychological or spiritual welfare of a child. These concerns can extend to a parent's relationship with a third party, a parent's sexual preference, the presence of physical (e.g., drug/alcohol) or mental (e.g., gambling/cults) addictions and, in one recent Ontario case, whether the parent smoked to such an extent that it aggravated a child's asthma. In this case, a judge ordered both parents to not smoke around the child. I think we will see this issue grow in importance as courts come to understand the risk posed from secondhand smoke (you now have another good reason to quit).

It is not uncommon when speaking with a parent seeking custody of a child to hear the parent's invitation to "speak with the child," as if there must be conclusive evidence of who should have custody of this particular child. Both parents may well have received assurances from the child that the child wished to be in the custody of that particular parent. Upon subsequent investigation, it may be found that the child is really attempting to communicate that he or she wishes to be in the custody of *both* parents and does not wish to see the separation take place. Similarly, some children do not wish to be seen to be preferring one parent over another and often express a preference that they feel the parent wishes to hear.

Courts have had to deal with the issue of whether a spouse can be violent with his or her partner and, yet, still be a good parent. Courts are beginning to understand that violence in the home is mutually exclusive of good parenting and provides a horrible role model for the children.

Another issue that the courts have been forced to deal with is the role of new partners. In some cases, a mother or father has moved on to a new relationship that puts the children at risk when they are in that particular household. In some cases, drugs, criminal activity or other high-risk behaviour has put the child at peril. This places the other parent at odds with the former spouse's new partner. Remarkably, lawyers do see parents who are prepared to put a new partner ahead of their children's interests and thereby lose an opportunity for custody of their children.

At the other end of the spectrum, lawyers have seen cases, such as one in Saskatchewan, where the court considered the father's new wife to be the best parent of the three adults involved and was grateful that she had arrived on the scene to offer parenting to these children. So, in some cases, a new partner can be a stabilizing force that enhances an opportunity for custody of children post-separation.

Increasingly, we see cases of interference with a parent's relationship with a child. I mentioned earlier the friendly parent rule. This is the other side of that coin, where a parent actively poisons a relationship between a parent and child and undermines it at every opportunity. The court takes a dim view of this behaviour and, in extreme cases, will change custody from one parent to the other, if that is the only way in which a child can be guaranteed to have a relationship with both parents.

Unsubstantiated allegations of abuse are almost routine now for family law lawyers. Children's aid societies regularly spend millions of dollars in valuable time and resources investigating weak, unsubstantiated or malicious reports of abuse in the context of a separation and divorce. Not only is this a waste of precious resources by agencies that are already terribly underfunded, but it jeopardizes the credibility of those who report genuine abuse. I have recently been involved in two long-standing cases in which parents made numerous false allegations to children's aid societies over a period of years. In both cases, the false allegations ultimately resulted in that parent losing any prospect of custody of the child involved. The parent simply lost all credibility with any authorities and with the court.

The Child's Views and Preferences

This raises the question of the value of the child's views and preferences. The answer lies in the particular child's age and level of maturity. There are two ways of looking at this question of age and maturity. First, as the child grows older, he or she is better able to articulate his or her wishes. On the other hand, as the child grows older, it is more difficult to impose on him or her a situation in which he or she does not wish to live. The court recognizes this and makes an effort to ascertain the child's wishes and preferences and to give follow-through on them if the court feels that the child was able to objectively form the opinion.

The court is very conscious of the ability of a parent to "assist" the child in forming an opinion. In extreme situations, this is sometimes called "poisoning the child's mind" against the other parent. In most cases, it is simply a case of undue influence, with a parent pressuring a child to pick them over the other parent. Here, we have seen all manner of pathetic behaviour by parents, including outright bribery, vague hints at suicide and even threats to terminate the relationship and move away, never to be seen again. Where it is evident that a parent is pressuring a child, the court will reevaluate the weight that it wishes to give to the child's desires. In other words, the court will try to take the pressure off the child and let them know that their views will be downplayed because of suspected parental influence.

When the court considers it necessary, the child's preferences can be obtained by:

- calling the child as a witness in court, although most courts discourage children as witnesses in a courtroom,

- arranging a private interview between the child and the judge in chambers (a recent Ontario case saw a judge arrange for another judge in the courthouse to meet privately with the children to obtain their views and preferences and then had that judge report back),

- having an assessment done by a childcare professional who would later report back to the court (more on assessements in a moment) and

- providing the child with his or her own lawyer to assist in determining and describing the child's wishes.

Siblings

Another consideration in custody and access matters is the presence of brothers and sisters. The general rule, whether under the Divorce Act or provincial law, is that brothers and sisters should not be separated. A strong effort is made to preserve the family despite the absence of one parent. Children often see the presence of brothers and sisters as a very important support during difficult times.

It is difficult to imagine the court concluding, in any but the most unusual circumstances, that the separation of children could be in their best interests. Unusual circumstances where it has occurred include one Alberta case, where a court separated a 15-year-old daughter and a 14-year-old son because they simply wanted to live with different parents. In one New-foundland case, a judge separated siblings because one parent wanted to move and a child wished to go with that parent. Even when this happens, the courts will try to ensure that some arrangement is made to keep the children in contact with each other and with the other parent.

This raises an interesting point where there is more than one child: If one child expresses a strong preference for a particular parent and the other child expresses a strong relationship with the sibling, then one child's views and preferences may end up governing the outcome of the custody arrangement. For example, a younger brother may be very attached to an older brother and equally attached to both parents. If the older brother insists on residing, for example, with his father, the younger brother may be pulled along as a result.

Tender Years Doctrine

An interesting concept that is described in custody and access cases is the "tender years doctrine." This doctrine considered it to be a general rule that the mother was entitled to custody and care of a child during its nurturing years. This came to mean that any child, regardless of who was actually his or her psychological parent, would be given to the mother until at least the age of seven years.

Obviously the tender years doctrine has undergone some revision over the last decade, with the emphasis now being almost exclusively on what is best for the child, regardless of the child's age. Some courts have commented that the "tender years doctrine" is now irrelevant given the "best interest" test. I still consider this doctrine to be a factor in decisions around very young children.

At the other end of the spectrum, we see a reluctance in the court to even make custody orders where children are clearly approaching the status of being an "adult child" or a "mature minor." In one British Columbia case, a judge was asked to make a custody order in respect of a disabled child who was, in effect, an adult. In another B.C. case, an adult developmentally delayed child was permitted status in the parents' litigation. I suspect we will see more and more of these unusual situations as families struggle to deal with older dependent children.

ASSESSMENTS

One method that the court will use to address these questions is called an "assessment." It can be ordered by the court against the wishes of the parties or it can be arranged on a voluntary basis. During the assessment, a skilled professional, often a social worker or psychologist, will meet with the family and the child(ren) to assess the child's needs and the ability of the parents to meet those needs. The assessment can take several visits with those involved and will often produce a recommendation for the court.

Whether through the court process itself or through an assessment, some of the issues that the court and the assessor look for include whether the child's needs are being met in a positive environment, who the child has bonded most closely with, the sexual orientation of the parents, the child's relationship with brothers and sisters and other family members, the child's religious and moral upbringing and his or her biological ties with each parent.

Assessments should be used only in difficult cases and will not be ordered automatically. Assessments are also very expensive and very time-consuming. It is not unusual to see an assessment cost several thousand dollars and become very intrusive to the child's and parent's lives. Assessors will meet with the children's teachers, friends, aunts, uncles, coaches, doctors and anyone else that may have some insight on what would be best for this particular child and this particular family.

CUSTODY

Before examining the circumstances in which custody is ordered and the methods by which it is ordered, it is important to understand the full meaning of the term. One judge defined custody as follows: "To award one parent the exclusive custody of a child is to clothe that parent, for whatever period he or she is awarded the custody, with full parental control over, and ultimate parental responsibility for, the care, upbringing and education of the child, generally to the exclusion of the right of the other parent to interfere in decisions that are made in exercising that control or in carrying out that responsibility."

The distinction between custody and access is the difference between having the right to make *all* decisions regarding a child as opposed to simply being entitled to information about the child's health, education and welfare and occasional time with the child.

The changes that have occurred in the area of custody and access over the last few years have been directed towards a sharing of this formerly exclusive decision-making power by the parents. Non-custodial parents have sought to enhance (1) their entitlement to information, (2) their entitlement to an opinion in decisions affecting the child and (3) to be able to share or have sole responsibility for important decisions affecting the child.

The traditional expressions "custody" and "access" have been challenged of late and separating couples have begun to use terms such as "co-parenting," "shared parenting" and "cooperative parenting." Each of these new terms is an attempt to describe the new division of responsibilities for the child.

However, the bottom line is that there are two types of orders with respect to custody of a child: sole custody or joint custody. Sole custody gives all of the aforementioned decision-making power to one parent and leaves the other parent with an entitlement to time with the child and information. As we will see in a moment, these sole custody orders are becoming increasingly laden with conditions and stipulations that detract from the full traditional custodial power.

Joint Custody

The other type of custody order is joint custody. Where a joint custody order is made, the parents (or other persons, if that is the case) share the custodial decision-making responsibility. Some parents have made a distinction between "joint physical custody" and "joint decision-making responsibility" over a child. In the case of joint physical custody, the child resides in two homes for fixed periods of time. These arrangements can include splitting a week, where the child resides with one parent for half of the week and the other parent for the other half of the week, alternating weeks, alternating months and, in some cases, alternating six-month periods or alternating years.

While the child is in the physical custody of one of the parents, that particular parent has all necessary custodial decision-making power and vice versa when the child changes homes. If the arrangement is expected to work in a way that meets the child's needs, there is a requirement for a high level of cooperation between the parents.

The case law on joint custody continues to evolve, but the current state of affairs generally sees the court ordering joint custody in circumstances where the parents consent to such an order. In other words, the courts are unwilling to impose a joint custody arrangement on the parents or the child if there is evidence of a lack of cooperation and if it would be against the wishes of one of the parents.

A recent case from the Ontario Court of Appeal sent a chilling message to parents seeking joint custody: If you cannot cooperate, then there will be no joint custody orders from the court. The facts of that particular case were unfortunate. One of the individuals involved was an extremely uncooperative parent, constantly arguing with the other parent, yelling and unable to control emotions. The court easily concluded that this particular parent was not a good candidate for a joint custody arrangement and, therefore, refused to order it. Based on those facts, the overriding message that went out to families was if there is no cooperation, then there will be no joint custody.

This decision had at least one unfortunate consequence in that parents who did not want to enter into joint custody arrangements suddenly realized that there was an incentive to not cooperate. By not cooperating, they were, in effect, exercising a veto over the opportunity for the family to have a joint custody arrangement. In reaction to that, there have been cases where joint custody was ordered over the objections of one parent. If the court determines that the only reason joint custody is not possible is because one parent is, in effect, holding out in the hope of having sole custody, then the court may impose it in any event.

In some cases, the physical custody of the child is not shared and the child resides with one parent exclusively, *but* important decisions are made jointly by the parents. This is sometimes called joint legal custody—as opposed to physical. In some circumstances, a family will call their arrangement "joint custody" and share the major decisions concerning the children, but have a schedule of time that looks much more like a traditional custody-access arrangement. In these situations, the non-custodial parent may see the child every second weekend from Friday night after school to Sunday evening or even Monday morning, dropping him or her off at school. This non-custodial parent might have an overnight visit in the alternate weeks. Even though they are not sharing time equally, the parents still call it joint custody to acknowledge their commitment to parenting.

JOINT CUSTODY AND CHILD SUPPORT

Joint custody orders, particularly those for joint physical custody, may result in a corresponding reduction in the need to pay child support. So, for example, where the parents are of a relatively equal earning power and there is joint physical custody, it is unlikely that child support from one parent to the other would be required.

I recently completed a case in which the parents of the children were police officers. They had been with the force for almost exactly the same period of time, earned the same money and had the same pension contributions. They worked shifts and were able to share responsibility for the children on an almost exact 50/50 basis. As their responsibilities were identical, it made no sense, economic or otherwise, to have child support flowing from one household to the other.

The Child Support Guidelines contemplate this effect of joint custody on the child support obligation. The Guidelines suggest that if the actual division of responsibility for the child on a day-to-day basis is a 60/40 split or more, then the Child Support Guidelines do not apply. (For more information about the Child Support Guidelines, see Chapter 7). This has caused some people to oppose joint custody on the grounds that it is simply a means by which non-custodial parents can avoid obligations for child support. No doubt some parents have been motivated by financial considerations, but generally the advantages of joint custody exceed such disadvantages.

Some recent court decisions have considered this issue of altering the amount of child support to take into consideration the existence of a joint custody arrangement. The court has a number of choices. It can simply leave the child support as is. In other words, one parent pays full child support even though he or she has the children more than 40 per cent of the time. Alternatively, the court can order a modest adjustment in the level of child support to account for the increased time that the children may be spending with one parent. Finally, the court can simply calculate a setoff, whereby the court calculates what the respective parents would be paying to each other if either of them had sole custody and then offsets the two amounts. If one parent is earning more than the other, then they pay the difference in child support. This will be considered in more detail in the child support section coming up in Chapter 7.

The reason I mention this now is that the obstacle to joint custody for some families is the fear that there will be a corresponding reduction in child support and someone will be unable to run their household. In such circumstances, I recommend to families that they simply consider paying the full amount of child support, even though one parent may have the children more than 40 per cent of the time, and then see how matters evolve. It is a small price to pay for one or two years to see if the children actually stay in that routine. If they do, and a reduction in child support is called for, the parents can then budget for a reduction.

Simply chopping child support off the minute one parent's time with the children exceeds 40 per cent makes no sense for either the household budget or the children. In addition, the legal fees spent arguing over whether there should be a child support reduction for a couple of years exceeds the amount of support that would flow to the children in any event. The bottom line here is that being flexible with each other around the joint custody arrangement and the child support arrangement makes a lot of sense.

ADVICE ON JOINT CUSTODY

A word of advice for those who would attempt joint custody arrangements: They do not work unless there is a high degree of cooperation and flexibility between the parents. Where a child alternates between two homes, it can be particularly difficult to manage the child's affairs, whether they be with respect to clothing, sporting activities, hobbies, visits with friends, visits with relatives or other pursuits, unless there is maximum cooperation. The goal of joint custody is not the convenience of the parents, but to maintain maximum contact between the child and the parents in pursuit of the child's best interests.

In every lawyer's practice there are cases in which the parents clearly cannot cooperate or even where there is violence, and then it is obvious that joint custody would not be appropriate. However, I can state on the basis of my experience over the last 26 years that most contemporary families are well-suited to joint custody arrangements. They may or may not divide the child's time equally between two households, they may or may not decide to share all of the decision-making, but with a little effort and cooperation they are more than able to work out an arrangement by which they agree to share the parenting of the children. In some cases, they even end up with a traditional "sole custody-access arrangement" but choose to call it joint custody out of respect for the level of involvement both parents have in the children's lives.

Where there is the absence of violence or some other grossly inappropriate behaviour, I strongly urge most families to enter into a joint custody arrangement and spend their time, effort and legal fees to craft the meaning of joint custody for their family. As you will see from the upcoming section, in any event, most families negotiate restrictions on the traditional meaning of sole custody. Why not show respect for the parenting that has been done by calling the future arrangement "joint custody" but tailoring it to your own needs?

CONDITIONS ON SOLE CUSTODY

Even where sole custody awards are made, it is not unusual for the courts to impose conditions upon the arrangement. For example, it is now common to see a restriction placed on the mobility of a custodial parent. Non-custodial parents who wish to protect their access visits have been seeking, in Separation Agreements and in court orders, specific geographic restrictions on the custodial parent's mobility. These terms can take the form of specific references to living within a radius of a city (e.g., residing within a 10-kilometre radius of the city of Calgary).

The Divorce Act provides the court with the power to impose a condition on the custodial parent that requires him or her to notify the other parent, at least 30 days in advance, if he or she intends to change his or her place of residence, and provide the planned date and location of the move. The court can require an even longer period of notice.

The Supreme Court of Canada has made an important decision in the area of mobility rights in a case known as Gordon v. Goertz. In this case, the Supreme Court said that there was no legal presumption in favour of the right of a custodial parent to move away from their traditional residence. The custodial parent has the right to decide where the child will live, but that right is subject to the right of an access parent to apply for a change in custody if the move is considered a material change in circumstances. If the child's needs are likely to be well served by remaining with the custodial parent, and if that offsets any loss in contact with the other parent, then custody will likely not be varied and the custodial parent's move will be permitted by the court.

However, the courts consider a number of factors, including the existing custody and access arrangement, the relationships between the child and each parent, the desirability of maximizing contact between the child and both parents, the views of the child, the custodial parent's reason for moving, the expected disruption to the child of a change in custody and the disruption to the child upon the removal from his or her traditional family, schools and community.

There is a debate emerging as to how much emphasis should be placed on the custodial parent's reason for moving. Initially the courts were only interested in this as it relates to the parent's ability to meet the needs of the child. In such cases, the courts were prepared to defer to the wisdom of the custodial parent in deciding to move. Lately, there is a trend of cases showing a greater willingness by the courts to look over the shoulder of the custodial parent and second-guess the need for the move.

The approach in these mobility cases is for the custodial parent to alert the non-custodial parent of the intention to move. The non-custodial parent then asks the court to block the custodial parent's move. The court then makes a preliminary decision as to whether the move would be a material change in circumstances for the child. If it would be a material change in circumstances, then the court undertakes a fresh inquiry into what is in the child's best interest. These cases can be very emotional and sometimes require an assessment to assist the court in making a decision about whether a child should be allowed to move.

Another restriction that the courts are prepared to place on the custodial parent concerns the effect of moving on the non-custodial parent's ability to visit the child and the cost of such visits. Where a custodial parent expresses a wish to move farther away from the non-custodial parent and has good reason (e.g., new and better employment), the court may order a reduction in the amount of child support that corresponds to the increased expense of travelling to visit with the child. In one case, where a mother moved from Toronto to Calgary, the father's child support payments were reduced to compensate for travel expenses he would now incur.

Another restriction that non-custodial parents seek concerns the name of the child. It is quite common for parents in negotiating settlements to agree that the child's name will not be changed without the consent of the other parent. This can be an emotional issue. The vast majority of separating couples simply agree to keep the child's name as is.

ACCESS

"Access" has been defined in court cases as being an entitlement to spend time with a child, and during that time to exercise some of the limited powers of a custodial parent. Other jurisdictions, particularly in the United States, call access "visitation rights." It is improper to characterize the time a parent spends with a child as being merely a visit.

Aside from the right to spend time with the child, the right to access can include, at least under the Divorce Act, the requirement as described earlier that a custodial parent give 30 days' notice of his or her intention to move the child. This new provision is in keeping with the emphasis on giving a non-custodial parent information about the child, whether it be with respect to their health, welfare or education. If a non-custodial parent received such notice of the custodial parent's intention to move, he or she would then have the opportunity to request a variation of the custody order.

Other entitlements to information include the right to be kept abreast of the child's performance in school, the child's medical needs and care and the child's general welfare. It is not unusual for courts to provide the non-custodial parent with an opportunity to make a contribution to the child's religious upbringing. In fact, there are many cases in which the non-custodial parent was given an opportunity to expose the child to his or her religion.

The wording and details of an access order can be extremely important. For years it was common for the courts and for lawyers, in drafting Separation Agreements and orders, to stipulate simply that one parent would have custody and the other parent would have "reasonable access" or "liberal access" or "generous access" at times to be agreed upon by the parents. Such provisions might be satisfactory where the parents are co-operative and where they can agree on times to be spent with the child. However, the moment such cooperation breaks down, the non-custodial parent is left in a very difficult position, since it is impossible to obtain court enforcement of these vague expressions. In fact, the non-custodial parent is left in a position of returning to court for a variation of the access provision to provide for specific dates and times.

Parents who anticipate difficulties or require some predictability often stipulate the precise days and times for the access to take place. An example could be as follows: every second weekend from Friday at 6:00 p.m. to Sunday at 6:00 p.m.; alternating Wednesdays from 5:00 p.m. to 8:00 p.m., alternating birthdays, Easter vacations, Christmases, New Year's Eve or other important family events. In the event the access is then denied, the non-custodial parent can point to the specific entitlement when seeking enforcement (for a description of access enforcement difficulties, see Chapter 12—Enforcing Family Law Orders).

Supervised Access

Supervised access is a means of watching the exchange of the child between the parents. In some provinces, facilities will supervise the exchange as a service to the court. It can be ordered or arranged voluntarily and is useful where one of the parents has been accused of sexual or physical abuse. Sometimes the supervision is needed because the custodial parent suffers abuse or the parents cannot be civil with each other at the time of the exchange.

Even where facilities are not available, it may be possible to have an objective, trusted third party supervise the visits. This could be a family member, priest, rabbi, community worker or so on.

STRATEGIC CONSIDERATIONS

Fortunately, fewer and fewer parents are putting their children through the trauma of a full custody trial. The success of mediation in solving custody and access disputes is well known. For a more detailed description of mediation, see Chapter 11—Alternatives to Court. For a description of the type of process your child will experience, should you decide to go to trial, see Chapter 10—Not Settling Your Differences.

On the issue of a trial, or any disputes with respect to custody, cost is an important consideration. When I mention cost here, I mean the financial not the emotional cost. It is not unusual for lawyers, when taking on a custody dispute, to ask for an advance on fees of between $10,000 and $15,000. Custody trials can consume a great deal of court time with absolutely no promise of a monetary recovery at the end. Consequently, lawyers are anxious to ensure that their fees are secure in advance, as the loser of a custody trial is a notoriously unhappy client.

Another consideration in this chapter is the tactical aspects of custody and access. In order to appreciate the tactical considerations, we need to understand the difference between an interim order and a final order. Interim orders are orders that are made pending the final decision of the court. Naturally, it is necessary to make temporary orders with respect to custody of a child until the court has an opportunity for a full consideration of the dispute. This means that the court must consider on an interim basis where the child should reside and who should have full decision-making power with respect to the child's needs.

The courts have, in the past, been very reluctant to move the child from the home of whichever parent has what is known as "*de facto* care and control of the child." This means that whomever has the child at the time the interim application is made is very likely to have custody of the child until the trial. The court will only depart from this general rule if it is clearly not in the child's best interest to remain with that parent. At the trial, the judge will often ask, "Where has the child resided pending this hearing?" "How has he or she been cared for?" "Are the child's needs being met?" "Is the child comfortable?" "Does the child go to a neighbourhood school?" "Are friends near by?" "Is daycare near by?"

You can see that the court will be very reluctant to disturb the child's world if it has been meeting his or her needs. As a result, interim custody often means final custody.

In the chapter dealing with property division (Chapter 5), I mentioned the strategic importance of the matrimonial home. You will recall that the home can be important in deciding which parent will get custody. The parent who gets custody will in turn get full child support under the Child Support Guidelines. I mention here again the important strategic connection between remaining in the home until a custody arrangement has been concluded. Hasty departures from the home will make it difficult for you and your lawyer to negotiate a fair settlement of the custody-access arrangements and the possession of the matrimonial home. You may wish to take a moment to review that section at the end of Chapter 5.

Sadly, there has been an unseemly development in the area of custody and the matrimonial home concerning trumped-up allegations of domestic violence. Domestic violence is a real and a serious concern in Canadian society and we should enforce the Criminal Code quickly and effectively against anyone who is violent towards their spouse or their children. When charges are laid against a violent spouse, that individual is immediately removed from the matrimonial home, usually placed in jail at least overnight and then released on conditions restricting his or her contact with the spouse and, in some cases, children. In many cases, the release restrictions will prohibit the spouse from going within a fixed distance of the matrimonial home. These rules are designed to protect the victim of the domestic violence and the children. The police are involved, the Crown Attorney's Office is involved and, because criminal charges have been laid, the matter becomes an issue to be sorted out in the criminal justice system.

In some such cases, in the context of the separation and divorce proceedings, lawyers will seek, on behalf of a client, a restraining order. This is an order from the civil courts requiring a spouse to stay away from the other spouse, the children or the home. It is also possible to obtain what is known as an order for exclusive possession of the matrimonial home, which effectively gives one spouse control of the matrimonial home until the matter is concluded. These concepts are explained in more detail in Chapter 12, which deals with enforcement. The cost of obtaining a restraining order or an order for exclusive possession in the civil justice system can be expensive. Both clients attend, both lawyers attend and a judge must make a decision. It can cost thousands of dollars to obtain those orders. If criminal charges are laid, lawyers are not involved at the outset, because it is essentially a police matter.

It did not take unscrupulous individuals long to figure out that a false or trumped-up domestic violence allegation would result in a free restraining order and order for exclusive possession of the home. Why go to court and argue in front of a judge when you can simply have the spouse picked up and removed by the police?

I would not raise this issue unless the matter was now prevalent. In the last two years of my own practice, I have seen over a dozen incidents in which the police were called to deal with alleged domestic violence under the flimsiest of circumstances. Individuals were arrested, detained in jail, charged and ultimately acquitted after spending great sums of money on criminal defence lawyers when, clearly, the charges should have not been laid in the first place. In at least one incident that I am aware of, when acquitting the alleged perpetrator, the criminal judge commented in his ruling that the charge should have never been laid in the first place.

I am including these comments in this edition of the book for a number of reasons. First and foremost, this is a gross abuse of scarce resources that genuine victims of domestic violence need. An individual who calls the police and accuses another parent of domestic violence because that parent knocked on a car window and asked for the baby's car seat (true) or because the other parent was unwittingly at the same movie theatre (true) or, in one particularly horrible case, the parent showed up at a police station with self-inflicted wounds accusing the other parent of having attacked them, only to find out that the alleged perpetrator had an airtight alibi showing he was far away with a group of people at the time of the alleged assault (true). These kinds of allegations are preventing police and Crown attorneys from working on real cases of domestic violence.

The second reason I deal with this in the custody section is that these types of false or trumped-up allegations are usually designed to block a parent's attempt to obtain custody or joint custody of children. This means that the children are being punished by the actions of one parent. In some cases, courts are using the presence of unsubstantiated allegations of violence or abuse as a reason to not give that parent custody. False allegations are an abomination in the family justice system and are no different than looking a judge in the eye and lying outright. It is an attempt to mislead the justice system and thereby undermines the work of many good people in the system.

The third reason I raise this in the context of custody is that I have now met too many individuals who have been arrested, jailed and ultimately acquitted—individuals who should have never been charged in the first place. Many have been devastated by their time in jail. I have sat with men while they cried about their experience in a jail. I have met people who have been absolutely shaken to their core by their arrest and became changed people as a result, and I do not mean changed for the better. These people lose confidence in our justice system. They have a hostility for the police and they have a hostility for the justice system, even if they are ultimately acquitted. This is not right. Lawyers, courts and our policy makers need to apply their minds to how to deal with situations in which false allegations and misuse of our criminal justice system contaminate the family law system.

In conclusion, whenever I read the news about the system's inability to enforce a restraining order and protect a genuine victim of domestic violence, I think of the resources wasted on trumped-up or false allegations and wonder if those resources had been targeted more appropriately, whether that individual or those children would have been safer.

The long and the short of it is that family law lawyers are now advising clients to be extraordinarily cautious at the time of marriage breakdown, for fear that inappropriate use of the criminal law process will spill into a family law dispute. It is all well and good to eventually be acquitted, but our criminal justice system is slow, and until the changes are eventually dealt with by a court, perhaps many months or even years later, custody determinations and possession of the matrimonial home may be merely academic.

As I said at the outset, custody is *the* issue in marriage breakdown and therefore may be the most emotionally charged. People under the stress of a collapsing relationship may be hard pressed to put their children's best interests first. At a time when they may need to look out for themselves, they must consider someone even more vulnerable. It is a time not for showing how awful someone else may be as a spouse or parent, but rather how good you are as a parent and how you can offer the softest landing to the children displaced by divorce.

PATERNITY

While not an everyday occurrence, the question of a child's paternity does arise from time to time. In some circumstances it may be a man hoping to establish that he is the father of a child or it could be the mother of a child alleging a man's paternity. In a few cases, it has even been the child attempting to establish paternity.

The reasons vary for undertaking such a procedure in court. One of the very first cases I had when I began to practise involved a young man who had not yet finished high school being confronted by his parents about a neighbour's grandchild. His parents had been enjoying a cup of coffee with the neighbours, admiring their 18-month-old grandchild, who was over playing for the afternoon. When they commented on how cute the baby was, the neighbours dropped the bombshell. "He should be—your son's the father!" When everyone regained consciousness, a paternity suit was launched by the mother of the child alleging that he was indeed the father due to one act of intercourse two years earlier.

In another case, a child needing money for university tracked down her biological father and attempted to prove paternity so she could obtain financial assistance. In another case, a woman who had divorced her first husband and moved away with their two children denied that he was the father of one of them in an attempt to block his access. In return, he sought to prove that he was the father of both of the children.

The law of paternity varies a little from province to province, but the Ontario approach provides a good example of how such issues are tackled by the court. Part III of the Children's Law Reform Act sets out a procedure for "establishment of parentage" by two types of applications:

1.   any person having an interest may apply to the court for a declaration that a male person is recognized in law to be the father of a child or

2. any person may ask for a declaration that a female person is the mother of a child.

It should be noted that the law has eliminated any distinction—in law at least—between children born inside and outside of marriage.

Once the court makes a "declaration" of parentage, it is good for all purposes and binding on third parties. So, if a man was accused of adultery by his wife and she proved he was the father of someone else's child (while still married to her), that would be conclusive proof of the grounds for her divorce.

The Act establishes several "presumptions" designed to assist the court in reaching a conclusion about paternity. If one of the following circumstances exist, then the court will presume that the man in question is the father of the child. It is up to the man to then disprove the presumption.

- The person is married to the mother of the child at the time of the birth of the child.
- The person was married to the mother of the child by a marriage that was terminated by death or judgment of nullity within 300 days before the birth of the child or by divorce where the *decree nisi* was granted within 300 days before the birth of the child.
- The person marries the mother of the child and acknowledges that he is the natural father.
- The person was cohabiting with the mother in a relationship of some permanence at the time of the birth of the child or the child is born within 300 days after they ceased to cohabit.
- The person has certified the child's birth, as the child's father, under the Vital Statistics Act or a similar Act in another jurisdiction in Canada.
- The person has been found or recognized in his lifetime by a court of competent jurisdiction in Canada to be the father of the child.

The following points should be kept in mind.

- If the presumptions apply to more than one man, then no presumption can be made and the court will need to consider the evidence.
- Both the alleged father and child must be alive at the time of the application.
- The standard of proof is "balance of probabilities" not "beyond a reasonable doubt."
- Any written acknowledgement of parentage by a person may be used as proof of the fact of parentage.

- More often than not, blood tests or DNA testing is used to try to narrow down the evidence.

- If an alleged father tries to abscond (run away), the court can issue a warrant for his arrest.

In the Ontario Act, a procedure is used to gather blood for testing. A person cannot be forced to give blood or to undergo any test. In fact, the order is for "leave" or permission to go and voluntarily obtain blood tests. If leave to obtain the tests is given and the alleged father, referred to as the "putative father," refuses to go, the court can draw an inference. In other words, the court can conclude that therefore, he must be the father.

The test itself involves the father, mother and child submitting blood samples, which are examined for red and white cell features. The cost can range between $700 and $1,000 for all three. It is not possible to establish with 100 per cent certainty that a man is the father of a child through such testing. Instead, a "plausibility of paternity" is expressed. The result may be that he is 95 per cent likely the father and so on.

If the people are not satisfied with the blood tests, they may decide to try "DNA Finger Printing," which is now available with a simple mouth swab. The turnaround is about four to seven business days. It is more reliable (99.9 per cent proof of paternity, 100 per cent proof of non-paternity) and costs about $700 to $1,000. For more information, check out www.mdslabscanada.com or call 1-877-849-3637 toll free.

The goal of paternity proof is often to establish a claim for financial support and the court will consider making an interim support order pending the gathering of the evidence.

PATERNITY AGREEMENTS

In some cases where the "paternity writing is on the wall," the couple may wish to avoid the embarrassment of blood or DNA testing and the arguing in court and simply agree to paternity. The provincial family laws provide for what are known as "paternity agreements" by which a man and a woman, who are not spouses, may enter into an agreement for

- the payment of expenses of a child's prenatal care and birth,
- support for the child or
- funeral expenses of the child or mother.

Whether you are the mother or the father of the child, it is important to consult a lawyer before signing such an agreement. Your lawyer can design clauses specific to your own case.

WHAT WILL WE TELL THE CHILDREN?

In this section I would like to deal with what will likely be one of the most difficult moments that you'll have during the separation and divorce: telling the children about your decision. This is a particularly tough challenge for most adults. At a moment when they must summon the most diplomacy and skill, they are also feeling heartbroken, angry, confused, frightened and embarrassed. It is also a time when there is an overwhelming, irrational desire to lash out and hurt the other spouse. Ironically, during this difficult time when some actions are clearly motivated by all the wrong reasons, parents assume that their horrible actions are in the best interests of their children.

I strongly recommend that neither parent discuss a separation and divorce with their children unless they have a clear and honest plan for how this very difficult conversation might unfold. Depending on the age of the children, there may be some difficult questions to answer. This is not a conversation that can be held two or three times in order to get it right. It has to be done properly the first time. This means thinking about your children, their individual needs and concerns and your own abilities.

A great starting point in planning this discussion with your children is to try to look at it from their perspective. While divorce is very common in Canadian society, children still feel a sense of shame, embarrassment, confusion and, strangely enough, blame. It is a remarkable feature of divorce that children blame themselves for the divorce itself. Certainly children will have questions and try to assign the responsibility between the parents for the marriage breakdown. They want to know which parent is causing the separation. They want to know who's to blame. They may even ask if one of the parents is having an affair. In many cases, the children have already picked up the vibe and may have preconceived notions about what is going on in their parents' marriage. If there has been fighting, they will have heard it. If there has been a chill in the air, they will have felt it. If there's anger and seething beneath the surface, they will have sensed it. I have been struck in my conversations with children of divorce by how much they knew about the problems in the marriage and how little credit their parents gave them for being aware of the difficulties.

You must be aware as you prepare for this conversation that beneath their probing questions they harbor a distinct impression that they are actually responsible for the marriage breakdown. This seems bizarre to many parents. How could the children possibly think that they're responsible? If we think about it for a few minutes, it actually makes sense. The children have received no explanation for this happening in their home. They know that their parents are angry. They know that they're often the subject of these angry discussions. They know that their parents' anger is often taken out on them. They begin to notice that they rarely see their parents together. Activities seem to be alternated between the parents. No one does anything as a family anymore and, if they do, it can be tense and unpleasant. They are at the centre of the conflict and they somehow must be responsible.

Sadly, these children, who've received no explanation for the problems and who are now blaming themselves, begin to think that if they change their behaviour perhaps the marriage can be saved. I've seen cases in which children begin to act extra good; they do unnatural things to save money for the family; they take on the role of clown, trying to please and cheer up their depressed parents. Of course, none of this can change the problem, and their sense of responsibility deepens.

Eventually these children, especially if they're in the middle of high conflict between the parents, become depressed; their schooling suffers; they begin to act out and misbehave; they may engage in self-destructive behaviour, and they may have generally unhappy lives. Some children find the best answer is to remove themselves from the home, so they end up spending most of their times with friends. This can be particularly difficult if there are younger children who are home and depend on older siblings.

Make a Plan

The way to avoid these problems is to make a plan and provide children with a coherent explanation for what is happening to the family and for what is happening to you as a husband and wife. A part of this coherent explanation must be an express statement to the children that *they're not to blame in any way for what is happening*. It does not matter how confident you are that the children will not blame themselves. You must expressly tell them anyway and ask them to specifically acknowledge that they do not blame themselves in any way for what is happening.

When dealing with younger children (say, under the age of seven), it can be very difficult to explain the separation in anything but the most simple terms: "Mommy and Daddy will have separate homes. You'll be spending time with both of us, and we will continue to be your mommy and daddy. We are going to work very hard to make sure that you are happy because you are most important person in the world to us. Don't worry. We are working on this and everything will be fine." As they grow older, further refinement of the message may be needed from time to time. They will have questions and you should be ready to answer them. I'm not saying that all the gory details must be shared with them, but be prepared to be honest. This is no time for stonewalling and being evasive. Ignoring them and hoping that their questions will blow over will only make matters worse. Give them short, straight answers.

Sometimes families try trial separations. They may honestly tell the children that the separation is temporary. In my experience, few of these separations are really temporary. What the parents are really trying to do is ease themselves and the children into the reality of two households. Unfortunately, the children end up with a false hope that a reconciliation is possible. When the reconciliation does not materialize, the children get a second heartbreak and disappointment. If the separation is genuine and reconciliation unlikely, then be straight with the children so that there are no false hopes.

With older children, parents can be more frank and provide detailed explanations about what is happening to the family. These children are rarely shocked by the announcement. That is not to say that there are not families with children who are absolutely floored by the parents' statement that they will be separating and divorcing. I've seen some modern families where the kids have been kept so busy speeding from one activity to the next that they really have no sense at all of what is going on around them. These children live in a pinball machine rather than a family. They are rarely seeing their parents act as a team in any event, so they do not have many opportunities to witness an actual dysfunction. For them, separation and divorce can be a total shock; however, in most families where the children are over the age of 11 they have a pretty good idea about what is going on. This doesn't mean that they like the idea. They may even say that they knew it was going to happen and wondered why it hadn't happened sooner. They still won't like the idea, but they had a sense it was inevitable.

Older children will have questions about where they will live, how they will stay in contact with both parents, how they will stay in touch with their friends, where their stuff will end up, whether they will continue to go to the same schools and play on the same teams and so on. Their concerns are very practical. What is your separation and divorce going to do to their worlds?

While it is not always practical (in situations where the parents cannot possibly cooperate, for example, where there is violence), it is better if both parents can sit down with the children with a common plan and give a consistent explanation and support each other and the children. I repeat:

both parents should be involved. One should not do all the talking. One should not take all the blame. One should not appear to be a victim, nor should one appear to be the villain. A simple, straightforward explanation about a need to end the relationship of husband and wife should be given. Similarly, it should be explained in a straightforward way that the roles of mother and father continue forever. Take your time. Watch their expressions. Be attentive to their needs. Be in control of yourself and the meeting. Listen to their questions and be prepared to give them answers.

Now, here's the interesting part—ask them not only for their questions, but ask them for their suggestions, for their wishes, for their ideas about how this new living arrangement can be made to work in a way that makes everyone happy. Be prepared for them to say that they do not want you to separate and divorce. Stick to your message. Separation is happening. Two households will be created and you need to know what they want and what they need to make that work well.

In the vast majority of cases, the children will tell both parents point blank they want to see them equally. They will want to spend time at both homes. This will be their number one concern. You must be prepared to address it and assure them that, of course, they will see both parents and spend time at both homes.

It is quite possible that a second and third meeting will be required to deal with their questions. Don't forget to follow up with them. Don't leave them hanging. It's easy to get busy with the details of separation, work and all the other day-to-day chores. Schedule a second meeting.

Perhaps in your family it will be appropriate to meet with the children individually. Some may speak more frankly if they are alone with you. This is when you will need to use your listening skills. They will want to know what their choices are. You can bet that kids in their circle of friends have already experienced separation and divorce. This can be good if those friends will provide a sympathetic shoulder. It can be very bad if those children have been through high-conflict divorces and provide precisely the role model that your children don't need. The more information you give your children, the less likely it is that they will pick up misinformation on the street.

Don't forget that there are many professionals in your community who are skilled in helping children cope with separation and divorce. Some children may need regular counselling. There may be things on their minds that they're not prepared to discuss with their parents. The earlier this type of intervention is used, the easier it will be for the children and the less likely that intervention will be needed on a long-term basis. It's when things are left to the boiling point that the counselling ends up being long-term, sometimes a lifelong, experience for your children.

To this point I've been speaking to the parents who have a reasonable prospect of working cooperatively with each other to ease the pain for the children. Unfortunately, there are parents reading this chapter who cannot work cooperatively. There are parents who are too hurt or too angry or too immature to put a child's interests first. There are parents who will try to manipulate their children. I've seen cases in which a parent tried to make a child feel sorry for him or her; told a child that they will be lonely without the child; promised gifts; told their children that they'll be angry with them if they don't take their side; ran down the other parent; told their children that they (the parent) will be hurt; and told their children that they need the children to take care of him or her.

We hope that our children will intuitively know that they should live with the parent who knows how to look after them and has actually done so; who will make sure that the child stays in touch with friends and family on both sides; who will ensure that the child is able to stay in regular contact with the other parent, whether by telephone, mail, e-mail or in person; who will keep the child's life in place as much as possible by making sure that they attend the same school, if at all possible in the same house and neighbourhood, and enjoy the same friends, lessons, sports, hobbies and so on; who will have a healthy attitude about his or her own needs and who will be realistic about the changes that are going on in everyone's lives.

In my book *Surviving Your Parents' Divorce: A Guide for Young Canadians* (which is written for children between the ages of 10 and 16), I try to bring children into the picture of divorce by giving them information about their parents' emotional stages and about the system and process of divorce. I hope to ease their anxiety. Consider the following points, which I felt obliged to draw to the attention of the children of divorce:

- Grandparents, aunts, uncles and cousins are all worried about children who must go through the divorce of their parents. They can be a terrific source of support at a very difficult time. In particular, grandparents can be a great help.

- However, it can be difficult for relatives to stay out of the argument between the parents. Family members can also be a source of stress and difficulty as the family goes through the separation. I recommend that children find the aunts and uncles who are helpful and lean on them and avoid the ones who are simply picking sides and causing trouble. I recommend that the children take advantage of the opportunity to get away and stay with relatives if they can.

- Sometimes when one parent gets sole custody of the children, they cut off contact with the other side of the family. This is a very poor choice and is rarely in the interests of the children. I tell children quite frankly to speak up if they want to maintain a relationship with members of the extended family. Just because the roles of husband and wife are ending does not mean that a child should be cut off from half of their heritage.

- They will encounter practical problems when travelling back and forth between houses. Stuff gets lost or it never seems to be in the right place when they need it. I tell children that they have to be more organized. They have to start making sure that they have the right stuff at the right house. This is something they did not have to worry about before.

- Children will have to be careful in scheduling time with their friends or other important events because it may now interfere with an access schedule. The parents may be arguing over who will be seeing the children on a particular weekend only to discover that the children have made their own plans.

- The telephone can be a useful way of staying in contact with a parent. Some kids enjoy talking on the phone; some do not. Long distance charges can make it even more difficult. Frequent and uninhibited telephone access between children and their parents is an absolute must. Lately this has extended to e-mail contact. It can certainly take a lot of the stress out of the relationship if parents are open and allow free communication.

- It can be very difficult if the child is seeing a parent only on the weekend to catch up about an entire two-week or longer period in such a short period of time. The access parent may have been waiting for two weeks to see the child and may have made big plans and is really anticipating spending time with the child. The child may show up for that weekend dead tired from a tough week at school and just want to crash on the couch and watch television. It can be awkward for both the parent and the child. It can be even worse if the child turns out to be sick and does not feel like going for a visit when it has already been arranged. Access parents have a very difficult life.

- The child may find it difficult to keep up with an entire network of aunts, uncles, cousins and grandparents when they are seeing their parent only every second weekend. Sometimes the child just wants to spend time with the parent alone.

- Holidays can be a very difficult challenge for families. These include making arrangements around such things as religious holidays, Thanksgiving, March break, summer vacation, Christmas and other holidays and even the parents' birthdays. These are supposed to be happy times and all the child hears is argument. Holidays can become a very stressful, unpleasant time for children if the parents cannot work it out. This is never more true than on Christmas day, which, like the other 364 days of the year, has only 24 hours.

- Children may end up with a feeling of restlessness as they move back and forth between their parents' homes. Some children report that they are never able to really settle in before having to move again.

- Children often end up becoming a very cheap "courier service" between angry parents. I tell them point blank to avoid this unpaid job. If parents need to exchange messages, they should speak to each other or write and mail confidential notes.

- On the more positive side, some children do tend to notice an improvement in their parents once they are separate and set up into their two new households. Two houses can be special for children. They may have a new room with new stuff in it. They may also have new stepbrothers and stepsisters and, for many families, it means two sets of vacations, one with each parent.

- Children are sometimes a little bit surprised at how much attention they receive after the separation. One child told me that his parents had turned into a couple of "super-parents," each one trying to be the greatest parent ever. It's a shame that it took a separation to cause that to happen.

Here is a list of my suggestions for children:

- Try to remember that divorce is not your fault.

- It is the fault of the adults and it is their job to fix it—not yours. Be patient and let them work it out.

- Don't forget all the emotional stuff your parents are going through. They can get angry and depressed. So will you.

- Be as open and honest as possible with both parents. Once they know what you want, they can plan for what is in your best interest.

- If you are over nine years of age, you have a right to be heard. Your opinion is important and really can influence the way things are handled. Remember, there is more to custody than just where you sleep at night. It also involves making important decisions about your life.

- If you are moving back and forth between two homes, whether for access or because of joint custody, try to make sure everyone is working from the exact same schedule. Make a copy of the calendar each month showing where you should be on each night and weekend. If you see a conflict (your championship baseball game is on the same weekend that your dad is supposed to take you to the cottage), let your parents know as soon as possible.

- Make a list of the stuff you need for the next day or the Monday after a weekend visit. It can help you avoid forgetting stuff that you will need, like homework.

- Try to stay in contact with the other parent, if at all possible. A few little short telephone conversations can make the weekend visit a lot more enjoyable. The same thing applies for other family members. Just because your mom and dad split, it doesn't mean you should lose contact with all your cousins, aunts, uncles and grandparents.

- Remember, you cannot please everybody all the time. Don't panic if conflicts come up. Pick the solution that makes the most sense and that suits you best.

- Be good to yourself. Relax. If you need to blow off some steam, do it. Speak honestly to someone you trust.

- Don't get drawn into carrying messages back and forth between your parents.

- Don't get drawn into discussions about money or support. Politely tell your parents that you are not interested. It is the adults' job to solve the money problems.

STEPFAMILIES

Stepfamilies or blended families may be a part of the separation and divorce situation. Perhaps one of you is moving on to a new relationship immediately. This is very tough for children. Having more siblings around may initially seem like fun, but once the novelty wears off, children often resent having to share their parent. They can feel lost in the shuffle. It is my suggestion that families go slowly as they make decisions to blend families. Listen to your children and be aware of their reactions. The stress of leaving one family can be doubled or quadrupled by putting them into the stress of entering a brand new family immediately.

A WARNING

I want to state frankly to any parent reading this chapter that managing your divorce properly is going to be critical to the future happiness of your children. You face a choice, a very clear choice.

If you fight and put your children through a high-conflict divorce, I guarantee you that as your children grow up they will be depressed; they will do poorly in school; they will be more likely to smoke; they will be more likely to take drugs; they will be more likely to be self-destructive and suicidal; they will be more likely to get into trouble; they will be more likely to have trouble forming intimate relationships both with men and women; and they will be more likely to have eating disorders and other psychological problems. They will also get their revenge and make your life miserable.

On the other hand, you can work cooperatively to have as amicable as possible a separation and divorce. If your children are not exposed to the conflict, then they are more likely to come through your divorce as a survivor.

I'm not saying that they won't be stressed and that they won't be unhappy and depressed at times, but they will have a much better chance of surviving in the long haul than the kids who suffer through bitter divorces. Take my word for it; I have met kids who have been through the good, the bad and the ugly, and it all comes down to choices that were made by their parents. You've been warned. The choice is yours.

CONCLUSION

I hope from the foregoing chapter that you have realized that the custody decision and choices made will have a profound effect on your children's happiness in the future. In this area more than any other, you must understand the options that are available to you and your family. Custody choices are related to decisions about the matrimonial home, the division of property and, very importantly, decisions about child support. Prior to going forward with any decisions, make sure that you understand and that your lawyer has explained to you the relative advantages and disadvantages of proceeding. There is room for a great deal of flexibility in resolving custody cases. So much depends on making good choices that here, more than any other area, you must be an informed consumer.

CHECKLIST

1. Do you understand the definition of "child of the marriage" and the extent of your responsibility for your children?

2. Do you understand the extensive list of considerations that a court will look to when deciding what is in the best interests of a child?

3. Would an assessment be appropriate to assist the court in making decisions about what is best for your children?

4. Who is the psychological parent in your family?

5. Is there any behaviour in the past that would be relevant to your ability to parent or your spouse's ability to parent in the future?

6. Do you understand why a court is not interested in your spouse's bad behaviour unless that behaviour is relevant to acting as a parent?

7. Do you understand the meaning of the friendly parent rule and the idea of facilitating maximum contact?

8. Do you appreciate the importance of maintaining a child's contact with the extended family?

9. Do you appreciate the role of your child's views and preferences in making decisions about custody and access?

10. Do you understand the choices that are available to you now in the area of custody, including joint custody?

11. Do you understand that joint custody can be defined in any way that you and your spouse consider appropriate for your family?

12. Do you understand the relationship between sharing time with the child and the calculation of child support in accordance with the Child Support Guidelines?

(Continued)

13. Do you understand the likelihood of restrictions being placed on the mobility of a custodial parent and the way in which the Divorce Act requires notice of any plan to move?

14. Do you understand the limitations on access and the ability of the court to enforce it?

15. Do you understand the tactical relationship between the matrimonial home, the property settlement, custody and child support?

16. Do you understand the difference between interim and permanent orders and how an interim order can create a status quo that is difficult or impossible to overcome?

17. Is paternity an issue? Do you understand the various means of solving questions of paternity?

18. Would a paternity agreement be appropriate?

19. Have you read the section "What Will We Tell the Children" and do you understand the implications of your choices for your children's future happiness?

7

SUPPORT

~

Financial Assistance After Separation

We have seen in the preceding chapters the importance of property division and child custody issues. Just as important, however, is the question of support once the family has separated and gone off to create two new households. It is a difficult fact of life for most families that each spouse and the children suffer a reduction in their standard of living after divorce. Two households cannot be easily supported on the same money that once supported only one household. Discussions about dividing RRSPs, matrimonial homes, cottages and businesses are fine for those who enjoy such assets and wealth, but for many people, the financial burden of separation can only be met through a division of one spouse's income for the benefit of the two new households.

Questions about support, whether child support, spousal support or the relatively new issue of parental support, are important and challenging areas for lawyers and clients. In this chapter, we will consider each area, including when an entitlement to support arises, how it is paid and when it ends. We will also consider some of the very recent changes in the areas of child support and some of the strategic aspects of spousal support and child support claims.

Most seasoned family law lawyers have had the unpleasant experience of explaining to clients that, while fair property division is critical to starting over, child and spousal support obligations, in terms of total costs, can far exceed the value of a modest family home. Consider, for example, a father of three children who earns $100,000 per year. Assume also that the children are all under the age of 10 and that they will all complete university at the age of 22. If we use the Federal Child Support Guidelines in the calculation of child support, this man's minimum obligation for child support alone would exceed $250,000. If the man involved in this scenario also had to pay spousal support, then the cost of his support obligations could easily be double that figure. We can see why issues of child and spousal support can become so emotional for families at the time of separation.

As noted in previous chapters, the various laws of the provincial, territorial and federal governments have all provided for the possibility of support upon marriage breakdown. For legally married couples, spousal support is available under the Divorce Act. For common-law couples, provincial family laws provide the right to claim spousal support. In the case of parental support, claims are advanced pursuant to provincial law.

An entitlement to claim support arises upon the breakdown of a marriage or a relationship. In this chapter, I refer to "marriage breakdown" as a triggering event for the claiming of spousal support. In using this expression I intend for it to apply to common-law spouses as well when their relationship breaks down. Consequently, any references to spouses in this chapter apply to both common-law spouses and legally married spouses.

Before entering into a consideration of these various forms of support, recall the all-important financial statements that figured so prominently in the division of family property. Here again, in calculating support, these financial statements play a key role in revealing to the court not only potential sources of support for the two households, but also the budgets within which these households must operate.

As a part of my practice, I regularly meet with clients in advance of separation and divorce. With fairly basic financial information, it is possible to tell an individual how much child and/or spousal support they will likely pay if the separation occurs in the near future. Spending some time with an experienced family law lawyer in advance of your separation is a valuable exercise. As we have seen in the property division chapter, a mathematical calculation can be done there, as well. The court prefers to know how property will be divided before making an order for spousal support. This means that if you gather the correct information and consult with an experienced lawyer, you can obtain a very specific opinion on how much child support, how much spousal support and how much of a nest egg (we hope) each of the spouses will have post-separation.

CHILD SUPPORT

On May 1, 1997, the Federal Child Support Guidelines came into force by virtue of amendments to the Divorce Act. Related amendments were also made at the same time to the Income Tax Act. These Child Support Guidelines were updated as of May 2006 to increase the amount of child support payable in the context of separation and divorce.

The Guidelines are a mandatory formula that dictates the amount of child support based on the gross annual income of the non-custodial parent. The rationale for the mandatory formula is threefold: (1) the use of a formula will ensure fairness and consistency in the amount of child support; (2) it will reduce the likelihood of conflict between the parents and their lawyers; and (3) it will provide for a faster, less costly way of resolving the issue of child support at the time of marriage breakdown.

The application of the Child Support Guidelines formula involves the use of tables that establish monthly amounts for child support based on the number of children in question and the paying spouse's gross annual income.

To use the tables, one parent must be the custodial parent or the primary residence parent. This would generally mean that the other parent spends 40 per cent or less of his or her time with the child. We will see in a moment how situations of split custody and joint custody are handled when calculating child support.

Base Monthly Child Support

In most cases, however, the children are residing with one parent for at least 65 or 70 per cent of the time. The access parent is likely seeing the children every second weekend and during overnight visits in the alternate weeks, plus a portion of vacation time. In such circumstances, the gross annual income of the custodial parent is, generally speaking, not taken into account. The Guidelines focus on the gross annual income of the non-custodial parent. As stated before, the gross annual income and the number of children are the sole determining factors for the calculation of the base amount of child support. If the annual income of the parent paying child support is more than $150,000, then a further percentage calculation is added on to the base amount of child support. Your lawyer can assist you in doing this calculation.

The Child Support Guidelines only apply to divorces and agreements that are completed after May 1, 1997. The formula does not automatically apply for orders that predate 1997. It is only if the parents seek a variation of the amount of child support after the May 1997 date that the new Guidelines will be invoked.

Lawyers regularly encounter couples who reached their agreements prior to 1997 and are not covered by the Child Support Guidelines. In such cases, the child support is included in the taxable income of the recipient custodial parent and is tax deductible for the non-custodial parent who pays the support. Under the Guidelines, the treatment is quite different. The custodial parent does not include the income in taxable income each year, nor does the non-custodial parent deduct the amount. The figure that changes hands is a net amount. This makes matters much easier for families when completing their income tax returns.

Each province has enacted its own version of the Guidelines for application to the provincial support orders. The Guidelines were designed and tailor-made for each province's respective standard and cost of living. This means that a person paying child support in Ontario will have a slightly different figure on a monthly basis than a person paying child support in Nova Scotia, even though they may have the same gross annual income.

As clients and lawyers work to apply the Guidelines, they are attempting to answer six questions:

1. How many children are involved?
2. What is the custody arrangement?
3. What is the annual income of the paying parent?
4. What does the table set out as the amount?
5. Are there any extraordinary expenses?
6. Will there be undue hardship if the table amount is used?

The use of the Child Support Guidelines has reduced considerably the debate over how much child support should be paid. It is true that parents do get into debates about incurring and dividing special expenses, but for the most part the base amount is no longer controversial and courts will rarely entertain debate about whether the guideline amount should be used. In other words, lawyers would rarely recommend going to court to argue over whether the Child Support Guidelines apply to the usual custody-access arrangement.

In Appendix A of this book, I have included the full Federal Child Support Guidelines for Ontario as an example of the way in which the base montly child support is calculated. Locate the table with the correct number of children and then locate the correct gross annual income. By running your finger across the table, you will be able to see the amount of monthly child support payable.

Special Expenses

I have used the expression "base amount of support" in the previous paragraphs. This is the amount that is typically paid on a monthly basis to assist the custodial parent with expenses arising from housing, clothing, feeding and meeting the miscellaneous day-to-day expenses of the children. The base amount of support calculated under the Child Support Guidelines is provided by the table.

Over and above this base amount, the custodial and non-custodial parents also contribute to so-called special and extraordinary expenses. These special expenses are usually incurred in consultation and are divided between the parents in proportion to their annual incomes. So, for example, if a child is a talented figure skater and requires special lessons and custom skates and must travel to competitive events, this would likely be considered an expense over and above the base amount incurred each month by the custodial parent. The parents would typically consult with each other, agree on the incurring of the special expense and divide it between the two of them in proportion to their annual incomes.

With respect to special and extraordinary expenses, the Federal Child Support Guidelines offer a few details about what may be considered a special or extraordinary expense. Consider the following:

- Childcare expenses incurred as a result of the custodial parent's employment, illness, disability or education or training for employment.
- That portion of the medical and dental insurance premiums attributable to the child.
- Health-related expenses that exceed insurance reimbursement by at least $100 annually, including orthodontic treatment, professional counselling, social workers, psychiatrists, physiotherapy, speech therapy, hearing aids, glasses and contact lenses.
- Extraordinary expenses for primary or secondary school education or for any other educational programs that meet the child's particular needs.
- Expenses for post-secondary education.
- Extraordinary expenses for extracurricular activities.

The courts have been asked to interpret the appropriateness of certain special expenses for children, and they have consistently said that the expense must be "reasonable and necessary" in the particular case, having regard to the best interests of the child. The examples set out above were not intended to be exhaustive. The court will look at every situation to determine whether an expense is reasonable and necessary. In one case, the court ordered that vitamins and health supplements could be considered a special expense.

Generally, the higher the level of income, the more extensive the availability of extraordinary or special expenses can become. Private school, for some families, may be considered an appropriate special expense. On the other hand, in a Saskatchewan case, the court ruled that piano lessons were too expensive for the particular family in question. In one case (to the horror of the family, I am sure), a judge ruled that a drum set was a reasonable expense in the circumstances. Even though the family finances were tight, the judge thought a small indulgence for the child would help him to cope with the separation and divorce of his parents.

For most families, the typical special expenses that are being dealt with relate to medical costs such as orthodontics, education costs such as tuition or tutoring, and sports activities or camp. Decision-making with respect to special expenses cannot be unilateral. In other words, the custodial parent cannot simply sign a child up and send the other parent the bill. Life is a lot easier if parents work cooperatively around these expenses.

I wish to add a short word about expenses related to post-secondary education, because this is often a significant expense for families and many questions arise. No doubt, a non-custodial parent is required to contribute to a child's reasonable post-secondary education expenses. The child attending post-secondary education has an obligation to contribute to their own expenses as best as possible, and the custodial parent also has an obligation to share in this expense. So, for example, in one B.C. case, a court confirmed that money the children had received through a trust fund was taken into consideration in setting the amount that the parents had to contribute for post-secondary education.

These expenses include not just the tuition itself, but also the cost of residence, food plans and even a car if it is necessary for travel to and from school. Computers are taken for granted now as a necessary expense for children attending university. Musical instruments have been considered a special expense, if the child is registered in a music program. In one case, a special expense included a private room for the child, who needed a place to study and practise their music.

The most important question that arises, however, when children attend post-secondary education, is what happens to the monthly child support when the child lives away from the custodial parent's home and, perhaps, lives in residence? Courts do not expect parents to pay "twice," in other words, to pay a base monthly child support to the custodial parent and pay for residence costs while the child is away from home. The most common way of resolving this is for the custodial parent to not receive child support, or to receive a reduced amount of child support for the months that the child is away from home and full child support for the months that the child is home from university during the summer.

Changes in Income

As a parent's income changes and as that parent shares each year's tax information with the other parent, adjustments are made to the base monthly child support amount. In most cases, parents exchange their financial information on an annual basis. The non-custodial parent father, for example, will reveal his gross earnings for the previous year and the base amount of child support will be calculated. The custodial parent mother, for example, will reveal her gross annual earnings. Those amounts will be relevant to the proportional sharing of special and extraordinary expenses.

The Supreme Court of Canada recently dealt with this issue of updating the amount of child support as a parent's earnings increase or decrease. The motives and circumstances can change from case to case, but it is not uncommon for parents to not stay in touch with each other around their annual earnings. A Separation Agreement or a court order may have been obtained after a very acrimonious period of negotiations or litigation, and the parent may not be anxious to rush into an immediate renegotiation simply because somebody's income has gone up or down.

In some cases, parents continue paying child support that would be a little more than would be called for by the Guidelines and, in many cases, they do not report an increase in their income and, therefore, end up paying less than the Child Support Guidelines would stipulate. In this latter case, we have recently seen parents who did not reveal increases in their incomes being hit with extremely large retroactive obligations to pay child support. In other words, the courts looked at the situation and said (1) you should have told the other parent about the increase in your income; (2) had you told them about it, the child support would have been at an increased amount; (3) your former spouse and child have been penalized as a result of your failure to disclose increases in income; and (4) not only must you now pay the total amount calculated retroactively, but you must also pay interest and legal fees on top of it. This has amounted to tens of thousands of dollars in retroactive payments in some situations.

The message that the court has sent to families is update your financial disclosure annually. If you have an increase in your income, disclose it and pay the appropriate level of child support. If you have a decrease in your income, disclose it and recalculate the lower amount of child support immediately.

Variation Applications

In some cases, it is necessary to return to court to obtain a variation of the child support amount. This is known as a variation proceeding. Either party can return to court to have the amount either increased or decreased, depending on the circumstances of the parents. This type of variation proceeding is required where a parent has not disclosed income changes or is refusing to make a retroactive payment. The parent seeking the payment forces the matter back into court for a determination and a variation of the amount of child support to bring it into line, perhaps retroactively, with the Child Support Guidelines.

WHEN IS A CHILD ELIGIBLE FOR SUPPORT?

The Divorce Act contains an extended definition of the expression "child of the marriage" and includes any child for whom the person has stood in the place of a parent or any child of whom one is the parent and for whom the other stands in the place of a parent. Essentially this means that biological parents, step-parents and adoptive parents can be obligated to pay child support. In addition, even if a person has not actually adopted a child but has treated the child as his or her own, a support obligation may arise.

As a general rule of thumb, child support continues until the child is no longer considered a child of the marriage within the meaning of the Divorce Act. This means that the child has attained the age of majority. So, for example, if a child turns 18 and is no longer in full-time attendance at an educational institution or university, child support will usually end. If the child continues on to university, child support typically continues until the age of 22 or the completion of the child's first university degree. A safe rule of thumb is to assume that child support will continue until the child is 22 years of age.

To continue to receive support, a child need not reside with the custodial parent. In many cases, children have been required to leave home to attend university but still receive financial support via the custodial parent and the non-custodial parent because of their ongoing dependency. There is no firm requirement that a child live with the custodial parent in order to continue to receive support.

It can be tricky for some families if a child is not committed to his or her education. For example, a child might attend university for a year and be entitled to child support, but then decide that the program was inappropriate and take a year off. Child support might be suspended while this child thinks about his or her options and become reactivated if the child returns to school.

Child Withdraws From Parental Control

One aspect of provincial law is the termination of support when a child has withdrawn from parental control. In Ontario, for example, the Family Law Act provides that every parent has an obligation to provide support for his or her unmarried child who is a minor or is enrolled in a full-time program of education to the extent that the parent is capable of doing so. In assessing this obligation to provide support, the court considers the needs of the child. The Act goes on, however, to state that the obligation to provide support does not extend to a child who is 16 years of age or older and has withdrawn from parental control.

Withdrawing from parental control means a voluntary withdrawal; the exercise of a free choice to cut the family bonds and strike out on a life of one's own. The court will not assume that a child has voluntarily withdrawn just because the child no longer lives at home. The court will want to determine whether the child was, perhaps, forced from the home. Were there some unreasonable parental actions that made continued cohabitation with the parents impossible? Was the child driven from parental control by emotional or physical abuse? Perhaps the withdrawal was not voluntary and child support should continue with a direct payment to the child or to another family member who is caring for the child.

A parent cannot expel a child from the home and expect to terminate a support obligation. For this reason, the onus of proving that a child has withdrawn from parental control is on the parents. Case reports are filled with numerous examples of children who have been driven from their home by parents or step-parents to live with friends or relatives. They have then applied for financial support and received it on the basis that, while they do not live with their parents, they did not voluntarily withdraw from parental control.

In one Nova Scotia case, the applicant was a 14-year-old girl who had experienced difficulties with her mother. The child would not abide by the "house rules" and persisted in staying out very late at night, contrary to her mother's wishes. She then moved out to live with her aunt and uncle for almost a year, but the aunt and uncle soon had the same difficulties. After a brief attempt to live again with the mother, the child left on her own initiative to live with her girlfriend's family. When the child applied for support, the court considered her to have voluntarily withdrawn from living with the parents and the parents had a lawful excuse for not providing support.

Illness and Disability of a Child

The questions of illness and disability for a child can be important. If a child passes the age of majority but for reasons of illness or disability must continue to be cared for and supported by the custodial parent, there will be a corresponding ongoing financial obligation for the non-custodial parent to pay support.

Step-Parents

In attempting to determine whether a parent has acted as if he or she was a child's parent even though they are not the biological or adoptive parent, the courts have asked questions such as the following:

- Did this person provide a large part of the financial support necessary for the child's support?
- Did the person intend to step into the shoes of a parent?
- Was the relationship between the person and the child a continuing one with some permanency?
- Can any inferences be drawn from the treatment the child would receive were he or she living with their biological parent?
- Has the person pertinent to the claim for support ceased to act as a parent of that child?

The court will also consider such things as the affection between the person and the child, the length of time of the association and whether the child has taken the surname of that person and lives in the same dwelling.

Other Child Support Considerations

The Child Support Guidelines have brought a great deal of certainty to the area of child support calculations, whether the calculations are being made pursuant to provincial law or the Divorce Act; however, there are points of controversy that the courts have been required to deal with over the last few years. What follows is an overview of some of the common issues that have arisen now under child support. In approaching the issue of child support, consider the following:

- The basic Child Support Guidelines are designed to work with a traditional custody-access arrangement. One parent has custody; the other has access. One parent has the child the majority of the time; the other parent does not. The Guidelines apply. In situations of joint custody, where a parent has the child more than 40 per cent of the time, the Guidelines will not apply and the court has the discretion to vary the amount of child support on the basis that it would be unfair to have a parent pay child support when they have a higher level of expense in caring for the child during their joint custodial time. This is dealt with in section 9 of the Federal Child Support Guidelines. That section stipulates that the amount of child support must be determined by taking into account (a) the amounts set out in the applicable tables for each of the spouses, in other words, the Child Support Guidelines, (b) the increased costs of shared custody arrangements and (c) the conditions, means, needs and other circumstances of each spouse and of any child for whom support is sought.

A Supreme Court of Canada case dealt with this issue recently. The message to families was basically that determinations of the amount of appropriate child support in shared custody situations would be determined on a case-by-case basis. Many parents simply do a setoff calculation, whereby the mother calculates what she would pay to the father if he had custody, the father calculates what he would pay to the mother if she had custody and one pays the other the difference between the two monthly amounts. For straightforward cases, it works well. If one parent's income and asset picture is considerably stronger than the other, then the court may not think a simple setoff is appropriate. Discussion of joint custody arrangements will obviously have an impact on the amount of child support.

In the Contino case—where the parents shared the children about 60 per cent versus 40 per cent and could not agree on the appropriate level of child support—the court suggested an approach that would look at the actual spending patterns of the parents, the ability of each parent to bear increased costs of shared custody (this would mean looking at their full asset and liability picture) and also the standard of living for the children in each of the households. The court followed five steps when looking at this shared custody/child support problem:

1. determine the parties' incomes,
2. determine each parent's monthly expenditures attributable to the child,
3. determine the ratio of income between the parents,

4. consider the net worth of the parents and their ability to absorb increased costs and

5. consider whether there would be a variation in the child's standard of living if there was a change in the level of child support.

Most lawyers have concluded from the Supreme Court of Canada case that there will be less certainty in these shared custody/child support determinations and solutions will be needed on a case-by-case basis.

- The Child Support Guidelines also contemplate the possibility that parents may have split custody, that is, each spouse has custody of one or more of the children. Perhaps, the teenage son decides to live with his father and a younger daughter chooses to live with her mother. In such a case, the amount of child support is calculated in a setoff, as described earlier, so the child support order is the difference between the amount that each spouse would otherwise pay if a child support order were sought against each of the spouses.

- Questions have arisen around the motives of the parent seeking a reduction in child support, particularly in situations of shared custody. Some observers feel that parents seeking joint custody simply are attempting to reduce their potential child support obligations. In some circumstances, parents with joint custody arrangements have still paid a traditional full Child Support Guidelines amount. For example, a father may have the children 50 per cent of the time but still pay the full amount of child support pursuant to the Guidelines. This may be appropriate in circumstances where the other parent has little or no income at the time of separation. The parents will sometimes agree to use that arrangement until the other parent is able to make a greater contribution to their own self-sufficiency. The bottom line is that the courts have not developed hard and fast rules.

In the Contino case, the application to vary the child support amount was triggered when the father's joint custodial time exceeded the 40 per cent amount. The reason it exceeded 40 per cent is that the mother asked the father to have the children for an additional night so that she could attend school. The amount of litigation on that issue was, in my view, out of proportion for the money involved. I would certainly recommend that families not treat the 40 per cent level as a threshold that automatically triggers the need for a child support variation. Use common sense and avoid spending money—that might otherwise go for the children—on the lawyers fighting over it. There is little point in arguing about the base amount of child support pursuant to the Guidelines. Unless there are some extraordinary or exceptional circumstances or undue hardship, the Guidelines will be invoked by the courts.

- The Child Support Guidelines also contemplate the possibility that a parent will suffer undue hardship if the Guidelines are used. It is a difficult determination to make, but the court will consider special circumstances that affect a parent's ability to make the ordinary child support payment. So, for example, where a parent has extraordinary costs related to their personal health, or the parent had huge business debts that needed to be paid, then the amount of child support might be altered. Parents should work cooperatively on special and extraordinary expenses. I recommend that no special expenses be incurred unless there is an agreement reached between the parents about the activity being undertaken, the cost of it and the method of payment. It makes no sense for a custodial parent to register children for the most expensive extracurricular activities and simply pass the bill to a non-custodial parent. Cooperation must continue well past the point of separation. If you haven't done so already, you may wish to read the section in the chapter on custody entitled "What Will We Tell the Children?"

- The court also has the discretion to reduce the amount of support paid if the parent paying child support must incur very high costs in exercising their access. So, if a parent resides in British Columbia but exercises access to a child in Ontario and airplane tickets, hotel costs and so on are a regular factor in exercising access, there may be room for a reduction in child support.

- Problems will arise in the calculation of child support from time to time, if parents are secretive about their earnings. Typically problems arise for lawyers when one parent attempts to hide a bonus or special commission. The Child Support Guidelines contain rules for attributing income to parents. When it comes to hiding income in order to keep child support low, many have tried, but experienced family law lawyers will always find a way to obtain the true income figures and will ask a court to attribute those true figures to the parent. During the process, there is a great deal of acrimony and legal expense. It is far better to be open with earnings and fairly negotiate the amount of money that is needed to raise the children.

- The development of a second family for an individual paying child support is not typically considered to be a reason to lower child support to the first family. The courts will look at this on a case-by-case basis, but they have not been inclined to reduce child support.

ı some unusual circumstances, a lump sum for child support is possible. This is reserved for exceptional situations and has become rarer and rarer since the implementation of the Child Support Guidelines. In one case, for example, a stepfather was given the option of simply making a lump sum payment rather than continuing to make a monthly payment to a child with whom the relationship had ended.

- Indexing of child support payments is no longer a typical feature of a child support order. The Guidelines were intended to provide the method by which child support base amounts are calculated.

- The calculation of the income used for the Child Support Guidelines tables has been the subject of litigation. It is often not easy to calculate what a parent earns; however, the court will take income from all sources in assessing the meaning of total income. A starting point is to look at line 150 of the income tax form filed with Revenue Canada. The court will not stop there if it appears that, perhaps, income is being hidden, too many expenses are being deducted or full disclosure has not been made. In addition, where incomes have fluctuated, with a parent earning a great amount one year and then experiencing a decline only to have it return to a different level in a third year, the court may simply turn to an average income for the purposes of child support. And, if the court believes that an individual is under-employed or deliberately keeping their income low to avoid child support, the court has the option of imputing income to that individual and treating him or her as if they earned a level of income appropriate to their standard of living. This litigation can be quite expensive and often involves the need to retain forensic accountants to accurately determine a true level of income.

SPOUSAL SUPPORT

The area of spousal support has become a virtual minefield for lawyers and clients over the last few years. The Supreme Court of Canada and courts in every province of Canada have made a wide variety of orders in connection with spousal support. There does not appear to be any clear or definitive approach to the entitlement, quantum (amount) or termination date of spousal support.

To add fuel to the fire, more recently there have even been serious problems about enforcement of legitimate spousal support releases and the reintroduction of concepts of "fault." In this section, we will examine the area of spousal support and the ongoing issues that create so many problems for couples as they separate and divorce.

The Divorce Act lists four objectives for orders of spousal support made under the Act. It provides that an order for the support of the spouse should

1. recognize any economic advantages or disadvantages to the spouses arising from the marriage or its breakdown,

2. apportion between the spouses the financial consequences arising from the care of any child of the marriage over and above the obligation apportioned between the spouses with respect to child support,

3. relieve any economic hardship of the spouses arising from the breakdown of the marriage and

4. insofar as practicable, promote the economic self-sufficiency of each spouse within a reasonable period of time.

In making support orders, the court considers certain factors, including the condition, means, needs and other circumstances of the spouses. These may include the length of time the spouses cohabited, the functions performed by the spouse during cohabitation and any other arrangement relating to support of the spouse. The courts have used a variety of approaches to calculating spousal support at the end of a marriage. Some courts have used what is known as the "income security model," other courts have used what is called the "compensatory model" and other judges and courts have applied the "clean-break model."

In an "income security model" the support obligation is considered to be derived simply from the existence of a spousal relationship. Under a "compensatory model" the spousal support is considered to be a form of compensation for the economic consequences of the marriage, such as loss of career opportunity through the need to care for children in the past. Under the "clean-break model" the objective of the support order is the severing of economic ties between the spouses so that each may go his or her own way. Support is for a fixed period of time that is transitional and then is terminated.

Before considering the question of calculating the amount of support, we should make it clear that the Divorce Act, of course, only applies to legally married spouses, including same-sex couples. A common-law spouse's entitlement to support arises under provincial law only, as is discussed in Chapter 8. The principles described in this chapter, however, are applicable to both legally married spouses and common-law spouses. When the court is faced with the need to arrive at an amount for spousal support, it looks at essentially the same criteria regardless of the nature of the relationship.

Spousal support is generally made on a periodic basis, with a monthly payment of a fixed sum directly from one spouse to the other, most likely from the husband to the wife. Family law lawyers would agree that the vast majority of spousal support orders are made from men to women, but we are seeing, occasionly, cases in which husbands have stayed home to care for the children, have lost their job, have suffered health problems or other difficulties and sought spousal support from their wives.

To most honest observers in the family law justice system, there does appear to be a double standard for spouses applying for spousal support. We have seen some unusual situations where spousal support claims by men have been rejected by the court under unusual reasoning. In the examples in this chapter, I will be referring to the support as payable from the husband to the wife, but all of the principles described should certainly apply without regard to gender.

The making of spousal support orders, whether under the provincial family law or the Divorce Act, boils down to the consideration of two key factors: (1) the spouse's need for spousal support and (2) the other spouse's ability to pay. Thrown into the mix with these two factors is an increasingly controversial consideration—the spouse's ability to provide for his or her own support.

Before considering the issues of need and ability to pay, including self-sufficiency, one important aspect of the law should be understood. Family law lawyers often meet with clients who angrily refuse to pay spousal support because their former wife or husband is "undeserving." They also tell hair-raising stories of misconduct that would suggest to most people that spousal support would be completely unfair. However, for the most part, the conduct of the spouses during the marriage and, in particular, at the time of separation is not a factor in calculating the amount of spousal support or the entitlement.

There is a little used provision in Ontario's Family Law Act that allows a person to argue that no spousal support should be paid because the other spouse's behaviour constituted "a gross repudiation of the relationship." This section is rarely used. Until very recently, the courts had confirmed that they were not interested in stories about the misconduct of the other spouse, particularly in the context of setting spousal support. Conduct might be relevant to a person's ability to parent, but it was not supposed to be relevant to one's entitlement to spousal support, the quantum of spousal support or its duration.

Typically, the court wanted to know if there was a need for support and if there was an ability to pay; however, all of this changed dramatically with the Supreme Court of Canada decision in Leskun. This case arose in British Columbia and it involved a husband and wife who split up under very unpleasant circumstances. The wife was older than the husband by some 10 years and part of the reason the relationship broke down was that the husband had started a new relationship with a woman he had met through work. To add insult to injury, the wife lost her job and injured her back. She had made a contribution to the husband's improvement in his education, which, in turn, had led to improvements in his earnings.

Certainly, those facts are unhappy ones, but they are not, by any stretch of the imagination, extraordinary in the context of family law disputes. Experienced family law lawyers have seen situations that involve attempted murder or suicides, serious assaults, frauds and heinous behaviour.

What seemed to make the Leskun situation different from all other unpleasant divorces was Ms. Leskun's response to the separation and divorce. She became obsessed with the litigation against her former husband. That obsession, and what appeared to be her ongoing anger with him, kept her from returning to the workforce. In other words, the husband's behaviour leading up to and at the time of the separation contributed to her inability to become economically self-sufficient.

His behaviour, and its effect on her, therefore, became a consideration in the setting of spousal support. The Supreme Court of Canada specifically noted this in its decision and, as a result, tens of thousands of Canadian divorces were re-evaluated overnight as to whether the awful behaviour of a spouse was a contributing factor to the other spouse's inability to become economically self-sufficient.

The case received a great deal of publicity and clients immediately asked lawyers to comment on whether fault, indeed, had been returned to the Canadian law of divorce. The only answer that lawyers can give is yes, but no one is quite sure what impact it will have in the long run.

There are no happy divorces. Everyone is miserable as a result of the marriage breakdown. No one enjoys the litigation in cases where it cannot be resolved. Everyone is affected in their career by the separation and divorce. No one has a monopoly on horrible treatment of their spouse at separation and divorce.

If every divorce in Canada must now contemplate the impact of awful behaviour on the other spouse's ability to return to the workforce, then we will be seeing a great deal of litigation and acrimony for Canadian families over the next few years. In addition, the corollary of the Leskun decision must be true as well, that is, if a spouse's ability to return to the workforce and become economically self-sufficient can be impeded by the way in which they were treated and the way in which they responded to the separation and divorce, then so, too, must the ability to earn an income by the payor spouse. It cannot be long before we see claims by husbands alleging that their ability to earn income has been reduced by the effects of the divorce on them and that there should be a corresponding reduction in their obligation to pay spousal support. This is a development that we will all be watching carefully over the next few years.

In determining the spouse's needs, the circumstances of each case must be examined. Much can depend on the nature of the marriage relationship—whether it was a traditional or a more modern marriage. A dependant spouse is entitled to a standard of living that is equal to what she or he could have expected had the marriage continued (where the parties have had a long-term traditional marriage with the result that the dependant spouse is without job skills or income).

In the following section I will attempt to set out the key considerations in the area of spousal support, both with respect to assessment of need and calculation of the quantum. It should be noted that these are general rules that apply nationally, but there may be some variation on a province-by-province basis.

- In determining a reasonable standard of living, the court must consider the spouse's ability to pay. In one case, the court decided that it was unconscionable to reduce the husband's standard of living below the poverty level in order to provide the wife with a reasonable standard of living. This was so even though the parties were married for 30 years and the wife was unable to work on a full-time basis.

- A wife asking for support is not expected to take any job in an effort to meet her own needs.

- The objective of a spousal support order is not to equalize the incomes of the two spouses.

- The need for spousal support should be assessed after determination of the division of family assets. If the division of assets leaves the spouse with sufficient means to meet his or her reasonable needs, then the court will not order support, or it will order a lower amount than it might otherwise have done.

- The court will also consider whether the prudent investment of the assets through property division at marriage breakdown and the spouse's qualifications for work will reduce the need for support from the other spouse.

- Spousal support has been denied in cases where there was a lengthy marriage but both spouses were employed throughout and after the marriage breakdown, and the funds from the sale of the matrimonial home generated additional income.

When assessing a spouse's need for spousal support at the end of a relationship, the court is very interested in the outcome of the property division. You will recall from earlier chapters dealing with property division that my characterization of the share of a property settlement is the "nest egg" for future self-sufficiency.

The court has always expected spouses to use their post-separation assets to contribute to their own self-sufficiency. In particular, the case of Boston v. Boston, decided by the Supreme Court of Canada, states very clearly that spouses must take their property settlements and invest them in a way that contributes to self-sufficiency. The court went so far as to suggest that spouses post-separation have an obligation to take their assets and consider placing them in a capital-depleting, income-generating fund that would create the equivalent of a "pension." The court stated that they were not requiring spouses to have particular investment savvy or use their property in risky investments, but there is an obligation to use assets to generate self-sufficiency.

In one case, a wife received almost $900,000 in assets at the time of separation. She used some of the assets to purchase a new home; she used some of the balance to do renovations to her new home; and she invested the amount remaining after that in such a way that she could generate nearly $1,500 per month from investment income. The court was interested in her ability to contribute to her own support by making these investments. The question then became how much more spousal support should be contributed by her husband to ensure that her needs were met.

Generally where a spouse is in her late 40s it can be difficult to expect a significant contribution to her own self-sufficiency if she has been out of the workforce for some time. Perhaps part-time work or conservative earnings from some form of employment will help, but there is the possibility that the spousal support will continue indefinitely as the individual need will be continuing indefinitely as well.

For younger spouses in their 20s, 30s and even early 40s, the key question becomes how and when will that spouse become self-sufficient and their need for spousal support thereby terminated. It is these circumstances that lawyers and clients are fighting over daily across Canada. As a general rule, spouses in these age groups are considered obliged to eventually obtain self-sufficiency. This means that they must work and contribute to their own needs as quickly and as effectively as possible.

In some cases, these spouses will need retraining or skills development in order to re-enter the workforce. It is possible that a spousal support order will be made in such a way to allow that retraining to occur. So, for example, if a woman has been out of the workforce for 10 years, but with

retraining could return to her work as a nurse, spousal support will be tailored to finance that retraining, as it allows her to return to a position from
which she could become self-sufficient.

In some cases, this will call for occupational assessments or other employment reviews. The goal is to find the right occupation for this particular
individual and to put him or her on a most effective path to achieving
self-sufficiency. Many spouses are willing participants in this retraining.
They welcome the opportunity to get back to their earlier careers. Childcare needs must be balanced, and in some cases the retraining must even
await the children being in full-time attendance at school, but eventually
the retraining takes place.

For spouses who are reluctant to retrain, the courts have used a variety
of techniques to encourage the return to self-sufficiency. In some cases,
the courts have ordered that spousal support will simply be terminated on
a certain fixed date. In other cases, the courts have ordered that spousal
support is payable for a certain period of time, say three or five years at
the end of which the matter returns to court for review. Some courts have
even used the approach of ordering a spouse to pay spousal support at a
certain level for a fixed period of time and then gradually stepped down
the amount of monthly support to wean the spouse off spousal support as
his or her earnings increase.

It is now rare in Canadian courts to see the courts order a fixed termination date for spousal support. Generally, courts are ordering that at
the very least the matter return to court for a review. Payors of support
are understandably anxious to see their spouses pursue their retraining
and return to work. The sooner they attain self-sufficiency, the sooner the
spousal support obligation can finish. Recipients of spousal support are
understandably nervous about returning to the workforce after extended
absences. In my own approach, I try to encourage the payor spouse to invest heavily and at an early stage in the recipient spouse's retraining. Her
return to the workforce can be eased by agreeing to pay spousal support
even if earnings from part-time employment are steady and significant.

Remarriage/Cohabitation

A question that arises in the area of spousal support concerns the spouse
remarrying. In the past, remarriage has been considered a reason to automatically terminate the payment of spousal support. Lately, however, the
courts have not been firm in this regard, and in some cases spousal support
has continued even after a spouse has remarried. This comes as a shock to
most payors of spousal support.

Spousal Support Release

A very controversial issue that has arisen in the area of spousal support is the ability to release the entitlement to spousal support. A spouse may wish to make a lump sum one-time payment to another spouse in satisfaction of any and all future claims for spousal support. For some couples, this is a desirable way of making a clean break. A case in Ontario, however, in which a spouse accepted a lump sum payment in exchange for a full release of spousal support has blown up and completely undermined the confidence lawyers and clients have in spousal support releases. In that case, the wife had signed a release but had used up the lump sum payment. It was a possibility that she might lose her home and she returned to court to have the spousal support release thrown out. On an interim basis (pending the trial) the judge ordered that spousal support be paid even though a release had been signed. It became next to impossible to settle a case using a lump sum spousal support payment.

New wording for spousal support releases was drafted by the Law Society of Upper Canada and circulated to lawyers to ensure that model wording was used if clients wished to enter into a spousal support release. Now, if there has been full disclosure, independent legal advice and a generally fair result overall, the court will enforce spousal support releases.

This does not mean that lawyers do not remain uncomfortable with spousal support releases, terminations of spousal support and lump sum orders. Lawyers cannot guarantee clients that the release will not be completely disregarded at a later date. The decisions of the courts have injected a great deal of unpredictability to this area.

As a result, more and more emphasis has been placed on the periodic monthly support payment and the methods by which spouses can become self-sufficient. Lawyers and clients are not prepared to take the risk that the release will be completely disregarded at a later date. As a result, more and more emphasis has been placed on the periodic monthly support payment and the methods by which spouses can become self-sufficient.

One related consequence of the unpredictability of the spousal support area is that lawyers find themselves unable to recommend any settlements in the area of spousal support other than indefinite spousal support awards, which at the very most would be reviewed in several years. Few lawyers are prepared to recommend that a spouse accept a termination date for spousal support in the current environment. This, you can imagine, makes it extremely difficult for lawyers to settle cases involving spousal support claims, particularly where those spouses are in their mid- to late 40s and their chances for retraining are unknown.

The courts will usually include a cost of living allowance clause, which will increase the amount of spousal support in accordance with the cost of living each year. This reduces the likelihood that the parties will need to return to court for support increases at a later date.

Variation of Spousal Support

Just as in the case of child support orders, it may be necessary for a spouse to return to court for a variation of the amount of spousal support if a material change in circumstance has occurred. For example, where the payor of support has been laid off or has suffered health problems, it may be necessary to return to court to have the spousal support reduced. Similarly, if the recipient spouse's needs have changed, it may be necessary to return to court to have the amount paid varied upwards.

Earlier I mentioned the case of Boston v. Boston. This is precisely the situation that occurred. Long after separation, the payor husband retired and wished to reduce his monthly spousal support obligation. The case went all the way to the Supreme Court of Canada, where it was determined that his spousal support payments should be reduced and that only the portion of his pension that had accrued after the date of separation should be used for the purposes of calculating the monthly spousal support award to his ex-wife.

Spousal Support Guidelines

As you can tell from the foregoing paragraphs, there is a great deal of unpredictability around the entitlement to spousal support, its quantum and the appropriate date for termination. In response to that unpredictability, a committee of lawyers and judges developed a set of Guidelines known as the Spousal Support Advisory Guidelines. These guidelines are just that—guidelines. They are not binding on courts, they are not binding on lawyers and they are not binding on clients. They are, in some cases, persuasive and can be used to guide separating couples to a particular outcome.

The approach in the Advisory Guidelines is to use one of two basic formulas for the determination of spousal support. One formula deals with a situation where there are no children; the other formula deals with a situation where there are children. Both formulas use income sharing as a method for calculating spousal support.

They do not zero in so much on budgets as they do on the ability of the parties to share income. Use of the formulae provides a range for the quantum and duration of support. They do not deal with the entitlement to spousal support.

The financial obligation post-separation for a spouse can far exceed the value of the assets that change hands at the point of separation. The need for self-sufficiency and the methods by which the courts encourage spouses to become self-sufficient and the methods by which courts seek to review, reduce or eliminate spousal support will be the subject of many, many cases in the years to come. It is also expected that we will see a great deal of litigation in our courts over the effectiveness of spousal support releases that have been signed over the last 15 years.

On one final note, I have met with more than one client over the last few years who has described to me difficulties in their marriage and their concerns about the financial costs of separation. In some cases, those spouses returned to their marriages and encouraged their partners to retrain and return to the workforce in anticipation of separating from them after self-sufficiency has been achieved. In other cases, I have met with clients who have concluded that it is better to separate when their spouse is in their 30s then to wait until the children and the spouse are older and face the risk of having to support that spouse indefinitely. Tough decisions must be made in many families.

PARENTAL SUPPORT

The Divorce Act does not contain any provisions concerning parental support, but provincial family laws now provide in some jurisdictions that a parent in need of support can obtain it from a child of the marriage. The courts have had little experience with this type of provision, but some general rules of thumb have emerged.

There are nearly a dozen cases across Canada that have interpreted the parental entitlement to support. In some cases, the children have been ordered to make a partial contribution to their parents' monthly budget. For example, one daughter was ordered to pay her father's condo fees.

Ontario's provision states that every child who is not a minor has an obligation to provide support, in accordance with need, for his or her parents who have cared for or provided support for the child, to the extent that the child is capable of doing so.

As you can see, such an order could only be made against a child who has reached the age of majority and again the court looks at the parents' needs as well as the child's ability to pay. Support will only be ordered for parents who have cared for or provided support for the child from whom they are now seeking support.

The times at which this claim arises can be interesting. In a recent case, a long-standing common-law couple separated. The common-law wife sued her common-law husband for spousal support and the husband's response was to join into the family law case the common-law wife's daughter from a previous relationship. The common-law husband alleged that the daughter should be required to support the mother. In other cases, older spouses have sought spousal support from their legally married spouse or common-law spouse at the time of separation and the spouse against whom the support claim has been made has sought to join the children from the family in the litigation to have them contribute to the other parent's ongoing support. In one case, an adult child had won a million dollars in a lottery and a parent sued the child for support. The court commented that the parent was not entitled to seek an increase in his or her standard of living simply because the child had won a lottery, but it would be reasonable for a child in such circumstances to contribute to any necessary expenses of the parent that the parent was unable to meet on their own.

These cases are complicated, even more so where there is more than one child against whom the support claim can be advanced. Each child may have different financial circumstances, family circumstances and different complaints about the quality of parenting they received from the parent now seeking support.

Again, as we see our population aging, it may not be uncommon in the very near future to see parents seeking support from their children where pension plans and other forms of public assistance do not meet the parents' needs. This may well be the family law litigation of the 21st century. I expect this portion of the chapter to be significantly enlarged by the time I write the next edition of this book!

CONCLUSION

Child and spousal support orders are key components of families moving on to new lives after separation and divorce. Thanks to the Child Support Guidelines, the quantum of child support is more adequate and less controversial in cases of separation and divorce. Spousal support, however, will continue to be controversial and the subject of much debate between husbands and wives—and their lawyers.

CHECKLIST

1. Do you understand the difference between the Divorce Act and provincial law with respect to child and spousal support?

2. Do you understand the way in which the Child Support Guidelines operate based on gross annual income and the number of children?

3. Have you consulted a lawyer about the application of the Guidelines to your case?

4. Do you understand the difference between the base amount of child support and the amount for special or extraordinary expenses?

5. Do you understand the role of joint custody and the division of the child's time between two households in relation to child support?

6. Do you understand the significance of May 2006 and that the Child Support Guidelines apply to all child support orders, including variations of order that occur after that date?

7. Do you understand that each province has its own tables of child support amounts?

8. Do you understand that child support is payable until the child is no longer below the age of majority, or until the age of 22 if the child continues in full-time attendance at an educational institution?

9. Do you understand that child support can be varied at any time upwards or downwards and the court is never bound by any agreement between the parents?

10. Do you understand that biological and other individuals who have treated the child as if he or she was their own are required to pay child support?

11. Do you understand the meaning of withdrawing from parental control and how it can be used to terminate child support?

(Continued)

12. Do you understand the various taxation rules with respect to pre-1997 and post-1997 child support orders?

13. Do you understand the ways in which the court will approach the ordering of spousal support?

14. What is your likelihood of achieving self-sufficiency or of your spouse achieving self-sufficiency?

15. What is the role of post-separation assets in the calculating of spousal support in your case?

8

COMMON-LAW SPOUSES HAVE RIGHTS, TOO

~

THE MEANING OF "COMMON LAW"

In this chapter, we will examine the meaning of the term "common law" and the misconceptions that surround it, and identify the rights and obligations of a common-law spouse when the relationship comes to an end. These rights and obligations may include: support, property sharing, pension sharing, custody of and access to children and financial support of children.

What does it mean to live "common law"? Most people would say it means "living together as if you were husband and wife but not actually getting married." The expression appears in few, if any, statutes passed by either the federal or provincial governments. It seems to have its origins in the English term "common-law marriage," which was a marriage not solemnized in the usual way but created instead by an agreement to marry in the future, which was then in turn followed by cohabitation (living together).

Living in common-law relationships has become very popular in Canada, particularly in Quebec. The results of each census provide more and more evidence that Canadians are prepared to live common law, particularly as a way of checking out whether they want to ultimately marry.

Common-law relationships are also very popular among those who are entering second or subsequent relationships.

Common-law relationships are also volatile. Statistics have told us that, where someone's first conjugal relationship was a common-law relationship, it is twice as likely to break down as a situation where someone's first conjugal relationship is a marriage. So, first-time common-law couples break up twice as fast as first-time married couples. About only 12 per cent of common-law relationships ever get to celebrate a 10th anniversary. On the other hand, 90 per cent of first marriages last at least 10 years.

Common-law relationships do not always start in the most orderly or legalistic way. For some people, living together arises out of necessity and may grow into a more intimate relationship. For others, it is a conscious choice to avoid the legal obligations imposed by marriage. Still others live together unmarried because they have no choice—one of them is married to someone else and not divorced. They are, therefore, unable to remarry.

Rather than use the expression "common-law spouse" in their statutes, several provinces and territories have instead expanded the meaning of the term "spouse" in some limited circumstances to acknowledge that there are consequences for men and women, whether in heterosexual or homosexual relationships, when they choose to live together but do not marry. The definition of spouse for common-law purposes varies from province to province. The federal law, the Divorce Act, of course has no interest in common-law spouses. The Divorce Act applies only to those who actually took the step of getting married.

Ontario's Family Law Act, which provides for property division and support on marriage breakdown, deals with the common-law spouse issue in an interesting way. Part I of the Act deals with property division and for that part of the Act "spouse" is defined essentially as people who are legally married. However, Part III of the Family Law Act deals with support obligations and Part III defines "spouse" as including three categories of couples:

1. people who get legally married,

2. people who live together for three or more years (whether a heterosexual couple or a same-sex couple) or

3. people who live together in a relationship of some permanence and have a child (adopted or natural).

In Ontario this means that when property is being divided after a common-law couple separates, the sections of the Act dealing with property division *do not apply* to them because they are not legally married.

However, it also means that each person *will* be entitled to claim support from the other under Part III if they fit the expanded definition of spouse.

Let's now consider the rights and obligations of common-law spouses upon the end of the relationship in relation to three important areas: (1) children, (2) spousal support and (3) property division.

CHILDREN IN COMMON-LAW RELATIONSHIPS

All things considered, this is one of the less complicated aspects of common-law relationships. The Divorce Act, of course, does not apply, so all issues concerning the children are decided pursuant to provincial family law. Custody issues will be decided in accordance with the child's best interests, as will any access entitlement (see Chapter 6). Provincial law applies to the children of common-law spouses and there will be child support obligations if the relationship ends. The Child Support Guidelines apply to child support calculations, regardless of the existence of a legal marriage or a common-law relationship (See Chapter 7).

SPOUSAL SUPPORT

Most Canadian jurisdictions have defined "spouse" in such a way that extends an entitlement to or duty to pay support at the end of a common-law relationship.

The area of common-law relationships has been the subject of a great deal of reform over the last few years. If you are cohabiting with someone, I urge you to speak with a lawyer in your province to determine the exact definition of common-law spouse for your purposes. Each province is different, each province has been evolving its own provincial law and each province, therefore, has its own cases interpreting the treatment of common-law spouses.

For example, in Ontario and Manitoba, in order to qualify as a common-law relationship for the purposes of spousal support, three years of continuous cohabitation is required. The exception is a relationship of some permanence if the couple are the natural or adoptive parents of a child, then it doesn't matter if you have been living together for less than three years. In Nova Scotia, the period of cohabitation required is two years. British Columbia, as well, requires a two-year period of cohabitation.

Regardless of whether the period of required cohabitation is one, two or three years, the court must still consider whether the people involved have actually been cohabiting. This means evaluating the relationship.

When examining a common-law relationship, judges consider a set of criteria based on cases that have gone to court. The court will consider the following:

- Did the partners share accommodations?
- Did one render domestic services to the other?
- Was there a sharing of household expenses? (not necessarily equal sharing)
- Was there sexual intimacy between them?
- Are they of the opposite sex? (with the exception of some provinces that now offer support for same-sex couples)
- What was the nature of their relationship?
- Were they husband and wife for all intents and purposes?

The courts have found that where there has been a relationship of such significance that it has led to the actual dependency of one party on another or the expectation that one will support the other in the event of financial crisis, an entitlement to support arises where there is a case of need.

Assuming the individual qualifies, the amount of the support and its duration is calculated in the same way that it is calculated for legally married spouses who have separated (see Chapter 7—Support). Aspects that can make these cases different include the length of the relationship and the court's willingness to make support orders time limited, that is, not open-ended or indefinite.

It should be noted that in many jurisdictions, this obligation for support of a common-law spouse may also apply with respect to an estate. That is, if a person dies leaving a common-law spouse as his or her survivor, that person may be able to obtain an order of support from the estate.

To all outside appearances, a common-law relationship and a legally married couple may look exactly the same. However, that little piece of paper—the Marriage Certificate—makes a big difference. Married couples know when they get married because they have an official government document that records the date, establishing the beginning of their marriage. They may argue about when it ended, but they definitely know when it started. The same is not true for common-law couples. Their relationship many need to be put under a microscope to determine when it started, when it finished and if it was, in fact, common-law continuously for the required period. Once all the hurdles are crossed, the spousal support is calculated essentially the same way, but there can be some extra work getting there.

PROPERTY DIVISION FOR COMMON-LAW COUPLES

A common-law couple can acquire some significant assets over a few short years—a home, cars, furniture, RRSPs, CSBs, a joint savings account—all without so much as a discussion about what would happen if one of them died or if they separated. That is why lawyers hear the familiar "Well, I just assumed . . ." or "I thought we would just share it equally . . ." or even worse, "I never intended to share that . . ." and so on.

With so many Canadians living in common-law relationships and so many of these relationships volatile, the courts and legislatures have begun to struggle with the question of property division. No laws in Canada— until very recently—extended any property sharing to common-law couples. The presumption was that they would leave the marriage with what they brought in and would leave with anything that was in their name. If they owned a car at the beginning of the relationship and they still own the car at the end, they would be presumed to take that car with them. If they made a contribution to an RRSP during the course of the common-law relationship, they would be presumed to take that contribution with them. Jointly held property was presumed to be divided jointly unless they could prove that there was a good reason to not divide it jointly.

As I mentioned earlier, each province has its own way of dealing with common-law spouses and a patchwork has now developed across Canada. Just like with spousal support, it is absolutely essential that you consult directly with a lawyer in your province to determine exactly what your property rights may be as you head into a common-law relationship and, most certainly, as you head out of it.

We cannot review each province individually, but I want to illustrate in the following paragraphs some of the different ways in which common-law spouses are treated in Canada.

Ontario has a system that extends to common-law couples only spousal support rights. When a common-law couple's relationship ends, the various provincial laws have nothing to say about the way in which property is divided. They have no statutory property rights. In fact, most lawyers and judges would agree that Ontario takes probably the hardest line in dealing with common-law spouses at the time of separation. If common-law spouses are to gain a share of property that is in the name of the other spouse, they must not only prove that they made a contribution of some kind to that property, but they must also convince a court that it would be unjust to allow that other person to be enriched at their expense. We will talk a little more about this in a few minutes, but in Ontario the bottom line for common-law couples when dividing property at separation is that there is no statutory help for dividing their property.

Manitoba tackled the question of common-law couples and property division in a different way. They passed a law called the Common-Law Partners' Property and Related Amendments Act. It came into force on June 30, 2004. Before that date, a common-law couple splitting up in Manitoba was treated essentially the same way as a couple in Ontario. That is, spousal support rights would apply, but there was no statutory assistance in dividing property. After June 30, 2004, if a common-law couple splits up, each partner will be entitled to half the value of the property acquired by the couple during the time they lived together. This includes division of any pension entitlements. These new laws in Manitoba apply to common-law couples who register their relationship at the Vital Statistics Agency or couples who, if they have not registered, have lived together for a certain period of time (three years) or less if there is a child involved.

This is a huge change in the way in which common-law couples are treated. This means that a common-law couple who lives together three or more years in Ontario and then splits up has no statutory rights, but a common-law couple who lived together exactly the same way for the exact same period of time on the other side of the border in Manitoba will share full division of property.

Nova Scotia adopted a system of registered domestic partnership. In the year 2000, the Nova Scotia Legislature amended its Vital Statistics Act to permit two individuals who are cohabiting or who intend to cohabit to make a "Domestic-Partner Declaration." The Declaration must be signed by both people and it must be witnessed. Once the Declaration is made, it is then registered and certain rights flow. The net effect of the changes in Nova Scotia means that there are four categories of cohabiting couples, as follows:

1. There will be married people who have all the rights and obligations given by provincial law to legally married spouses.

2. There are common-law partners who live together for two or more years, whether the couple is opposite sex or same sex.

3. There could be a couple registered as domestic partners regardless of the period of time that they have cohabited. This would apply to opposite sex or same-sex couples.

4. And finally, there are likely in Nova Scotia some unmarried cohabiting couples who do not meet the statutory test for common-law partners and have not registered as domestic partners. They would not have any property rights.

You can see from the above examples that the treatment of common-law couples in Canada is now becoming more and more confusing. It is also becoming more and more critical for couples to consult with lawyers in their province to determine their exact rights. Do you meet the cohabitation test? Have you been in a conjugal relationship? Could you register your relationship under some provincial legislation and thereby gain rights? Can you sign a Cohabitation Agreement? If you have registered your relationship, can you de-register it? And so on.

These are all extremely important questions and, unfortunately, depending upon the province in which you reside, there will be very different answers. Canadians are also a mobile population. We move from province to province and for common-law couples this means that there could very well be a change in their status. Imagine the disappointment of a couple that moves from Manitoba to Ontario in the second year of their relationship. They may have been poised to gain property rights, only to learn upon separating in Ontario a few years later that there is no statutory recognition of property rights for the common-law couple.

The courts have also developed some general guidelines over the years to help common-law couples sort out such property division matters where the law does not do it for them:

- In the absence of an intention to the contrary, each person may leave the relationship with any assets they brought in and any acquired in their name alone during the relationship.

- The court will not allow one person to be "unjustly enriched" at the other person's expense.

- Where one of the persons confers a benefit on the other person and suffers a corresponding deprivation as a result and there is no other legal reason or justification for the enrichment, the court may "correct" the situation through the use of a device called the "constructive trust." A constructive trust is simply a fancy legal way of saying to the spouse who has the property in his or her own name (called having "title"), "You are actually holding that property or part of its value in trust for your partner." The court then orders the part considered to be held in trust to be paid over to the other person.

An example might be helpful. Let's assume a man and a woman decided to live together in Ontario. Over a couple of years, they each saved $10,000 to put down on a home. They bought the house in the man's name with a vague intention to marry someday and live in it. Over the next several years, they moved in, and both paid the mortgage and expenses as best they could, although not equally. A child was born and the woman agreed to stay home to care for the child and the home. She then inherited $50,000 and, rather than start a small business, she agreed to renovate the kitchen and build a playroom. They later separate, with the house still in the man's name. Would the man be unjustly enriched at the woman's expense if he kept the whole house? Did she confer a benefit on him and suffer a corresponding deprivation by renovating instead of starting a business? Would the court correct this by imposing a trust upon him to hold a share of the house's value for her? The answer is yes to all three questions.

The same approach is true of all property acquired by common-law spouses, whether it is the home or the furniture in it. The court will look at their intentions and their contributions and try to achieve a fair split that does not leave one enriched at the other's expense.

Other general rules used by the courts when dealing with such cases include:

- Each case is different. The size of an interest in a piece of property will depend on the facts of the particular case.

- A contribution does not automatically entitle a person to a half interest. The court will determine what is a fair return on the actual contribution.

- The court prefers a direct connection between the contribution and the property in question. It does not necessarily have to be a contribution directly to the acquisition of the property. It could be some act that preserved the property, maintained it or improved it.

- Merely being a supportive good partner or paying some household expenses will not necessarily entitle one to a share of a property. Remember, there must be the aspect of one being unjustly enriched at the other's expense. The case law is evolving on this point.

- There have been cases that found home, childcare and housekeeping services to have been a "contribution," but in such cases the spouse who cared for the child or did the house duties freed the other spouse to earn and acquire property.

- The court will consider the intention of each person, but does not insist that both have the same intention. It will consider what each person reasonably expected to happen or what interest in the property they reasonably expected.

- If the property in one spouse's name is there because it was a gift from the other spouse, then the court will not "correct" the situation. One cannot be "unjustly enriched" by a gift.

Matrimonial Home

It should also be noted, in the context of this discussion of common-law property rights, that since there is no "matrimony," there can be no matrimonial home. Again, the provinces vary in their treatment of the home owned by the couple. Some provinces now extend special rights. Other provinces, such as Ontario, do not extend any special protection for the homes of common-law couples. There is no such thing as a common-law couple in Ontario having the right to claim exclusive possession of the home in the same way that a legally married spouse would. This means that it is absolutely essential that a common-law couple preparing to split consults with a provincial lawyer to determine any special rights that may be afforded to their common-law "matrimonial home."

Pensions

Before leaving the area of property we should look at one special area that for common-law spouses requires protection—pensions.

Everyone acquires Canada Pension Plan benefits over their working life. The Canada Pension Act provides that persons of the opposite sex who had been living together for at least one year and who have been separated for more than a year may apply to the federal government for a division of pension credits. So, where a working spouse acquires credits, the other spouse may apply to share them. An application must be accompanied by the "necessary details" of course—birth certificate, Social Insurance Number, addresses (current and at cohabitation), relevant dates of cohabitation and separation and, for some reason, the reason for the separation.

FEDERAL LEGISLATION

While it is the provinces that determine division of property for common-law couples, there are many benefits and entitlements or obligations that may arise under federal law. The federal government passed the Modernization of Benefits and Obligations Act in 2000. This Act amended approximately 67 federal statutes so that the benefits, rights and obligations given to married persons would also apply in the same way to common-law couples. The definition of "common-law couple" was set at two persons who are cohabiting in a conjugal relationship, having done so for a period of at least one year. This means that federal legislation treats common-law couples (again, whether opposite sex or same sex) who cohabit for one year in pretty much the same way as it treats married couples.

COHABITATION AGREEMENTS

The best way, in my opinion, is to address the issue of common-law rights and obligations head on—"Honey, what would we do if something went wrong?" If the investments are significant or complicated (e.g., they involve money from either family), you should seriously consider a Cohabitation Agreement. This type of domestic contract is the equivalent of a Marriage Contract and is designed for people who will not be legally married but will live together.

Cohabitation Agreements are contracts. These contracts are not difficult to prepare (written, signed, witnessed), but like any contract that affects your property they should be prepared with independent legal advice.

Don't be reluctant to raise the subject. If your relationship is strong, then it will survive this type of planning. Look on the bright side: you can make Powers of Attorney and wills at the same time and save yourself a trip to the lawyer's office.

LEGAL ADVICE

It is particularly important to consult a lawyer about division of property when lengthy common-law relationships collapse or where significant assets are involved. Canada Pension credits should also be discussed with your lawyer.

What can be done in cases where the common-law couple wishes to make joint purchases or investments? The best route, of course, is to think in advance about what you feel should happen if one of you died or you separated. It can be a difficult subject to raise because it means confronting the possibility of two very unpleasant possibilities. Who wants to think about that when things are going so well? You do.

CONCLUSION

The purpose of this chapter is to open the eyes of people in common-law relationships or those thinking about being in one. The rights and obligations are very limited; the right to ask for support and the duty to pay it if the relationship has created a dependency. Sorting out property purchased jointly can be extremely difficult and confusing. If left to the courts, property division can be very rough justice. Custody and access issues are determined in exactly the same way as with the children of legally married spouses. The same is true of the parents' obligation to support their children.

In conclusion, let me add a caution once again about the importance of consulting with a lawyer in your province or territory to determine exactly what your provincial or territorial law provides for you.

CHECKLIST

1. Does your province or territory offer support or property rights to common-law couples? If so, do you meet the province's or territory's definition of common-law spouse?

2. Have you consulted with a lawyer in your province or territory to determine whether you qualify as a common-law spouse?

3. Do you own property with your common-law partner?

4. Have you discussed or considered how your property would be divided or protected if one of you died or if your relationship came to an end?

5. Do you understand that children of common-law relationships are treated exactly the same as children of legally married couples for the purposes of custody, access and support?

6. Do you understand the peculiar rules used to assist common-law spouses in dividing their property, including the constructive trust?

7. Do you keep records of your contribution to the acquisition of assets in your relationship? What evidence would you use to prove which property is yours?

8. Have you considered the possibility of using a Cohabitation Agreement to clarify your rights and obligations should the relationship end or one of you die?

9. Do you have a will? Do you have Powers of Attorney for personal care and for property?

SETTLING YOUR DIFFERENCES

~

Avoiding the Courtroom

One of the goals of this book is to help you make some intelligent choices about your family difficulties. Reasonable choices will lead, in the vast majority of cases, to settlement. So, I want to spend a few minutes looking at how and why settlements are reached.

We have already examined the potential emotional obstacles to settlement (see Chapter 1—Taking a Look at Ourselves). Assuming none of those problems are clouding your decision, at some point in time you and your lawyer will realize that a settlement is close, that your needs are capable of being met without going to court for an imposed court order.

A settlement should be reached because that is what the people involved want and because it is fair to both of them. Unfortunately, this is not the case for many lawyers and their clients. Some cases settle for other less satisfactory reasons. Consider the client who settles because she is emotionally tired or weakened or frightened of an abusive husband. She settles to avoid further conflict. Or, consider the client who settles because he cannot afford to go to court anymore.

There are too many clients who settle because the cost of proceeding outweighs the benefit of an immediate settlement. This can mean either that the client cannot afford to pay his or her lawyer to continue a valid case or that the net amount that can be recovered exceeds that which would remain after a trial.

Sometimes a case is settled because it has not been prepared properly. Necessary evidence was not provided, the case is called for hearing and the lawyer or client is not prepared to go to court or has been tactically outmanoeuvred. These are all less than satisfactory reasons for a client to settle a dispute.

A case that is settled on such uneasy ground is not settled for long. I have met too many family law clients who feel they were pressured into a settlement with which they were unhappy. In one case the client was summoned to her lawyer's office to discuss a settlement offer that had just been received by fax on the eve of the court appearance. The offer, as it turned out, was not very different from a previous settlement proposal. The lawyer reviewed the offer with the client after which the following exchange took place.

Lawyer:	"Well, basically that's it. I think you should accept it and avoid a trial."
Client:	"But, it's not what I had in mind. I thought . . ."
Lawyer:	"Well, if you don't accept the offer I will need a $10,000 retainer before we go to court."
Client:	"What? $10,000? I can't write a cheque for $10,000. Could you wait until we win the trial? I'll pay you out of what we recover."
Lawyer:	"Oh I can't do that. There's no guarantee we would be successful. In fact, if we lose you may have to pay your husband's legal costs. Your case does have some weaknesses. There are no guarantees, especially in family law cases."
Client:	"But I thought we had a good case. You said . . ."
Lawyer:	"Do you want to go to court?"
Client:	"What should I do?"
Lawyer:	"It's your decision."

Suddenly the case wasn't as good as it seemed six months earlier and the client had the unmistakable feeling of a rug being pulled out from under her. This happens all too frequently, leaving clients unhappy with the process, thinking that the settlement had very little to do with what they wanted or what they were entitled to. Before long, the tainted agreement is being twisted this way and that way by a dissatisfied spouse looking for some advantage to compensate for their unhappiness. Of course, once the agreement is ignored or breached, the whole struggle begins again. Therefore, in this chapter I want to talk about the documents related to the possible settlement of your case:

- Offers to Settle,
- Minutes of Settlement,
- Orders on Consent and
- Separation Agreements.

It may not always seem obvious, but the lawyers handling the matter actually have a professional obligation to encourage you and your spouse to settle or compromise. Lawyers' rules of professional conduct tell us that we must advise and encourage the client to compromise or settle a dispute whenever it is possible to do so on a reasonable basis. We must discourage the client from commencing useless legal proceedings.

Keep that in mind as your case progresses.

OFFERS TO SETTLE

Offers to Settle come in two forms—informal ones, contained in letters exchanged by lawyers, or formal ones, contained in a document prescribed by the Rules of Court. Both are valid and binding, if accepted. As negotiations go on between your respective lawyers, bits and pieces of the case start to get resolved. One letter may confirm an agreement on the sale of the home, another may fix the amount of child support and so on. In some cases, settlement of one issue is conditional upon settlement of another. For example, a father may agree to pay a child's hockey camp expenses provided he has the child for two months each summer. If one part of an offer is accepted, then the other part can be resolved. After the exchange of several letters, a basic agreement may take shape.

Often an experienced lawyer will see fairly quickly an appropriate middle ground upon which the parties can settle. He or she may contact the client to discuss a possible settlement and seek permission to propose it to the other side. A first letter may contain proposals on several matters. With skill and correct timing, it may resolve the dispute; however, in many cases it does not, and more letters are exchanged or proceedings are commenced or moved to the next step. Settling demands a great deal of patience from everyone. Keep in mind the emotional stages discussed in Chapter 1—Taking a Look at Ourselves.

One caution I wish to offer is with regard to the famous "Without Prejudice" letters. Those words often appear at the top of each letter exchanged between lawyers. Many clients don't understand why those words appear on some letters but not others. The short answer is that we have a system that (we hope) tries to encourage people to settle their differences out of court. To do so, people, including lawyers, need to be able to speak to each other frankly without fear that some remark or admission will be used against them later in court if the matter doesn't settle.

Lawyers have developed a system of shielding discussions designed to settle the case from disclosure in court at a later date. For example, lawyers might say such things as "My client did not do what your client says he did. However, without prejudice to my client's case at a later date in court, I am willing to recommend that my client pay a fixed amount to your client to settle this matter." By using the words "without prejudice" he prevents the other lawyer from even mentioning the Offer to Settle at a later date.

Consequently, whenever you see a letter marked "without prejudice," it is usually an attempt to resolve the case without admitting the client did anything wrong or to prevent reference to it later.

A more formal type of offer is provided by the Rules of Court. There is even a prescribed form for it. This form is a relatively new innovation and was designed to end arguments that often developed between lawyers over who offered what in the informal letters discussed above. Usually, at the end of a trial, lawyers would stand up with their letters that offered to settle and say that the other person should have to pay all the costs of the trial because they had been offered the same thing (or better) long ago.

For example, a wife may have offered to accept $2,000 a month for support. If her husband rejected that offer, went to court and ended up paying $2,000, then it makes sense that he should pay for the cost of everyone going to court. The trouble was that letters marked "without prejudice" could not be used to tell the court what the offer had been and even if they could, lawyers frequently argued about what the lawyer's letter actually meant. Judges found it confusing and often ordered everyone to just pay their own lawyer and go home.

To solve these problems, the formal Offer to Settle was developed. It operates the same way as the letter but has some important differences. First, because of the Rules, all formal Offers to Settle look the same and follow the same format, meaning there is less to argue about.

Second, the Offer to Settle is made with the specific understanding that it will be drawn to the attention of the judge at the end of the trial. The Offer to Settle means in so many words, "I think the judge will decide the case as follows . . . so let's settle the case on that basis. If you don't accept my Offer to Settle and the judge orders the same thing or better for my client, then I intend to show him or her this Offer to Settle."

The Rules of Court provide that if an Offer to Settle is made but not accepted and the judge orders the same terms as the original offer, then the person who rejected the offer must pay all the costs incurred between the date the Offer to Settle was made and the end of the trial. This can be particularly onerous if an experienced family law lawyer makes a shrewd, but fair, Offer to Settle early in the proceedings.

One judge described family law cases as "extremely lengthy and ruinously expensive because of one or the other party's unreasonable and unrealistic demands upon the other." He went on to say that "extended family litigation has become unbearably expensive" and that he would insist on Offers to Settle being made. The Rules now require that Offers to Settle be made in such cases.

As you can see, the Offer to Settle creates a lot of pressure. It cannot be rejected out of hand and it forces the lawyer and the client to think about their own case and how it might turn out. Whether the Offer to Settle is formal or informal, a lawyer who receives one must tell his or her client about it and provide a recommendation about possible acceptance or rejection. Even if the offer is unreasonable, the client must be told about it. It is not up to the lawyer to judge what the client might or might not accept.

Assuming an Offer to Settle is accepted, the lawyers may recommend incorporating the agreement into Minutes of Settlement, an Order on Consent, or a Separation Agreement.

MINUTES OF SETTLEMENT

Anyone who has ever been to a business meeting knows that someone is usually asked to "take the minutes." This involves making as detailed a record of the discussion as possible. Minutes of Settlement are no more than the details of a settlement discussion that took place, often after legal proceedings have commenced. One of the lawyers might volunteer to draft up a summary of a settlement reached through the exchange of letters, Offers to Settle or even a face-to-face meeting between all the lawyers and the clients. In some cases, the clients have just finished a court hearing or a "pre-trial" (see Chapter 3—Taking a Look at the Process) and a consensus emerges while everyone is still at the courthouse.

Minutes of Settlement should always be signed by the clients themselves and are usually witnessed by the lawyers. In many cases they are completely handwritten or partially typed and partially handwritten. I have often seen lawyers sitting in hallways using their briefcases as makeshift desks furiously scribbling out a settlement just reached in another room. Their haste is often out of fear that one client or the other might change their mind.

Once signed, the Minutes of Settlement are binding and enforceable. To avoid any argument, many lawyers often incorporate the agreement reached into an order of the court made on consent.

ORDERS ON CONSENT

You will recall that the court makes orders in response to requests made by the lawyers and their clients. The request is often in the form of a Notice of Motion and is supported by an Affidavit. In many cases, the lawyers have scheduled competing motions to be heard at the same time so that several matters can be resolved at one time.

As the lawyers and clients wait for their turn to be heard, discussion may yield some common ground. By the time the lawyers are ready to stand up and argue in front of the judge, a settlement on one of several issues may have emerged. One lawyer may simply advise the court, "Your Honour, the parties have reached an agreement on this matter and we ask that you make the following order on consent." The lawyers are using the time booked at court to record the settlement in an actual court order. This saves time and protects the parties' settlement.

It doesn't always occur while waiting to be heard by a judge. Sometimes the exchange of settlement letters or Offers to Settle produces an agreement that is then incorporated into an "order on consent"—an order that everyone agrees should be made.

SEPARATION AGREEMENTS

The Separation Agreement is by far the most popular method of settling family law disputes. Essentially, the spouses, through their lawyers, sign a contract that sets out the terms of their settlement. We sometimes hear people refer to this as a "legal separation." The alternative, living separate from each other without a written agreement, is not an "illegal separation," as there is no requirement for people to have a written Separation Agreement. There are, as we shall see in a moment, several advantages to a written agreement. It is also worth noting that Separation Agreements are used whether the couple separating was legally married or not. In other words, a common-law couple will also sign a Separation Agreement.

Legal proceedings need not have been commenced in order to use a Separation Agreement. In fact, many people consult lawyers, negotiate and sign Separation Agreements without ever seeing the inside of a courtroom.

They are the lucky ones. Others feel obliged to experience the courtroom and its related expense and only turn to the Separation Agreement as a way out of the court system. Mediation (which is discussed in Chapter 11—Alternatives to Court) frequently yields an amicable settlement, which can then be incorporated into a Separation Agreement. So, while the use of Separation Agreements can arise in a number of ways, their purpose remains basically the same—to settle the dispute by contract.

The technical requirements for a Separation Agreement are not extensive. The contract must be written, signed by the parties and witnessed. All law firms have computer systems that contain thousands of model agreements and clauses. As the lawyer identifies the appropriate settlement, he or she simply picks and chooses from a precedent book the necessary clauses and paragraphs. A law clerk or secretary inserts the family details and related information. A hard copy (paper version) is produced and reviewed with the client. We will look at the agreement itself in a moment, but you can see at this point that there is no magic in the "legal separation." It is a contract like any other. If you wish to change or amend it later or even cancel (revoke) it, it must be done by the same method.

Let's consider the reasons for having such a contract. There are several advantages.

• The negotiations themselves have a way of making the couple consider things they might not otherwise have thought relevant. Not only must they resolve the disputes about the past but also think of the future—Where will I live? Can I move with the children to another province? What will happen to my estate if I die? And so on.

• A written agreement that the couple can refer to from time to time offers predictability in the future. There is less room for debate when it is there in black and white. A related advantage is the fact that those among us (you know who you are) who have trouble honouring their verbal promises (you say things like "I never said that!") are less able to walk away from a written promise.

• In every province, Separation Agreements can be enforced like any other contract. They are legally binding. An added advantage in many provinces is that support provisions in Separation Agreements can be filed with the court or "Support Enforcement Agency" (see Chapter 12—Enforcing Family Law Orders) and enforced as if they were court orders. This can be a great advantage to a person wishing to enforce a promise to pay support.

• Also related to the question of spousal support is the fact that tax advantages will arise if the obligation to pay support is in a Separation

Agreement. Revenue Canada permits a person paying spousal support to deduct the amount paid. (No agreement means no tax deduction.) This applies to court orders also.

- A written Separation Agreement can speed up considerably any subsequent divorce proceeding. The agreement can be filed and its provisions incorporated into the consent divorce judgment if necessary.

As you can see, the advantages outweigh the fears of having a written Separation Agreement.

I think that people sometimes avoid negotiating one because

- they don't want to rock a boat that may be steady for the first time in a long time,
- they are concerned about the expense of the lawyers,
- they keep saying they will do it themselves—but never get around to actually doing it or
- they worry that the lawyers will find something to argue about and get them into a battle they don't want and can't afford.

These are all valid concerns, but the first one may happen anyway, perhaps because you don't have an agreement. The second is controllable if you follow my advice or use mediation. Think of it as buying insurance. As for the third point, let's face it: if you haven't done it by now, you never will. And the fourth one is also controllable if you follow my advice.

Which brings us back to the advantages.

In terms of the content of a Separation Agreement, there are very few limitations on what a couple can deal with in the contract. In general terms, the agreement can deal with

- ownership in and division of property,
- support obligations—child and spousal,
- the right to custody of and access to children,
- the right to direct the education and moral training of children and/or
- any other matter in the settlement of their affairs.

I have reproduced a full Separation Agreement in Appendix A. You may want to take a moment to examine it now. You will note that like any standard contract, it begins by identifying the people who are entering into the agreement. Their names appear in full along with a statement as to their residences. The date of the agreement appears at the top of the first page.

After the introduction, several standard clauses appear. One sets out the particulars of the marriage (Where is that marriage certificate, anyway?) or the period of cohabitation, if it was a common-law relationship. Another paragraph sets out the date and circumstances of the separation. The couple will acknowledge that they intend to continue to live separately and will not interfere with the other person's life.

Each agreement is tailored to the individual needs of the couple and can include paragraphs on the following subjects (check if any apply to you and refer back later if necessary):

- custody,
- access,
- division of household contents,
- division of the matrimonial home (sale),
- possession and maintenance of the matrimonial home,
- future use of property (e.g., cottage sharing),
- child support,
- spousal support (amount and duration),
- indexation of support,
- restrictions on the mobility of custodial parents (e.g., can't move more than 30 kilometres),
- restrictions on changing a child's name without consent,
- methods of solving future disputes (mediation or arbitration),
- release of interest in other's estate,
- general releases,
- releases of interest in specific property,
- division of pensions,
- interpretation provisions (e.g., definitions),
- health and medical expenses,
- dental coverage,
- automobile division or use,
- Canada Pension Plan,
- life insurance,
- responsibility for debts,
- tax consequences,
- effect of recohabitation,

- effect of default,
- financial disclosure,
- independent legal advice and
- responsibility for legal fees.

There is no limit to the terms that can be incorporated into such an agreement.

Signing (or "executing," as lawyers like to say) the Separation Agreement can be quite an experience, although many people have commented that it seems anticlimactic after all the tensions of negotiating it.

The law office staff (law clerks and paralegals) will prepare four identical versions of the agreement, one for each client and each of the lawyers. At the end of the signing "exercise" there will be four duplicate originals. I call it an exercise because it is a bit of a marathon of signatures and initials that goes like this:

- You will sign your name on the last page on the right-hand side above a line and typewritten version of your name as it appears on the first page. In other words, the last page will have a line with, for example, "Michael George Cochrane" typed under it. Place your usual signature on the line. You do not have to write your name out in full—your usual signature is fine. A witness will sign beside your name. This may be a paralegal or other office member, although your lawyer may be the witness to your signature.

- You will then place your initials on each page of the agreement and beside any handwritten changes that have been made at the last minute. (Sometimes a name is misspelled or a birthdate is incorrect.) The same witness will place his or her initials beside yours wherever they appear. The pages are marked with initials for two reasons: to acknowledge that you've read each page, and to prevent anyone from trying to substitute a new—and perhaps different—page later.

- Both people must sign the agreement as I've described it above. This is often done on different days at different times. The last page, where the signatures appear, will often show the dates upon which the couple signed the agreement.

- It is the lawyers' task to ensure that the agreement has been signed properly by both sides.

- Once it has been signed by both sides, the agreement is a legally binding contract.

Wait—there's more.

There are some additional documents that are signed at this stage: A Certificate of Independent Legal Advice and an Acknowledgment by Wife/Husband. The Certificate is a sworn statement by your lawyer that he or she is the witness to your signature, that they believe you are the person whose signature they witnessed and that they believe you understood what you were signing and did it voluntarily. The lawyer will often sign a Certificate of Independent Legal Advice, whereby he or she acknowledges that they explained the nature and consequences of the agreement and that the client signed it voluntarily. The client will then be asked to sign an acknowledgment that they hired the lawyer to advise them about the agreement, that the lawyer did so and that they are fully aware of the consequences of the agreement. It will also state that the person is signing voluntarily. Lots of paper, lots of signing.

You should also note that in some provinces, where Separation Agreements are enforced by the court, you may also need to sign an affidavit at the time of the final signing of the agreement that will facilitate filing with the court or with the police.

The signing exercise takes place only after the agreement has been reviewed, line by line, by you and your lawyer. (Not by you and the secretary, or the paralegal, or the articling student, or the junior lawyer, but the lawyer who negotiated it.) Do not be shy about asking questions. Look at each paragraph carefully. Do you know what it means? What does it accomplish? Don't accept statements like, "That's standard—it's in every agreement." Remember, you are going to be asked to sign the Acknowledgment I mentioned earlier. You are paying a lot of money for this contract, so understand what it does for you. If you don't, you may end up "paying" for years.

Don't be rushed. Sometimes law firms have little interview rooms or a library that can be used. Or, ask the lawyer if you can take the draft agreement home to read. Review each draft from beginning to end. Review each new change. Does it do what you thought it would do? Does it accomplish what your lawyer said it would accomplish? If not, he or she should have a good explanation.

This brings us to another area—setting aside (or cancelling) an agreement at a later date. Following the technical rules for assembling the agreement will not make it immune to a charge that it was entered into "improperly" or that a special circumstance has changed. An agreement entered into "improperly" could include an agreement signed under duress. In other words, one party forced (through threats) the other person to sign an agreement that they would not otherwise have signed. This is why there is so much emphasis on both people having independent legal advice and acknowledging it in the document itself. It is difficult to challenge an agreement as being involuntary when a lawyer was consulted and gave advice. But it happens.

Another "improper" agreement would be one that was brought about by fraud. For example, if a person has hidden or lied about the presence or value of assets, then any calculations for the division of property would be inaccurate. If it was done to mislead the spouse, the court may set the agreement aside.

The courts will also set aside agreements entered into because of undue influence, material misrepresentation, unconscionable bargain and something lawyers call "non est factum." Briefly, "undue influence" occurs where one person uses his or her power over another in such a way that the more powerful person acquires a benefit. A "material misrepresentation" occurs where one person hides a fact or lies about a state of affairs with the effect of inducing the other person to sign the agreement. In one case, a husband told his wife the agreement was for "tax purposes." In another case, a husband was told it was only "temporary." Both were misrepresentations.

An "unconscionable bargain" may be set aside by a court if it finds that the parties were in unequal bargaining positions and, as a result, the deal was improvident for one of them. This would likely be in cases where no legal advice had been obtained. I know of a case where a husband told his wife that she was entitled to one-seventh of the property because there were two adults and five children. She signed the agreement without legal advice.

Non est factum is a special legal term for what can be quite straightforward—a person signs a document thinking it is one thing but finds out it is something else. It used to be reserved for the blind and illiterate but can now apply to document switches.

To avoid these types of problems, lawyers now insist that the clients exchange sworn statements about their assets and their value. This discourages fraud and allows the lawyers to negotiate a fair agreement. As much as this exchange of information makes sense, there are still clients who will ask lawyers to prepare agreements without having first exchanged full financial information with their spouse. These clients are usually in a hurry, want to save costs or think they already know everything about finances. If this type of client subsequently discovers that the other spouse was not completely honest in his or her disclosure, it is very unlikely that the court will set aside the agreement. The moral of the story is: Don't sign a Separation Agreement without seeing a full, sworn financial statement from your spouse.

You should also understand that the court does not consider itself bound by any agreement that affects children. The amount or duration of child support, for example, can be changed by the court at any time regardless of what the agreement says. The same is true of custody and access. The court will always try to do what is best for the child.

In the case of spousal support, Separation Agreements often provide that in the event of a "material change of circumstances" (essentially a significant change in some way), the amount and duration of the support can be changed. So, if a wife was receiving $800 per month while working part-time but was laid off, then her support could be increased by the court until she finds a new position.

One special situation deserves mention—what if the people get back together after the Separation Agreement has been signed? The answer is like many in law: it depends. The court will look to the agreement itself and see if that situation was contemplated. It often was and the agreement may provide that its terms expire if reconciliation occurs. It is obvious that there are reconciliations that don't last. The couple may have second thoughts and begin to cohabit again. After a few months the old problems surface and everyone is left wondering what happens now.

Generally, a reconciliation of the spouses will terminate the Separation Agreement with respect to future dealings. If the couple acquire a new matrimonial home or joint savings again and then separate again, they will need to re-divide under the family laws. However, all transactions that were intended to be complete are not undone by the cohabitation. Property that was transferred stays transferred. Reconciliation, however, may terminate provisions dealing with spousal and child support.

The intention to resume cohabitation must be bilateral—that is, both spouses must wish to reconcile. Evidence offered of such an intention in one case was the occurrence of several acts of intercourse, but the court disagreed. One of the spouses testified that they had no intention of getting back together; it was just sex.

Separation Agreements are valuable tools for settling family law cases. Their value is found in recording the agreement the couple wants and needs. This result can only be achieved by understanding the process and giving informed instructions to your lawyer.

CONCLUSION

In conclusion, there are a number of ways to document the settlement of a family law case—Offers to Settle, Minutes of Settlement, Orders on Consent and Separation Agreements. Each method has its own value depending on the circumstances of your case, but all are based on arriving at a settlement that meets your needs and the needs of your children. Making sure your needs are met is the only valid criteria for settlement. Fatigue or cost or other factors will enter the picture, but they should not obscure your needs. Remember the settlement must last for a long time—maybe forever.

CHECKLIST

1. Where are you at, emotionally? Are you ready to settle for the right reasons?

2. Has your lawyer explained all of the options and the advantages and disadvantages of each choice?

3. Has an Offer to Settle been made? Why not?

4. Do you understand the role of Minutes of Settlement and Consent Orders?

5. Is your agreement legally binding? Was it written, signed and witnessed?

6. If you have avoided wrapping up your divorce in a Separation Agreement, is it because you are you afraid of something? The cost? Rocking the boat? Procrastination?

7. Have you obtained independent legal advice?

8. Do you have full sworn financial disclosure?

9. Separation Agreements can be set aside if there is fraud, undue influence, duress, misrepresentation or other tricks. Remember, independent legal advice may help you avoid these problems.

10. The court reserves the right to reopen issues of child support and child custody when to do so would be in the best interests of the child. Even spousal support may be reopened, but don't make dangerous assumptions that it will be. Contracts will be enforced.

11. Reconciliation attempts can have a big impact on such things as support and custody. If you are trying to "work it out," have you informed your lawyer?

10

NOT SETTLING
YOUR DIFFERENCES

~

Going to Court

In the previous chapter, we saw how cases can be settled when the people involved find a way to resolve their differences. Not settling means only one thing—going to court for a full trial. This aspect of family law is becoming less common, due in part to the expense of full trials and because clients and lawyers are using more creative methods of solving problems, such as mediation. But there are still many, many courtroom trials every year in every province and territory, at an appalling cost to the people involved.

A trial, at its most basic level, means that the people involved have not been able to agree on a solution to their problem and are left asking the court to solve it for them. All the issues discussed in the previous chapters can and have been decided by a judge in a courtroom. When people stand back from the process and consider, for example, the meaning of a custody trial, I believe they are in part ashamed of their inability to re-solve the problem. They are admitting that they, the child's parents, cannot agree on what is best for this child, so they will ask a complete stranger (the judge), who has minimal familiarity with their lives, to decide on this most important aspect of their lives for them. Yet this is precisely what happens with children, property, spousal support and even the entitle-ment to a divorce itself.

First, we have to separate reality from the misconceptions created by television. Family law trials in Canada bear very little resemblance to the trials we see on television. I'm always amused by how the TV clients who consult the TV lawyer for the first time at the beginning of the show are having a TV trial by the end of the program about an hour later. We should all be so lucky—most people wouldn't have their financial statements filled out by then, let alone a trial.

TV trials are fast, exciting, filled with tough cross-examinations, lying witnesses, surprise alternative theories ("Isn't it actually true that . . .") and the obvious "good person" winning over the obvious "bad person." On television, justice is black and white and no one ever seems to pay the lawyers.

Reality? The process is slow, very slow. Some people wait over a year for their trial (that's a whole TV season, never mind one episode), the process is filled with delays, it's often boring in the middle of a trial while technical arguments are made, the process is overblown with much posturing and, unlike television, it is a tense time for you and an even greater burden for your children if they are involved. I think many people justifiably consider a trial to be the most intimidating experience of their lives. You will never meet someone who brags about how great or how interesting or how rewarding their family law trial was. You never hear anyone say, "It was worth every penny . . ." If anything, most people think it was a complete waste of time and money, on top of which it was a very emotional experience that made them feel vulnerable and out of control.

Having said all that, we cannot simply ignore the trial as a painful lesson in living. Sometimes couples are forced to trial—one person takes an unreasonable position or some aspect of the law is so unclear that a judge's decision is needed. In this chapter, I would like to consider the trial from a few different perspectives so that those who simply *must* go through it can do so with a little more confidence and a little more control.

Before considering any of the technical aspects of a trial, we must consider what unfortunately becomes an overriding consideration—the cost. In advance of the trial, when it appears that a settlement is unlikely, you and your lawyer should discuss the likelihood of a trial. At that time, you should consider the preparation and review of a new retainer that authorizes the lawyer to conduct the trial on your behalf. At the time the retainer is reviewed, the lawyer will undoubtedly inform you that no trial will be possible unless a substantial advance on fees is received before the trial commences. The lawyer will likely explain that the legal fees for a trial are approximately $1,500 to $5,000 per day (minimum) and more if additional lawyers are involved on your behalf. It is not unusual for lawyers to request an advance on fees before the trial in the amount of $10,000 or $15,000. It is highly unlikely that you will find a lawyer who will conduct the entire trial on the understanding that he or she will be paid the legal fees out of the eventual recovery of property at the end of the trial. This is particularly so in cases where the dispute is over custody. The lawyer will insist upon his or her fees in full, in advance.

Assuming that the cost of proceeding to trial doesn't deter you from this option, let us now consider the physical setting of the proceedings.

THE COURTROOM

Experienced family law lawyers or one of their staff will often take their clients to the court for a tour in advance of the trial to familiarize the client with the layout of the courtroom and to remove any anxiety about the settings in advance of the proceedings.

It is misleading to think of the activity at the courthouse as being confined to the courtroom, although much of the action does take place there. Important things also occur in the court office, the judge's office (called chambers), the lawyers' lounge and even in the hallways.

The courtroom is laid out in a fairly standard fashion, with the judge at the head of the court (usually) on an elevated platform (called the bench). Immediately in front of the judge's bench is the clerk's table, where exhibits are collected and where the court reporter will sit during the trial. The court reporter will likely be a different person than the court reporter who assisted at the examinations for discovery. However, the court reporter's function at a trial is the same—to prepare a transcript of all discussions in the courtroom from beginning to end. A few feet farther away from the judge's bench is a long table called "counsel's table" (sometimes it is two tables, one for each side).

There may be three or four chairs at each counsel table. The lawyers will sit at these tables with their clients and any lawyer assisting on the case or, in some circumstances, a witness with whom the lawyer wishes to confer during the proceedings.

On the judge's left is the "witness box," which can literally be a box with a door at the back through which the witness enters and exits. Inside the witness box is usually a Bible for the administering of an oath and a glass of water for the witness.

On the judge's right will sit the clerk of the court. If the lawyers wish to give the judge anything during the course of the trial, they will often hand it to the clerk who in turn will pass it to the judge. The clerk will also mark exhibits during the trial and provide the judge with any necessary assistance upon entering and exiting the court. You may recall the marking of exhibits at the examinations for discovery. Those same exhibits will now be re-marked during the trial, while the new transcript is being prepared.

At the back of the courtroom is a seating area for the public. The proceedings are open unless they have been closed for some special reason, such as protection of a child, but the public is generally free to come and go during the course of any proceeding in a courtroom.

Some courthouses use special smaller courtrooms for family proceedings; however, in many courthouses, the same courtroom is used for family law trials as for murder trials and for other forms of litigation. This means that the courtroom may be equipped with a press box and a jury box, often on different sides of the courtroom. Reporters will take over the press box to cover some of the more spectacular and lurid cases, while the jury box, as mentioned earlier, will always sit empty during a family law trial.

The courtrooms are usually linked by hallways to which only authorized personnel have access. The judges will use these hallways to get to and from their chambers. Court staff and lawyers who have business with the judge will also use these hallways. In some older courthouses, the judge's office may be in another part of the building, so he or she is escorted from the office through the court hallways to the courtroom. In the judge's chambers, the judge works on judgments, reads the court file, makes telephone calls and dresses in his or her gowns in advance of trial. It is important to note that this particular judge has likely never heard of you or your spouse and has had nothing to do with the case before the trial. In some circumstances, the judge may have only read the court file a few hours in advance of the trial.

Generally the judge enters the courtroom through a private door behind the bench itself. A clerk will call out "All rise . . ." with a reference to the particular court in which the trial is taking place, and when the judge enters everyone in the courtroom will stand. The judge carries a large notebook that will be used for the taking of notes during the trial. Some judges take a great many notes, others appear to only take notes on the most important points. A few judges now use laptop computers.

Lawyers, too, have private dressing rooms in the courthouse. These are called "Barristers' Lounges" and sometimes look like no more than a locker room. It can be quite an experience in these lounges; settlements are negotiated, victories celebrated, losses mourned, war stories and anecdotes traded and a lot of socializing goes on. Clients are, of course, not welcome in the lawyers' lounge. It is akin to the local clubhouse in some communities.

When a trial is scheduled to be heard, a lot of time can be spent in the hallways of the courthouse waiting, waiting and waiting. Trials often run overtime, emergency hearings are scheduled, thereby throwing off the judges' plans, judges and court reporters must take breaks and any number of relatively minor but unpredictable events can cause delays. While in the halls, lawyers either prepare their witnesses, discuss possible settlements, make telephone calls or just sit and wait. In a busy courthouse, the halls can be a fascinating place to spend a few hours. However, those awaiting trial find it less interesting due to the stress of their own impending trial.

THE PAPER CHASE

You will recall that the courthouse maintains a court file with a copy of everything that has happened during your case. All motions, affidavits, claims, petitions, orders, transcripts and so on are all in the court file to provide a chronological history of the family dispute. In advance of the trial, the lawyers will have prepared a "record," which is a bound collection of all the important court proceedings that will be used like a summary book by the judge during the trial. The lawyers will often have duplicates of this summary in front of them during the course of the trial so that whenever a reference is made to a particular aspect of the proceedings, the judge and lawyers can all refer to the same material at the same time.

The lawyers will also prepare copies of important evidence and exhibit books for use during the trial. The financial statements completed by the couple will likely be out of date by the time the trial arrives and fresh ones will have been completed and filed for use at trial. As you can guess by now, the court file can be quite a monster by the time the trial has arrived. This is particularly so if litigation has taken place over a few years.

The nature of the remaining disagreement between the couple will have an effect on the paperwork in front of the court. If, for example, it is a divorce proceeding that includes a dispute over custody, access, property and the divorce itself, the form of the court proceedings will be dictated by the fact that a divorce is being sought. If some issues have been re-solved by the time the trial is to take place—for example, only custody is an issue—the paperwork put before the court may be pared down from the full content of the court file. The bigger the dispute, the bigger the court record and court file used by the judge. The court file is maintained by court staff and delivered to the judge in his chambers by the court staff. All this work goes on behind the scenes in advance of your case actually being considered by the court.

THE TRIAL ITSELF

The circumstances under which your case is "called for trial" can vary from province to province. Some courts use a "fixed date" method, which can add a great deal of convenience to your hearing. At a certain point, the lawyer must certify to the court that the particular case is ready for trial. In other words, the lawyer alerts the court to the fact that this case can be called at any time for trial and he and his witnesses will be ready. When judges are ready to book trials, they look at the list of cases that are ready (called "the ready list") and start to pick and choose trials that will be heard. This often takes place with a few dozen lawyers and a judge comparing their schedules over the next few months.

Depending on witness availability and the expected length of the trial, the cases are slotted into a judge's schedule. In some cases they are given a "fixed date," which means, for example, that Judge Brown will hear Porter v. Porter on November 20, 2007. This is very convenient for the parties since they know in advance the date of their trial and can plan accordingly for witnesses to be present and for parties to be available.

Another, but far less convenient, method is to just tell five sets of lawyers to be ready to go to trial "the week of November 20th." The cases are then listed one to five for that particular week. If case number one settles, then case number two must be ready to go. If case number two settles, then case number three should be ready and so on. The judges deliberately overbook and anticipate settlements in such a system. The look of panic on a lawyer's face when he or she finds out on a Friday that they are not number five for the following week but rather number one on Monday morning is unforgettable. There can be quite a weekend scramble in order to be ready for the trial. Unfortunately, this kind of system also forces some less-than-satisfactory settlements on the parties when the lawyers discover that they are not in fact ready for trial.

Regardless of the method of setting the case for trial, let's assume that your case is going to be called on a particular date. You will need to arrange time off work for the entire trial, which may in some cases be several days, and you may also need to arrange for childcare. Your lawyer will be arranging for subpoenas to be served on all the witnesses who will be giving evidence in support of your case. Even friendly witnesses, who have agreed to come to trial, will receive a subpoena and a small sum of money to cover their expenses travelling to and from the trial. While they will only be needed at the time they actually give their evidence, as a witness they are required by the subpoena to be available for the entire trial unless excused by the judge. This can be quite an inconvenience and requires some sensitivity by the lawyer in ensuring that witnesses do not waste their time sitting around in court on days that they are not giving evidence.

It is not unheard of for everyone to be at the court ready to go and suddenly discover that the judge who is supposed to hear their case is now hearing, for example, an emergency injunction application in a labour dispute or some other urgent matter. The trial coordinator tries to patiently explain that the trial cannot go ahead as planned. Sometimes it is put over for a day, sometimes indefinitely. Sometimes the trial begins but is then adjourned. I have even seen cases split in half, with part of the case being heard by a judge in November and the rest of the case being heard by the same judge in the new year. You should not assume that your entire trial will be done in one sitting.

However, let's be optimistic and assume your trial starts when it's supposed to start.

It can be divided into five main parts:

1. introduction and opening statement,
2. the petitioner's (or applicant's) case,
3. the respondent's (or defendant's) case,
4. summation and
5. judgment.

Let's examine each separately.

Introduction and Opening Statement

At the opening of the trial, after the judge has been ushered in, the lawyer for the petitioner/plaintiff (I am going to refer to the people involved as the petitioner and respondent during this section) will stand up and introduce himself or herself and the other client and other lawyer. This occurs whether the judge knows the lawyers or not and is simply for the record being prepared by the court reporter.

The lawyers will take turns describing the case very briefly to the judge by way of a "thumbnail sketch." They will also tell the judge about anything that has settled in the case or anything that they may have agreed upon to make the trial more expeditious, such as the preparation of a common exhibit book. The lawyers may even give the judge an idea about which witnesses will be called and when they expect to be finished putting evidence before the court. The judge may ask some questions or may simply say to the petitioner's lawyer, "Call your first witness."

The Petitioner's (or Applicant's) Case

The petitioner goes first and presents his or her story in whatever order he or she feels is most logical. The story is confirmed by witnesses. The rules of evidence are quite complex and dictate the type of evidence that may be given by particular types of witnesses. Expert witnesses are given a little more latitude in the types of things that they may testify about. Virtually all other witnesses may only testify about things of which they have actual knowledge.

Each witness is handled in the same general way. The lawyer or the clerk of the court calls the witness to the witness box. If an "order excluding witnesses" has been made, the witness may be in the hallway. These orders are often made at the opening of a trial to keep the waiting witnesses from hearing each other's evidence and tailoring their answers. While in the hall, the witnesses are not allowed to discuss the case with any witness who has given evidence.

Once in the witness box, the witness is sworn in (or affirmed) and asked preliminary questions, such as their name, address and relation to the parties. The lawyer who has called this witness then asks the witness "open-ended" questions. By open-ended I mean that the questions cannot be leading. For example, the lawyer could not say to this witness, "Is it true that you have worked for the petitioner for 10 years as a chartered accountant and concluded that his 100 business shares are worth only $1 each?" This is a leading question because it suggests the answer to the witness and therefore leads him in a particular direction. The question must be open-ended: "How long did you work for the petitioner?" "Did you calculate the value of his business shares?" "How many shares did he have?" "What method did you use to calculate their value?" "What conclusion did you reach about the value of each share?" The witness is taken step by step through the information he has that is of value to the court and to this particular party's case.

Before the trial, the lawyer should spend some time with the client and the witnesses explaining how to give evidence. The evidence should always be given in a clear voice and directed to the judge if at all possible. One should only answer the question that is asked and never guess or speculate about a particular answer. It is an absolute must to review the transcripts from the examination for discovery in advance of the trial as a way of preparing and refreshing one's memory about the evidence.

Once the petitioner's lawyer's questions are complete, the lawyer for the other side has an opportunity to test the witness's story through cross-examination. In this situation, if the lawyer is doing the job properly, every question will be a leading question requiring only a "yes" or "no" answer. The conventional wisdom is that a lawyer should never ask a question on cross-examination to which he or she does not already know the answer. Nor should questions ever be open-ended during cross-examination. This can mean hours of preparation for even the briefest of cross-examinations.

One method that a lawyer can use on cross-examination is contradiction of the witness's evidence at trial by demonstrating that the witness made a statement on a previous occasion that is inconsistent with his or her most recent evidence. In other words, the lawyer says to the witness, "What you are telling the court today is not the same as what you told us on a previous occasion under oath." This type of contradiction is called an "impeachment" and is most frequently used against the parties themselves who have had their evidence recorded at the examination for discovery.

Once the cross-examination is complete the petitioner's lawyer, who called the witness in the first place, is given the opportunity to re-examine the witness on any new issue that has arisen during the cross-examination. The lawyer may not ask something that he forgot to ask during the direct examination. It must be something new and it must have arisen during the cross-examination. Re-examination does not take place in every case, but it does allow the lawyer who called the witness to tighten up weak aspects of the evidence that may have been established during cross-examination.

Remember that the judge is making notes through all of this evidence. If he or she does not have any questions, the witness is excused and another witness is called to the witness box. The above process is then repeated, with the direct examination followed by a cross-examination, followed by a re-examination if necessary and questions from the judge. This applies to the witnesses called and to the petitioner. All witnesses are treated in the same way, although obviously the evidence of some is more important than the evidence of others.

The Respondent's (or Defendant's) Case

Once the petitioner has called all of his or her witnesses the respondent takes over. Sometimes the respondent's lawyer will open with a brief statement about the evidence to be called and any other clarifying remarks. The respondent's lawyer then calls all his or her witnesses and the same procedure described above is repeated with respect to each witness.

As witnesses identify documents, each one is marked and entered as an exhibit. The judge examines each document and makes notes about its importance in his or her notebook (whether paper or computer).

That is the procedure in theory, but let's add a small dose of reality.

Consider that the following things may happen while this is under way:

- A witness who was subpoenaed does not show up and the case is adjourned for a day or the order of witnesses is changed.

- A witness shows up but has forgotten to bring important documents with him or her and is excused to locate the documents. Again, either an adjournment is triggered or the order of witnesses is changed.

- People are wandering in and out of the court. They may be lawyers waiting to be heard by this judge in another proceeding, law students monitoring the court lists for their offices, university or high-school students on courthouse tours and even people from other trials. Every time someone walks in, the proceeding is disrupted while everyone turns around to take a look. Why? Because the person might be a witness who should be excluded from the proceeding. The judge or lawyers then ask the person why they are in the courtroom. Once they are satisfied that it is not a witness who has been excluded, the proceeding gradually returns to normal.

- The trial that was originally estimated to take no more than two days is suddenly at the end of its second day and five witnesses have not yet been heard. The trial is then adjourned for six weeks until the next time that the judge is available to continue hearing evidence.

Returning to the trial process itself, once the respondent's case is finished, the petitioner has an opportunity to call evidence in "Reply." This is like a re-examination of a witness and means that if something new came up during the respondent/petitioner case that the plaintiff needs to reply to, he or she can call a witness to provide the court with new information. The petitioner is not permitted to call a witness who should have been called at the outset as a part of the petitioner's case, but if something new has arisen, the petitioner will have an opportunity to put that evidence before the court. The process is then repeated for that witness or witnesses.

Summation

After all the evidence is before the court, the lawyers then stand up and take turns (petitioner first) summarizing their case for the judge. The lawyers trace through the evidence, emphasizing strong points and playing down weak ones. They also weave the relevant law through their summary. This will involve pointing out cases or sections of legislation to urge the court in a particular direction favourable to their client. At the end of each summation, the lawyer suggests to the judge the appropriate outcome in very specific terms.

The lawyer for the respondent repeats this process for his or her client. Once the judge has both versions before him or her, the three of them may engage in some detailed discussion of the finer points of the law or the facts of the particular case. The judge will sometimes thank the lawyers for their work and adjourn the case indefinitely. The judge will then pack up his or her notes and the evidence and sit down later to figure out what should happen in this particular situation. Rarely will the judge give a decision on the spot, and this adjourning indefinitely while a decision is written is called "reserving judgment." It can put the case on hold for several months.

The people involved leave the courtroom, the couple goes back to their lives, the lawyers go on to other cases, and the judge goes on to new trials, while everyone waits for a decision.

The lawyers may send their clients reporting letters at this stage, providing a detailed synopsis of what happened and what can be expected in the judge's decision. Sometimes, but not always, the bill is enclosed for the work to date.

The Judgment

Just when the client thinks things have returned to normal, the lawyer calls to say that the "Reasons for Judgment" are available. This means that the judge has written out—usually typed—the reasons why the case has been decided in a particular way. The judge will often trace his or her reasoning, making it clear that he or she has accepted either the petitioner or the respondent's theory of the case. Sometimes the judge develops his or her own theory.

The Reasons are related to but different from the judgment itself. The lawyers identify what the judge has actually decided by reviewing the Reasons. For example, the petitioner gets custody, the respondent gets access on particular terms, the cottage is divided in a particular way, the shares are valued at a certain amount and so on. These essentials are extracted from the Reasons and typed into a separate judgment, which is then approved by the lawyers. If the lawyers cannot agree on what the judge has decided in the Reasons, they arrange an appointment to see the judge and settle the dispute. Once they have arrived at an agreed form for the judgment, it is recorded at the courthouse and becomes effective.

The lawyers will then usually make an appointment to see the judge to discuss costs (i.e., who will pay the winner's costs and to what extent). This is an important aspect of the case, because the offers to settle that were made earlier (see Chapter 9—Settling Your Differences) are now compared with the actual judgment. If the loser rejected a favourable offer to settle, the costs can be considerable.

Once the court decides who must pay whom, a "bill of costs" is prepared in which the winning lawyer sends his bill to the losing lawyer for approval. If there is a disagreement about the amount, it can be settled by consulting the judge. The court official uses a tariff set by the Rules of Court to decide what is a fair bill from the winner. Losing a trial of four or more days can be an expensive proposition. Not only must the person pay their own lawyer, but they must pay the winner's lawyer as well.

Someone out there is undoubtedly saying "Yes . . . but if I win, then the loser pays my legal fees and I'm off the hook." Not quite. The "winner" may get about 50 per cent of his or her actual expenses of the trial. So while the loser pays part of the "winner's" bill, the "winner" still has to pay his or her own lawyer the remaining amount.

APPEALS

Before leaving this area we should deal briefly with appeals. It is not unusual for the lawyers, upon examining the Reasons for Judgment, to discover what they consider to be an error in law by the judge. The judge may have decided the case by using an incorrect principle of law or misinterpreting a section of an Act. It is not unheard of for each lawyer to discover a different mistake and develop two or more reasons as suggested grounds for appeal. These will be pointed out to you in the lawyer's reporting letter. In such cases, the lawyer will often say that he or she has reviewed the judgment and respectfully feels that the judge "erred in finding as a fact that . . ." or "erred in interpreting the law . . ." It amounts to a difference of opinion and the lawyer is suggesting that if he or she took it to a higher court, that court would agree with his or her opinion.

Appeals are not free. In fact, they can be very expensive. The cost of a transcript alone, for a trial of several days, can be thousands of dollars. Something very important or valuable must be at stake to even begin to think about an appeal. It should be treated as seriously as your original decision to begin the case, with emphasis on the costs of the appeal and the likelihood of success. As with the original trial, the losing party will pay the winner's costs again if unsuccessful on the appeal.

Appeals do not occur quickly. Depending on the province and level of court to which one is appealing, they can add several months and in some cases more than a year to the litigation. Ask your lawyer how long it will take.

The first appeal is not necessarily the last of the court. If the appeal court changes the trial judge's decision, the other side may be able to appeal that new decision to a higher court. If important new legal concepts are involved, the appeals can go all the way to the Supreme Court of Canada and take years to resolve.

The only advantage to appeals is that they occasionally do correct decisions that were made improperly, and they often enable the law to be "stretched" a little to offer fairness to a new situation perhaps not contemplated by the law. For example, some cases concerning common-law spouses went all the way to the Supreme Court of Canada but made a significant new interpretation of the law available to thousands of people. It may have resulted in numerous settlements of cases that were working their way through the legal system across Canada.

Another small advantage of the appeal process is that there will be minimal involvement by you in the case. The lawyers take over for appeals and clients need not attend the argument of the appeal at the higher court. The lawyers will appear before that court with entirely new, fresh paperwork developed specifically for the appeal. The appeal may be argued before as many as three judges, at which time the lawyers will argue the law as interpreted by the trial judge. Rarely do the appeal judges give their decision on the spot, so yet another "reserved" decision can be expected. The appeal judges will deliver a complete set of Reasons for their decision, just as the trial judge did. These decisions are considered most important by the lawyers and are often published in legal reporting services so that other lawyers are aware of them (so much for your privacy).

CONCLUSION

So, do you still want to go to trial? Are you being forced to go to trial by an unreasonable person on the other side? I don't ask such questions lightly, because the first question you must answer is "Why must I go to trial?" At the beginning of this chapter I noted that people go to trial when they have not settled their differences. Why haven't you settled yours?

CHECKLIST

Consider the following questions once you have answered the one above:

1. Have you received a full written opinion about the case and the issues involved?
2. Does the opinion letter discuss the likely time of trial and expected cost?
3. How long will the trial take?
4. Is it a fixed date?

(Continued)

5. Are you available when the trial is scheduled?

6. What is the theory of the case? How will it be presented to the court? Do you understand the structure of the trial? Have you been briefed in the methods of giving evidence? Have you reviewed the transcripts from the examinations for discovery?

7. Which witnesses will be called?

8. Have you executed a new retainer specifically authorizing the lawyer to conduct the trial?

9. What is the likelihood of success?

10. What Offers to Settle have been made? What effect will they have on costs at the end of a trial?

11. How much of a new retainer will you be required to provide in advance of the trial?

12. If successful, will the retainer cover the costs of collecting the judgment?

13. If custody is an issue, what role will your children play in the proceedings?

14. Do you understand the physical setting of the court? Will your lawyer arrange for a tour of the court in advance?

15. Have all the undertakings (promises to do something like provide copies of documents) been fulfilled and have you done your best to locate any missing pieces of evidence?

16. Have you completed updated Financial Statements?

17. Do you understand the likelihood of adjournments and delays once the trial is scheduled?

18. What is the difference between your likely net on the last settlement offer and your likely net at the end of a trial?

19. If custody and access are the issues, have you considered the use of mediation to resolve these particular disputes?

20. Once again, why are you going to trial?

21. What happens if you lose?

11

ALTERNATIVES TO COURT

~

Mediation, Arbitration and Collaborative Family Law

It is fair to say that until recently we, in Canada, have had a one-dimensional approach to solving family law problems. Our legal system, as you have seen from previous chapters, requires families to solve delicate issues such as custody of children or division of the family home in the same way that responsibility for car accidents, breached contracts or defective products is decided. This adversarial process leads only to one place—the courtroom. It is not a creative process. On the contrary, it encourages lawyers to promote one solution for the entire case and then battle to have their vision prevail.

This approach is particularly unsuited to families in crisis. Like labour disputes, family members must continue to deal with each other after the dispute is finally resolved. It was recognized many years ago that relations between labour and business were important enough that special methods were needed to resolve disputes quickly, inexpensively and without burning every bridge in the process. Mediation and arbitration are techniques well-known to those in the labour field and are becoming increasingly popular in family law. In this chapter, we will examine these two methods of dispute resolution with special emphasis on mediation. We will also look at something new called Collaborative Family Law.

MEDIATION

In mediation, the couple facing a family problem related to their separation uses a skilled third party to assist them in discussing the issue to reach a mutually satisfactory solution. Instead of having a judge impose a solution, the people design their own. There is no limit on the type of issue suited to mediation: Who should have custody? How should access be structured? Where will we live? How can we divide our furniture and other property?

Mediation's approach is different from the adversarial courtroom approach because the mediator encourages the parties to look at the problem from different angles and to develop an understanding of each person's needs and interests. The goal is not to develop two competing positions but to determine whether everyone's interests—especially the children's—can be met through some creative solution. Who is better able to develop such a solution than the parties themselves?

Mediation is voluntary and non-adversarial and works best when a skilled impartial mediator guides the discussion. Not surprisingly, those who have used mediation note that it provided them with new negotiation skills that permitted them to resolve subsequent disagreements. In a nutshell, mediation seems to be faster, less expensive and makes people happier with the agreement to the point of finding increased compliance with it. Mediation has the potential to be the most important development in family law in decades.

Before looking at mediation in more detail, we should understand what it is not. It is not marriage counselling, which is designed to help a couple sort out difficulties in their relationship with a view to staying together or easing the emotional strain of ending it. Mediation is also not therapy, which is designed to help an individual sort out personal, emotional or psychological problems that affect them and their relationships with others.

Assuming a decision to separate has been made, mediation can offer a family a more humane method of tackling any issue, no matter how big or small. Its goal is joint planning for the future, not argument over the past.

Mediation has become more popular in Canada over the last decade through a combination of word-of-mouth and encouragement of its use by legislation. The federal Divorce Act, for example, was amended in 1986 to place a positive duty upon lawyers to advise clients of the wisdom of negotiating support and custody issues and of the availability of mediation services in their community. This provision has resulted in lawyers encouraging clients to try mediation for these issues.

Provincial laws also encourage the use of mediation. For example, Saskatchewan's Children's Law Act (in force as of October 1990) now mirrors the Divorce Act and requires lawyers involved in custody and access disputes governed by provincial law (you will recall that this happens when the couple is not seeking a divorce but still needs help with custody matters) to inform their clients about mediation facilities that might be able to assist in negotiating a solution. As in the case of the Divorce Act, the lawyer must certify that he or she has complied with this requirement.

Ontario's provincial family laws—the Children's Law Reform Act and the Family Law Act—do not require lawyers to specifically inform clients about mediation, but they do facilitate the use of mediation by allowing the court to order the parties to use it when they both consent.

Most provinces have such a provision in their provincial family laws and every province is governed by the Divorce Act. So, at the very least, husbands and wives who are divorcing and need assistance with custody and access will have mediation drawn to their attention.

Let's look more closely at the actual mediation process.

Family mediators are not regulated in any way by either federal or provincial legislation. There are national and provincial associations, however, that organize the membership through voluntary guidelines, accreditation levels, continuing education and so on. There is no requirement that a mediator join these associations prior to offering services to the public, so you must be cautious in selecting a mediator who is experienced and qualified.

An ongoing debate concerns whether mediators need any special educational background in order to assist a family with a problem. Some "mediators" seem to have no other qualification than having gone through a bad divorce themselves. They may be empathetic but they are not qualified. Many of the best family mediators are lawyers, social workers or psychologists. At the end of this section we will discuss how to find a good mediator, but for now you should understand that the neutral third party who will conduct the mediation should be a qualified professional who brings some special skills to the dispute-resolution process.

The mediator's role includes a variety of functions and obligations. He or she must

- be impartial (both you and your spouse are clients),
- control the mediation (mediators act more as chairpersons and will never impose a decision).
- keep the discussion on track,
- work out a schedule for the meetings,
- coordinate the sharing of information between the couple, such as financial information related to support,

- keep the process confidential,
- be vigilant to ensure that you get help from other professionals as needed (therapists, accountants),
- be careful to act only as a mediator and not, for example, give legal advice (if they are also a lawyer) or psychiatric advice (if a doctor),
- promote cooperation by helping to build goodwill and by reducing tension,
- help you to develop your own negotiating skills,
- ensure that domestic violence is not present,
- compensate for subtle differences in the bargaining positions and abilities of the parties and
- stay in touch with your respective lawyers to keep them up to date on developments.

Within these general parameters, the mediator leads the couple through the mediation process.

Do mediators exclude the need for lawyers? In a word—no. Even if the mediator you have selected is also a lawyer, you and your spouse should still each have your own independent legal advice. The mediator is not there to provide legal advice. He or she facilitates the discussion and helps discover solutions and options. Your lawyer (so carefully selected at the outset, remember?) is there to make sure you understand your rights and obligations under federal and provincial law. He or she will also advise you on the merits of any agreement reached with the help of the mediator. It has been said that people negotiate in the "shadow of the law." This means that people should negotiate a settlement based in part on what would happen if the matter went to court. Lawyers ensure that a fair deal is achieved, one that will hold up over time.

The lawyer's role, therefore, also includes a number of functions and obligations. He or she must

- meet the obligations imposed by the Divorce Act and, in some cases, provincial law with respect to available mediation services,
- keep up to date on qualified mediators and their professional qualifications and accreditation,
- explain to clients the relative advantages and disadvantages of mediation,
- be cautious to ensure that clients unable to negotiate effectively are not placed at an unfair advantage in negotiation with their spouse,

- stay in close contact with the mediator and client once mediation begins and

- be careful not to undermine the mediator's work (he or she must scrutinize the agreement to protect the client but also protect the consensus that was achieved).

As you can see, the lawyer and mediator must work together closely to ensure a fair and lasting agreement. You may recall my suggestion about retaining a lawyer who is well versed in the area of mediation.

Assuming you have found a mediator, for example, through a recommendation from your family lawyer, and both you and your spouse are willing to give mediation a try, the mediation process will generally move through different stages: identifying the issues, developing options and choices, making choices, developing the agreement and recording it after legal advice on its fairness.

At the outset, the mediator will ask whether you would like to have the mediation "open" or "closed." If the mediation is "open," then statements made in mediation may be admissible later in court if the mediation fails to achieve an agreement. "Closed" mediation is the opposite—it's confidential. Nothing said in the sessions can be used in court (unless, of course, it related to evidence of child abuse, which provincial law requires be reported). Some people feel that if the mediation is "open," the people using it will be less willing to speak openly—something that is essential. Mediators, however, report that open mediation does not seem to inhibit the discussions and that people speak freely regardless of it being open or closed. The choice is yours and it is an important one. Consider the choice carefully and discuss it with your lawyer and spouse.

One case I am aware of involved a husband and wife who were separating because the husband had developed a relationship with a woman he met through a new church he had joined. There were two children involved, boys aged seven and 10 and they were justifiably anxious about what was happening. The father wanted joint custody (see Chapter 6—The Children) of the boys, while the mother, who was quite angry, felt she should have sole custody. To complicate matters, the father wanted the boys to convert to his new faith, while the mother vigorously opposed any further disruption in their lives. Child support was, of course, linked to custody. The mother wished to move to her hometown to be near her family. Unfortunately, that was 2,000 miles away and the father opposed any move away from his good job and new church. A tough, but not unusual, problem.

The mediator helped this husband and wife to organize these issues into a logical agenda that could be discussed without losing sight of the children's interests. That is exactly where they began, with a discussion of past childcare routines and parenting for the boys. The father's new faith was explored so the wife understood his new needs. The need for a move was explored again with the focus on the children and their existing routine.

They agreed to postpone the move and entered into a joint custody arrangement. This freed the mother to retrain to develop job skills with support from the husband. The boys continued in their regular church but received some exposure to the father's faith, with a view to letting them make their own decision down the road.

This couple learned that it is possible to settle problems without one person winning and the other losing. The mediator kept track of the developing agreement and prepared a written memorandum of the final decision. The mediator's memorandum formed the basis of a more detailed Separation Agreement, which was prepared by the lawyers in consultation with the couple and the mediator.

Why, you may ask, did the couple not just sign the agreement prepared by the mediator? It's because there are often technical matters that the lawyers need to build around the clients' basic agreement. The mediator may not have discussed with the couple, for example, the precise wording of releases concerning property claims and so on. The lawyers will ensure that the agreement is legally correct, fair and what you want.

The advantages of mediation seem clear:

- You, as opposed to a court, make the decisions.
- The discussions are private and confidential.
- The process is faster than waiting for court dates.
- The solution is tailor-made for your circumstances.
- It can be less expensive than going to court.
- The agreement can be renegotiated if circumstances change.
- The process can teach you new negotiating skills that will help you resolve disputes in the future.
- You still have the benefit of a lawyer scrutinizing your agreement to ensure fairness and legality.
- It is a dispute resolution method that leaves its users feeling better about themselves and happy about their agreement.

Having said that mediation holds great potential for families that are separating, it is not for everyone. It is a process suited to people who are in a relatively equal negotiating position. If one spouse is at a clear disadvantage, mediation may not produce a fair result.

For example, people who come from homes where there has been violence are unlikely to be able to negotiate with a spouse who has beaten or harassed them. So, violence that puts one spouse in fear of the other and unable to negotiate can prevent mediation. We will briefly examine domestic violence later in this book (see Chapter 14).

Similarly, if for any reason, one spouse does not wish to mediate, it is not the appropriate method of dispute resolution. It must be voluntary by both parties and undertaken in good faith.

Finally, where child abuse is present, the mediator will be unable to honour any request for confidentiality. All provinces require persons learning of child abuse to report it to authorities so they can intervene to protect the child.

And now, a brief word about those who oppose mediation in family law. Some women's groups, some feminists and related groups have opposed the use of mediation in family law. They argue that mediators promote joint custody of children, that mediation is a method of taking women out of the public court system to deprive them of hard-earned rights in a private setting and that many women are in an inherently weak bargaining position vis-à-vis their spouses (in many cases due to violence). Their concerns about violence are legitimate; great strides have been made to promote the message that mediation is not suited to those rendered incapable of bargaining as a result of violence in the home. But to suggest that mediation should not be available for those who wish to use it and are capable of negotiating is, I believe, very unfair. It would deprive many women and men of a very humane method of solving family problems.

Not every province delivers mediation services in the same way. Some provinces have publicly funded mediation services available for free. Other provinces and territories only have private mediation services on a fee-for-service basis, paid in full by the parties. Still others have a combination of free public services and private mediators.

While mediation is generally available in each province, it may be difficult to find a qualified and experienced mediator close at hand. You have a couple of options when searching for a mediator. First and foremost, if you have selected a good family law lawyer, he or she should have experience with local mediators, and should have a list of three or four from whom you can select. In fact, your lawyer will likely provide a recommendation.

When you finally have a list of names to pick from and are meeting with mediators, do not hesitate to ask probing questions about the mediator's background, qualifications, experience and specialties. Some mediators do not deal with financial matters and some will only do custody and access, while still others prefer to do comprehensive mediation—tackling all the issues facing the family. Remember, the mediator is also anxious to see if the "chemistry" is right, so take full advantage of the introductory meeting, which is often free of charge.

You will wish to discuss costs. Most mediators charge an hourly rate ranging between $50 and $500. The cost is often much less than lawyer's fees because the process is faster and less protracted by paperwork and court dates. At the outset, most mediators will have an agreement with the couple about who will pay, how and how much. Usually the cost is split equally and billed directly to the clients. In some cases, the mediator may send the bill on to the lawyers, who in turn pass it on to the clients.

I recommend spending as much thought on hiring the mediator as you did hiring your lawyer.

ARBITRATION

A few words should be added about arbitration, which has been available for hundreds of years in commercial matters but has only recently found its way into family law. It is another alternative to going to court and is not unlike the use of a private judge. The parties select a private individual, often an experienced lawyer or a retired judge, to hear their dispute in private. After the hearing the arbitrator renders a decision, sometimes within 30 days.

Arbitration is attractive for a variety of reasons. It is completely private. The public and press (if that is a concern) do not have access to your private affairs. It can be significantly faster and more predictable than the public courts, which are busy and subject to delays, such as summer breaks, adjournments and other interferences.

Proponents of arbitration also point to the desirability of being able to select the "private judge" and to be able to have someone preside who is truly interested in a family law matter. This is not the case in the public courts, where judges are assigned to all sorts of cases, family law being about the least popular. Many judges are very devoted to family law cases but some are not, and assignments can be random.

The expense of arbitration is its weakness. The parties are still paying for two lawyers and now "the judge" as well. In the public courts, judges are "free" due to tax dollars paying their salaries. A private judge can cost between $2,000 and $3,000 per day for each day of a hearing. This cost is shared by the parties. However, for those who can afford it, the privacy and speed of the arbitration process can be attractive. Your lawyer will be able to arrange for an experienced arbitrator if you decide to go that route.

MEDIATION/ARBITRATION

With advice from their lawyers, some people enter into a process that combines mediation and arbitration. In this approach, the individual selected to help the people reach a conclusion acts as both a mediator and an arbitrator. This person will spend the first part of the process meeting with the people and their lawyers, trying to resolve the whole case by agreement. In some cases, they are able to help the parties narrow the issues for the arbitration. However, if they are unable to come to an agreement the mediation portion ends and the mediator's role changes to that of arbitrator. He or she will now consider the matter that remains in dispute as if he or she were a private judge.

In this process, which has advantages and disadvantages, the individual selected to help resolve the dispute works as hard as he or she can to resolve it through mediation. But if one or both parties cannot come to an agreement, the role switches and the person trying to mediate suddenly turns into an arbitrator who simply imposes a decision.

One of the advantages is that it certainly encourages people to work things out in the mediation phase. One of the disadvantages is that it can be difficult for an arbitrator to forget some of the things heard in the mediation and become a neutral decision-maker. If this process is being recommended to you, review these advantages and disadvantages with your lawyer prior to entering the process.

RELIGIOUS ARBITRATION

An issue arose in Ontario about the use of religious arbitrations. For many years it has been well known in the legal community that priests or rabbis will often conduct mediations and in some cases, arbitrations, for members of their faith going through separation and divorce. Some members of the Muslim community have expressed a wish to use Sharia law as a code for determining the outcome of family law disputes within their community. Concerns were expressed that Sharia law might lead to unfair results, and that if Sharia law was applied in private in a family law arbitration, unfair results would never be discovered and rectified. In addition, under the Provincial Arbitrations Act, individuals could give up the right of an appeal of the arbitrator's decision. This, too, could lead to unfairness.

In Ontario, a set of amendments to the Arbitrations Act and the provision of special rules for "Family Arbitrations" have been developed as the solution. There is a requirement for independent legal advice prior to signing arbitration agreements. There are limitations on the ability to waive a right of appeal, and there is a requirement that family arbitrations take place under the provisions of the laws of Ontario or another Canadian jurisdiction. In other words, parties to an arbitration cannot oust the law of Canada. I expect that other provinces in Canada will enact similar limitations and those individuals going through separation and divorce will feel confident that the same rules apply to everyone, whether they are in a courtroom or a private arbitration.

COLLABORATIVE FAMILY LAW

Over the past few years, there has been a great deal of discussion about a new approach to practising family law. This approach has been called Collaborative Family Law Practice. It bears enough resemblance to mediation that I decided to include a discussion of the approach in this chapter.

Collaborative family law practice is a blend of soft-advocacy on behalf of a client and well-known mediation techniques. A mediator, a neutral third party, is not employed by either client. Instead, the clients and their lawyers enter into an agreement committing themselves to reach a negotiated settlement.

Importantly, the clients and the lawyers expressly forego any entitlement to litigate the matter in court while the negotiation is under way. This means that the threat of going to court over a particular issue is removed from the negotiations. A lawyer using this approach will undertake not to represent the client if the negotiation is unsuccessful and the matter proceeds to court. The parties are not releasing their entitlement to eventually take the matter into court if it is not settled. Rather, they are making a firm commitment to a negotiated process and are agreeing not to litigate or to threaten to litigate so long as the process is under way and is productive.

The role of the lawyer stays much the same as a usual law practice. The client's rights and obligations are researched and presented in the ordinary course, but the negotiations are characterized by respect among the parties and the lawyers, and good faith and voluntary disclosure of information, documentation and other evidence. The approach includes laying all of one's cards on the table in the hope that a settlement is achieved quickly, inexpensively and in a way that meets the needs of the clients, not to mention their children, if custody issues are involved.

I add this caution about collaborative law practice: everyone must be certain that it is not used to simply delay the inevitable. It could be a major disappointment if a great deal of effort and time is placed on a collaborative negotiation to discover that a new lawyer must be hired to start all over again if the matter does not settle. Discuss the appropriateness of collaborative law with your lawyer. In order to use the process, your lawyer will have gone through a special training program as a collaborative family law lawyer.

STRATEGIC CONSIDERATIONS FOR ALTERNATIVES TO THE COURT

It's no secret that I am of the opinion that the Canadian justice system is letting Canadian families down in the way in which they handle family disputes. While there are certainly exceptions in some courts and in some provinces, for the most part the family law system is slow, insensitive, ineffective and not cost-effective for anyone.

Evidence of this can be seen in the fact that hundreds if not thousands of people are opting out of the justice system and using mediation and arbitration and collaborative family law. Just a few years ago, it was common to hear lawyers and clients discussing the advantages and disadvantages of opting out of the system. One of the disadvantages that a lawyer would be required to discuss with the client was the increased cost. Let's face it—your tax dollars have already supposedly paid for the justice system. It is, for all intents and purposes, "free." When a lawyer discussed with a client the possibility of opting out, he or she would have to explain that there would be an added cost for the mediator or the arbitrator or for the collaborative process, so the cost of opting out was a factor.

Around the time that I was preparing this latest edition, I had an interesting meeting with a very good judge, a person who really knows family law and has always shown great sensitivity on the cases before him. Another lawyer and I explained to this judge that our clients, who were involved in a very high-conflict dispute, were opting out to use a private arbitration. This judge raised his eyebrows and said, "That's acceptable if they can afford the expense of an arbitrator."

I explained to him that while they could indeed afford an arbitrator, the problem was that they could not afford to *stay in the justice system*. He looked alarmed and I explained that two lawyers and two clients had basically spent the entire day for the second time waiting to meet with a judge so that they could obtain permission to schedule other days for re-attending at the court. In other words, the clients had spent thousands of dollars paying lawyers to simply sit around waiting for meetings at the court. That money, the lawyers and clients had decided, would have been better spent paying an experienced and sensitive family law arbitrator to simply deal with the case quickly and effectively. So, ironically, we are now in the position where more and more Canadians are opting out of the justice system because they cannot afford to stay in it.

I fear that we are headed toward a two-tier justice system, where poor, self-represented people stay in the publicly funded justice system (Judge Judy—paid for by taxpayers) and middle-class and well-to-do people simply opt out and "buy a decision" from an arbitrator.

This raises some strategic considerations. Discuss carefully with your lawyer the wisdom of participating in a mediation. The process should be conducted in good faith—it should not be used as a fishing expedition. I have participated in mediations where it became clear after just a few hours that the lawyer and client on the other side were simply using the mediation process to fish out useful information and try to determine our bottom-line as an advantage in negotiations. I have also participated in mediations where it was clear the other side was using it as a method of delay and a method to run up costs. I mention these aspects of mediation/ arbitration so that you will review these advantages and disadvantages with your lawyer before you go into the process. It must be conducted in good faith or it can be abused.

Another problem that we have seen in the mediation/arbitration area is the very common requirement that the decision be kept confidential. As the process is private, the decision is private. This means that we no longer have a large base of published court decisions to help us resolve cases. Many legal observers are concerned that a vast body of law is disappearing into the private closed files of lawyers and arbitrators. Sadly, this is a price that the justice system is paying because it is driving people out.

Mediation/arbitration and collaborative law have a lot to offer Canadian families. They are certainly more responsive and at times more creative in the way in which problems can be solved. They are certainly a more humane process for families. For a variety of reasons, we will see more and more mediation/arbitration and collaborative law used over the next decade.

CHECKLIST

1. Do you understand the purpose of mediation?
2. How is it different from marriage counselling and personal therapy?
3. Would you participate willingly and in good faith?
4. Are you capable of negotiating with your spouse?

5. Has there been violence between you and your spouse that would prevent you from negotiating effectively?

6. Does your lawyer feel you are suited to mediation? Is he or she supportive?

7. Will you use an independent lawyer to double-check the agreement and advise you during negotiations?

8. Will the mediation be open or closed?

9. Are public (free) facilities available?

10. Will legal aid cover the mediation?

11. Is the mediator qualified and experienced?

12. Is the mediator a member of a mediation association?

13. Does the mediator have a specialty?

14. What is the hourly rate and billing arrangement?

15. Will the mediator stay in contact with the lawyers and report to them as well as you?

16. Will the mediator prepare a memorandum of understanding of any agreement reached and work with the lawyer to see if it can be implemented in a Separation Agreement?

17. What kind of schedule is proposed for meetings?

18. What references do you have for this mediator?

19. Do you like the mediator? Does the chemistry feel right?

20. Will the speed and privacy of arbitration be worth the added expense?

21. Have you discussed the availability and appropriateness of collaborative family law with your lawyer?

12

ENFORCING FAMILY LAW ORDERS

~

Making an Order Stick

Obtaining a court order for custody, access, support, property division or any other aspect of family law is one thing—enforcing the order can be another experience altogether. One cannot assume that the other person will simply abide by the order of the court; remember, they may have "lost" in court and this order is an unwanted imposition. When faced with a spouse who refuses to comply, the spouse with the order may wonder, having gone through the expense and tension of the court proceeding, what the point was.

Enforcement issues can arise in some odd circumstances. Perhaps a parent will refuse to allow a child to go for an access visit, or an access parent may refuse to return a child on time. Sometimes, child support is not paid or it is not paid in full. In other situations, families rely on restraining orders or orders for exclusive possession of the home and police enforcement may be required. In the most serious situations, children are abducted by a misguided parent and both the criminal and the civil justice systems are asked to respond.

In this chapter we will examine each of the family orders from the perspective of enforcement.

CUSTODY ENFORCEMENT
Criminal Law Custody Enforcement

It is a criminal offence in every part of Canada to abduct a child who is under the age of 14 and who is the subject of a custody order. If the child is taken from the custodial parent with the intention to deprive that parent of the child, then the abducting person (95 per cent of abductions are by non-custodial parents) may be found guilty and punished with up to 10 years in jail. This is the case whether the parent has a custody order or not, except that when the parent does not have a custody order, charges cannot be laid unless the Attorney General of the province gives his or her permission. The court will look at the terms of the order—either sole custody orders or joint custody—and decide whether there was an intention to deprive the other parent of custody at a time when they were entitled to it.

A "no-order" situation can arise in cases where the parents simply separate; it can arise where they have separated and agree that the child will live with one of them but they never obtain an order from the court, and it can apply to situations where there is a court order for custody that was not made by a Canadian court.

A Wisconsin father who abducted his children to Winnipeg after the Wisconsin court had ordered that the mother should have custody was charged under this part of the Canadian Criminal Code and the children were returned to their mother. These children had been told that their mother was dead and we can only imagine the consequences for them.

If the custody order was made by a Canadian court, it can be enforced immediately anywhere in Canada through the abduction provisions of the Criminal Code; however, it should be noted that, if caught, the abducting parent may have a couple of defences available. First, no conviction will be obtained where the person with custody consented to the child being removed by the other person. It is not uncommon for parents to live in direct contravention of the court's custody order. The order may say that the mother is to have custody, but the child actually lives with the father. This could happen if circumstances change and, for example, the mother became ill and could not care for the child. There may have been little reason at the time to amend the court order if the intention was that the child would eventually return to the mother's custody. However, if the father decided to move out of the province, the mother would have difficulty alleging that the child was being abducted if she had originally consented to the child being in the father's custody.

It is also a defence to an abduction charge if the child was taken to protect him or her from "imminent harm." This situation would arise where the non-custodial parent discovers that the custodial parent is mistreating the child. I heard of a case where the father had custody but had lost his job and began to drink heavily. He could not care for the child and the mother refused to return the child after an access visit for fear that the child might meet with harm. An abduction conviction would be unlikely in such a situation.

It is, however, no defence to a charge of abduction that the child consented or suggested that the change in custody take place. This prevents the parent from pressuring the child to agree with any suggested changes.

The benefit of the Criminal Code provisions is that once a charge is laid, a Canada-wide warrant for the abductor's arrest will be issued to all police forces. The criminal enforcement route is faster, which is critical when the person may be attempting to flee the jurisdiction.

Many provinces have adopted a standard protocol for responding to an abduction of a child. In most, if not all, cases the custodial parent will require a lawyer's assistance. Start with the custody order itself. A legible copy of the order, certified by the court if possible, should be kept in a safe, accessible place at all times.

One of the issues addressed in the standard protocol concerns domestic violence. How can the police and a Crown attorney (who would be called upon to lay the charges) distinguish between an abduction and a parent who is fleeing domestic violence and is simply taking the children with her? Such determinations are made on a case-by-case basis.

Even if the abducting parent is located with the child and criminal charges are laid, it can be difficult to arrange the return of the child. The warrant only brings the abductor back. It is often necessary to involve the local child-protection agencies, which can take custody of the child until the custodial parent or his or her designate can arrive. The best solution, of course, is for the police to coordinate their arrest of the abductor with the presence of the custodial parent.

Parents faced with abductions should also contact Child Find (Canada), a non-profit organization with offices across Canada that locates missing and abducted children, at 1-800-387-7962 or visit their website (which is particularly helpful) at www.childfind.ca. Child Find will assist in reuniting the child and the custodial parent.

Civil Justice Enforcement of Custody Orders

In its own way, the civil justice system can also be used to respond to a parental child abduction. The two primary considerations in a civil enforcement case are the child's welfare and a fair and proper administration of justice. Not every case is a clear-cut abduction and in some circumstances the custody order simply needs to be enforced in another jurisdiction.

The provinces (except Quebec) and territories have all passed laws to speed enforcement of each other's custody laws. The goal is to enforce, with minimal fuss, the other province's custody orders and return the child to the jurisdiction that made the order. Each province enforces the other province's orders as if they were its own, to discourage the abducting parent from trying to have the order reconsidered in the new province. There are exceptions, of course. If the court thinks the first order was made by a jurisdiction to which the child did not have a strong connection or everyone is now present in a new jurisdiction and a review is appropriate, the court may reconsider the whole matter of custody. Also, if the child might meet with harm if the custody order was enforced, the court may choose to substitute its own order for the other province's order.

All of the provincial legislatures have adopted the Hague Convention on civil aspects of international child abduction and enacted legislation to facilitate enforcement of extra-provincial custody rights. This Convention, which has been accepted by many countries, attempts on an international scale to secure the prompt return of children wrongfully removed to, or retained in, a country that has signed the Convention. It also attempts to ensure that rights of custody or access under the law of a country are respected by other countries. It applies to children who are under the age of 16 years. If a child is wrongfully brought from the country in which he or she habitually resides into Canada, then the Hague Convention can be used across the country. These laws attempt to prevent the re-hearing of custody cases in the new jurisdiction.

The following is a summary of major countries that will enforce the child abduction provisions of the Hague Convention:

- Argentina,
- Australia,
- Austria,
- Belize,
- Bosnia and Herzegovina,
- Burkina Faso,
- Canada,
- Croatia,
- France,
- Hungary,

- Luxembourg,
- Netherlands,
- Norway,
- Portugal,
- Spain,
- Sweden,
- Switzerland,
- United Kingdom (England, Northern Ireland, Scotland and Wales) and
- United States (extends to American Samoa, Guam, Northern Marianas Islands, Puerto Rico, and the U.S. Virgin Islands).

Some countries that do not offer enforcement of the Hague Convention include:

- Belgium,
- Czechoslovakia,
- Egypt,
- Finland,
- Italy,
- Japan,
- Surinam,
- Turkey,
- Venezuela and
- Yugoslavia.

MORE ON ABDUCTIONS

If faced with the abduction of a child, consider the following.

- It may be necessary to hire a private investigator to locate the child. Private investigators can be very effective and often have sources of information available to them that others do not. In some provinces, legal aid will pay for the cost of the private investigator if the need for one is reasonable in the circumstances.
- Provincial law often provides for an order requiring others to assist in the search for a child. This can enlist the help of other enforcement agencies, such as a local sheriff's office.

- It is a criminal offence to obtain a Canadian passport falsely listing a child as one's own, contrary to a custody order. Sometimes a parent will forge the custodial parent's signature in order to spirit the child out of the country. The penalty for such an offence is two years in jail.

- While the custodial parent may be able to recover costs of locating and recovering the child, he or she cannot sue for damages for emotional distress that may have been suffered as a result of the abduction.

- The federal government enacted the Family Orders and Agreements Enforcement Assistance Act, which will help a custodial parent trace an abducted child through the federal information banks. However, access is not direct for individuals; a provincial enforcement agency must request the information for reasons of confidentiality.

This is as good an opportunity as any to provide advice to parents who have considered abducting their own children. First, as justified as you may think you are, the courts will take an extremely dim view of the abduction. If caught, and there is a great likelihood that you will be caught, the court will be under pressure to make an example out of you to discourage other parents from making similar abductions. Few people will see you as a martyr if you are imprisoned for abducting your own child.

Second, barring some life-threatening situation, it is next to impossible to characterize the abduction as being in your child's best interest. Robbing a child of the other parent can be catastrophic. Lying about the other parent's death or whereabouts will seriously undermine your credibility and the child's confidence in authority figures. Abduction is very rarely a realistic alternative.

CANADA CUSTOMS AND TRAVELLING OUTSIDE CANADA

When travelling outside Canada, carry identification for your child regardless of his or her age. This can be a birth certificate, baptismal certificate or passport. Parents who have custody should carry relevant court orders, Separation Agreements or other legal documents. An adult who is not a parent or guardian should have the written permission of the parent as well as the child's identification.

Family law lawyers are often contacted on the eve of a vacation because the parent who will be travelling with children wonders whether there will be a problem at the border. More and more often, there are big problems. It is not unheard of to have families turned around at the border or at airports because they do not have the permission of a non-custodial parent or a custodial parent to be travelling with a particular child after separation and divorce. These permission letters should be obtained in advance of travel. They are not complicated and could read as follows:

To Whom It May Concern:

Re: Travel of (name of child and birth date as it appears on a passport or birth certificate)

This is to confirm that the above-named child will be travelling with (name of parent as it appears on a passport or birth certificate) in (for example, the United States) between March 15, 2007, and March 24, 2007. I wish to confirm that (name of parent again) is travelling with (name of child again) with my permission. If you have any questions or comments, please do not hesitate to contact me at (telephone number).

Signed this _____ day of _____ , 2007.

_____   _____
Witness   (Signature of Parent)

Do not take a photocopy of this letter, but have an original ready with your passport if the question arises. In some more acrimonious cases, the lawyers will provide a notarized copy of such a letter to ensure that the travel takes place without difficulties.

Canada Customs uses a national database of high-risk travellers, known as the Primary Automated Lookout System (PALS). It is able to verify traveller information. They will also use, in some cases, a hand-held computer system that provides photo-images of missing children. Their computer also has access to the United States Immigration database. Everyone is painfully aware of the increased security around travel.

You are well-advised to plan ahead and ensure your travel will take place with the other parent's consent. If that consent is not available, it may be necessary to apply to the court for an order authorizing the child to travel with you. These orders will be made to allow the travel, unless there is a very good reason to not permit travel. The courts will not frustrate family vacations simply because someone is being vindictive. If the consent to travel is unreasonably withheld, more often than not, the court will also order legal fees against the parent who is trying to block travel. In other words, if you oppose your child travelling outside the country with the other parent, you should have a very, very good reason, such as fear of abduction.

ACCESS ENFORCEMENT

The news with respect to access enforcement is mostly bad. To begin with, many non-custodial parents have orders that entitle them to "reasonable" or "liberal" or "generous" access. When access is denied, these terms are virtually impossible to enforce. The parent holding such an order will be required to return to court to have the access converted into something more specific. If the specific access is then denied, the non-custodial parent is in a position to try to enforce the order.

In most provinces, when access is denied, the non-custodial parent has one remedy—that is to request a finding of contempt of court against the custodial parent. This means that the non-custodial parent must convince the court that the denial of access was a wilful interference with the non-custodial parent's entitlement to access.

It should be noted that the police will rarely, if ever, assist with the enforcement of an access order, knowing that there are civil remedies available for the enforcement of the access order. They will generally refer you to your family law lawyer.

The standard of proof required on a contempt hearing is higher than for normal civil proceedings (which is on the "balance of probabilities"). The non-custodial parent must prove the wilful denial beyond a reasonable doubt. If successful, the court has two options: jail or a fine for the custodial parent. Neither is appropriate in most cases, since the fine is only depriving the family of much-needed money and the jail sentence is often out of proportion to the access denial itself. The result is that neither penalty is imposed and the access denial goes unpunished.

Courts have been struggling to find ways to improve access enforcement. In some provinces (e.g., Manitoba and Ontario) the court has permitted a custodial parent to avoid punishment for contempt by giving them an opportunity to purge their contempt through the provision of "make-up time" with the child. Make-up time is simply giving back the time denied with the child on another occasion, thereby making up for the time that was lost. If this is done, the contempt is ignored and no penalty is imposed. In other cases, the courts have restructured access to ensure that the contact occurs and that there are regular pick-up and drop-off schedules.

The latest and most serious way in which access can be enforced against an interfering custodial parent is to reverse custody. A parent who finds his or her access continually frustrated or denied is sometimes left with the only option of returning to court and asking for custody. As a part of that application, the parent undertakes to the court to ensure that the other parent has regular contact with the child. This is considered an absolute last resort, but it has been done.

So, with a few exceptions, access enforcement is not effective in Canada, with contempt power threatened but rarely enforced. The contempt power is slow, expensive (one motion can cost as much as $3,000), burdensome and those who use it must seek penalties the court is reluctant to impose.

Two unfortunate consequences of poor access enforcement concern child support and custody-order compliance. The courts of three Canadian provinces have now made orders suspending child-support orders until access provisions are complied with. In these cases, the court, frustrated by a custodial parent's refusal to permit access, ordered the non-custodial parent not to pay support. This, of course, is a double punishment for the child. Poor access enforcement has long been an excuse used by non-custodial parents for the non-payment of support. This connection may become stronger if non-custodial parents turn to withholding support as a means of access enforcement. Those faced with access denial should not withhold support from the family unless a court has ordered it. Similarly, those with custody should not withhold access because support has not been paid.

The other issue, which is more difficult to assess, is custody-order compliance. There is little or no research available on why non-custodial parents abduct their children. Perhaps it is an act of anger designed to punish the custodial parent for their perceived failings in the relationship. There is no doubt that it is harmful to the child, and a non-custodial parent would be hard-pressed to justify any abduction. Some people are now asking whether poor access enforcement influences the non-custodial parent's decision to abduct a child. They note that parents who are happy with access are not likely to abduct. Good access enforcement provisions in provincial laws would certainly help.

To avoid problems, consider the following:

- Avoid access orders that provide only for "reasonable," "liberal" or "generous" access. Have an access entitlement specified, right down to the days, times and specific holidays. The parents can always agree to more access, but at the very least set out a minimum amount of access for reasons of certainty if enforcement is needed.

- Consider calling the arrangement "joint custody" rather than access. The provisions can be the same, but the change in terminology can result in easier enforcement should difficulties arise.

Remember that the custodial parent may also wish to have access enforcement. What can be done about the non-custodial parent who does not come to see the child in accordance with the terms of an order made by the court? There are many parents who are entitled to see their children, many children who are entitled to see parents and many courts that have decided that such access is in the child's best interest. Yet these parents do not exercise their right or responsibility to time with the child.

Part of the procedure used in Manitoba, Saskatchewan and Newfoundland assists children to see the non-custodial parent who does not visit. If the court has ordered access and it has not been exercised, the court can order reimbursement of expenses incurred as a result of the failure to exercise the access, impose supervision on the access or, if the parties consent, order them into mediation. This can be important in the situation where a custodial parent has planned a two-week vacation and the non-custodial parent cancels their scheduled summer access at the last minute. In such a case, with this remedy, the court could order reimbursement of the expenses incurred by the custodial parent.

As you can see, the enforcement of access orders is a difficult undertaking. Let's now take a look at an area of enforcement that has seen a great investment of time, energy and money and has still yielded little compliance—support enforcement.

SUPPORT ENFORCEMENT

It seems that compliance with support orders is still a problem in many provinces. Numerous studies have been done that suggest that non-payment of support orders ranges from 50 to 80 per cent. Non-payment includes paying the order late, not paying the full amount or not paying the order at all. A quarter to one-third of all support payers never make any court-ordered payments. The consequences for the family awaiting the support can be overwhelming. As tens of thousands of marriages break down every year and tens of thousands of new single-parent families are formed, many of these families live below or close to the poverty line.

So why don't the non-custodial parents pay? Studies suggest it has nothing to do with their ability to pay. One study found that 80 per cent of separated or divorced spouses had a disposable income sufficient to discharge their obligations to their spouse and child. So why don't they pay? It would seem that they do not pay because they do not want to pay. In particular, self-employed people are very difficult to enforce against, particularly those who are working in jobs that are paid in cash or under the table.

Virtually all provinces and territorial governments, with support from the federal government through complementary legislation, have established "support enforcement programs." These programs have been established at a cost of tens of millions of dollars to provide support creditors with free enforcement of their orders. (By "support creditor" I mean a spouse who is awaiting either spousal support or child support and by "support debtor" I mean the person who is supposed to be paying either the spousal support or the child support.) Governments have an obvious stake in this service because those who do not receive support tend to rely on public assistance at a cost of further tens of millions of dollars to taxpayers. The justice system is also drawn into disrepute when its orders are considered unenforceable.

Before examining some of the individual features of the provincial and territorial services, we should consider the methods used by the services themselves to enforce support orders. These techniques may vary slightly from province to province, but they are all basically the same.

The most popular method of enforcing a support order is through the attachment or garnishment of wages. The court in this situation allows the deduction of a fixed amount from the pay of the support debtor on a continuing basis. The amount requested is remitted to the Support Enforcement Office, which then sends the cheque on to the support creditor.

Many people are under the mistaken impression that the Support Enforcement Office issues a cheque each month to the support creditor for the full amount of the support order and then begins to enforce the order. This is not the case. The Support Enforcement Office only sends a cheque for the amount actually collected. If nothing is collected (perhaps due to a lack of employment), then nothing is sent. If only half the amount owed is collected, then that amount is remitted to the support creditor. The attachment or garnishment of wages can be an effective method if the support debtor has a regular job. Most jurisdictions place a limit on the amount of wages that can be taken through this method (usually a maximum of 50 per cent). This leaves the support debtor with money to live on while at the same time allowing him to meet his obligations to the family.

Another method of enforcement is the "Writ of Execution" or "Warrant of Distress." These are essentially orders of the court to the local sheriff to seize any land or property owned by the support debtor in order that it be sold to pay the debt owed. This applies to land, furniture, cars, bank accounts and so on. It is effective only against property in the particular province that is enforcing the court order. Few debtors are foolish enough to let property be lost in such a way. When push comes to shove, they make a payment. Even fewer seem to have property available against which the writ can be executed.

The court has the power to imprison a support debtor for non-payment, but this is rarely used unless the debtor can clearly pay but wilfully refuses.

The few cases in which I saw this used were quite effective. After the support debtor spent a few hours in jail, the money was found. Judges are reluctant to jail people for non-payment.

Other methods for collection of support orders include ordering the support debtor to post security that would then be forfeited if he or she does not pay as ordered. Some provinces now permit the support order to be registered on title to property owned by the support debtor. This could, for example, block a refinancing of the property until a support order is paid and could ultimately force the sale of the property to meet the support debt. Drivers licence suspensions are also used in some provinces.

British Columbia, Manitoba and Ontario, through their various Support Enforcement Offices, have the power to arrange for the appointment of a Receiver for the support debtor's property or business in order to facilitate payment. But as you can see, the above remedies are only effective when the person actually has property or money. If support enforcement is to be effective, Support Enforcement Offices will need to be able to seize wages quickly and efficiently to impress upon a support debtor the need to pay. Only tough enforcement will form the habits necessary for ongoing compliance.

THE SUPPORT ENFORCEMENT OFFICES

Through Support Enforcement Offices, support enforcement is automatically initiated, monitoring and tracing are available, and government computers and lawyers are available to track down and enforce the support order at no cost to the support creditor.

The type of system may vary from province to province. For example, Ontario, Manitoba, Saskatchewan and Alberta have a system by which all support orders made by the court are automatically entered on the system for enforcement. The support creditor need not do anything other than get the support order in the first place. For example, in Ontario, every order made by the court is required to have a direction in it to the Director of the Support Enforcement Office. The couple can opt out under very limited circumstances, such as posting three months' support as security.

By contrast, British Columbia has an "opt-in" system, which requires the support creditor to take the support order to the office and ask that it be enforced. It is the only privately run Support Enforcement Office in Canada.

Clients of these services should be scrupulous in filling out the necessary forms and be certain that all information in the enforcement services is up to date . . . and then they must wait.

Regardless of which system is used, it is always open to creditors to enforce the order themselves with the help of a lawyer in private practice. They do so at their own expense, of course, and would only consider doing so if the Support Enforcement Office was failing to respond to their immediate needs.

Once in the system, the support debtor must make all payments to the Support Enforcement Office, which, as already mentioned, remits the amount collected to the support creditor. As you might have guessed, computers play a large role in this type of system and payments are recorded as they are made. If one is missed, the computer notifies the enforcement personnel, who respond with the most appropriate enforcement procedure—usually a garnishment or wage assignment. In some cases, a "show cause" is needed, whereby the support debtor is summoned before the court to explain his failure to pay the order. The support debtor must, in other words, show the cause of his failure to pay.

An important function of the Support Enforcement Office is the tracing ability. Provincial and federal data information banks can be searched to locate the address, place of work, sources of income and other important information of support debtors. These tracing powers were put in place with great emphasis on the protection of privacy, and the information obtained may only be used for the purposes of enforcing a support order or custody order and nothing else.

At the federal level, the Canada Pension Plan data banks and Canada Employment and Immigration Commission data banks are available for searching. Provincially, driver's licence information, health insurance data and other provincial benefits can be searched if they will assist in the location of a support debtor.

Assuming the search of federal data banks turns up some information, federal monies that may be owing can be garnished to satisfy the support order. Money that can be seized includes:

- income tax refunds,
- EIC benefits,
- interest on Canada Savings Bonds,
- CPP benefits,
- Old Age Security benefits and
- a variety of agricultural benefits payable to farmers.

At the provincial level, similar benefits have been identified for diversion if the support debtor is not meeting the support obligation. In Ontario, a large lump sum payment to a doctor under the provincial health insurance plan was intercepted for non-payment of support (yes, even doctors don't pay their support).

One would think that with so much effort, support orders must surely now be paid routinely. No such luck. The reality is that most of these services are overburdened and cannot begin to enforce as vigorously or as effectively as needed.

It is my own personal view that we need to go back to the drawing board on support enforcement in each of the provinces and across Canada. I was involved in the development and implementation of Ontario's support enforcement system, and the current approach is well beyond anything that was ever originally imagined when the service was created. In many cases, the enforcement systems simply processed cheques that might otherwise have been paid from one party to another.

It's my opinion that the support enforcement system should return to a concentration on difficult enforcement cases and should provide incentives for people who pay directly, in a timely way and in full. I have never understood why our income tax system allows a parent who has been delinquent with child support to still deduct spousal support that has been paid. In my view, there ought to be a comprehensive system that allows the tax system to penalize those who do not pay when they are quite capable of paying.

Ontario's service, which is by far the busiest in the country, reports a 30 per cent rate of total non-compliance with support orders, even though they have been enforcing at taxpayers' expense for several years. In some cases, support creditors must seriously consider taking their support orders to private lawyers if they wish to have immediate attention paid to their needs. Unfortunately, the collection incurs legal fees, which can be self-defeating.

PROPERTY ENFORCEMENT

The litigation over the family property may produce a judgment in favour of one spouse for a significant amount of money if the family assets were of considerable value. As we saw in Chapter 5—Dividing the Family's Property, some potentially large assets are now subject to division on marriage breakdown: pensions, homes, cottages, bank accounts, GICs, cars, boats and so on are all available for division. Judgments can be in the hundreds of thousands of dollars, but, again, the judgment is of little use if it cannot be enforced.

For spouses who are legally married, this can be a relatively easy exercise if the family property is still owned by one of the parties. Most provincial family laws permit the court to order, at the time of judgment, the method by which the judgment is to be paid (or satisfied, as lawyers like to say). So, for example, if at judgment the wife is owed $250,000, then the court can order that certain pieces of property be transferred to her in order to pay that debt. The husband may be ordered to transfer his interest in the matrimonial home to her, for example, in satisfaction of the judgment. This method is very practical and saves the couple further time and trouble with the enforcement of the judgment. Unfortunately, this power is not available for common-law spouses.

Assuming property is not transferred at the time of judgment, a spouse who is entitled to money may use a number of different enforcement procedures. These procedures include a Writ of Execution, which is registered on title to land owned by the debtor spouse, garnishment or attachment of wages and, if no assets are readily available, the creditor's spouse's lawyer can arrange for an examination in aid of execution. This is also sometimes known as a "judgment debtor exam."

In this procedure, the lawyer summons the debtor spouse into an inquiry (like the discoveries) whereby the lawyer is given an opportunity to examine, under oath, the debtor spouse as to his or her ability to pay a particular judgment. A transcript is prepared and the debtor's assets can be pursued with the information obtained during the examination.

Each step can be expensive and time consuming. This type of enforcement should not be undertaken unless the creditor spouse has a detailed discussion with his or her lawyer about the cause of this predicament (that is, of having a judgment and no property to seize), what the expected cost of the enforcement will be and what the likelihood of success is considered to be in the circumstances.

The "judgment and no property to execute against" situation raises an important aspect of property enforcement that begins long before the judgment itself is obtained, known as the "restraining or preservation order." At any point in the legal proceedings, a person concerned about a particular piece of property in dispute may ask the court for an order restraining the owner of the property from dealing with it in any way. For example, a husband who owned a valuable coin collection could be restrained by court order from selling that coin collection until the trial is finished and a judgment has been rendered. This preserves the property in case it is needed to satisfy the judgment or in case the property itself is ordered transferred to the other spouse. Restraining orders with respect to property should be obtained at the outset of any legal proceeding.

A restraining order may go beyond a prohibition of selling it to include even using it as security. So, for example, a wife could be prohibited from increasing the amount of a mortgage registered against a cottage that was in her name alone.

Orders for Possession

Another type of family law order is the order for exclusive possession of a matrimonial home. This type of order does not affect ownership of the home, but determines who may possess it or live in it during the period leading up to a trial. The criteria may vary a little from province to province, but the goal is the same—to give possession of the home to the spouse who needs shelter and could not find alternative accommodations. It is not uncommon for the parent who is given interim custody of the children to also have possession of the matrimonial home until the case is decided.

The order of possession of the home, as we have seen in Chapter 5— Dividing the Family's Property, prohibits the other spouse from being on the property. In Ontario, for example, the breach of an order for exclusive possession is a provincial offence punishable by a fine and/or a jail sentence of a considerable length. Subsequent offences are punished even more severely. To enforce such an order, the spouse in possession should always have a certified copy of the order for possession of the home and proof that it has been served on the other spouse. If that spouse then appears at the home in contravention of the order, the police will know in an instant that he or she is aware of the order and can be arrested and removed from the property. In Ontario, the officer may even arrest the offender without a warrant.

The order for exclusive possession is considered to be an important tool for the protection of spouses where there has been violence in the home.

PERSONAL RESTRAINING ORDERS

A different kind of restraining order is the type that restrains a person from doing something. This type of order may, for example, restrain one spouse from "molesting, annoying or harassing" the other spouse and children. It can be a blanket prohibition of contact or a more specific prohibition of contact at all times except those specified in the order. In the latter case, the order may prohibit contact except on, for example, Friday evening at 7:00 p.m. so that a father may speak with, or pick up for access, his children.

In jurisdictions where a specific punishment is not prescribed, the court may enforce such orders for possession of the home or restraint of a person through the use of its contempt power. In Ontario, this type of order is enforced the same way as the order for exclusive possession. A breach of the order is treated as a provincial offence punishable by fine or jail and places the offender in a position of being arrested without a warrant.

In some cases, the criminal-law procedure must be used to control a violent or unruly spouse. The Criminal Code allows the court to order that an accused person enter into a peace bond. This means that the spouse agrees to be on good behaviour and to have no contact with the other spouse, directly or indirectly. If the peace bond is breached, the recognizance—usually $500 or $1,000—is forfeited and the spouse can be convicted of breach of the peace bond. A peace bond, therefore, has the same effect as a restraining order.

This procedure has some advantages over the civil restraining order. For example, it is free. The Crown attorney prosecutes the case and the offending party must hire a lawyer to defend the charges. If a restraining order was sought in family court, then the person who wants the order must hire a lawyer, prove the case and then push for enforcement.

However, the criminal peace bond should be used for legitimate situations of criminal behaviour. Inappropriate use can cause matters to escalate out of control—especially if a spouse may face a criminal conviction and a record.

CONTEMPT

Television has familiarized everyone with the concept of "contempt of court." Usually a misbehaving lawyer is being warned by the judge about some courtroom antic. Again, reality is quite different. The power to find someone in contempt of court is the court's way of controlling its own process, of making sure that people follow the rules of court, whether big or small. This type of enforcement is necessary to ensure the smooth and respectful functioning of our courts.

If a person using the court process shows a wilful disregard for the court's rules, the court can punish that contempt in an appropriate way—through a jail sentence, fine or denial of access to the court's remedies. Most provinces have given the court this power through specific legislative provisions or through the rules of court themselves. Some courts are considered to have this power inherently and the judge may invoke the power on his or her own, but usually only does so if one of the parties before the court has urged a finding of contempt against the other spouse. Regardless of the source of the power of contempt, it is a potent method of enforcing the court's orders because the judge ultimately has the ability to jail someone he or she considers to be wilfully disregarding the court process.

Because someone's freedom may be at stake, the courts have developed very rigorous standards for making a finding of contempt. If a motion is brought asking the court to find someone in contempt because they have ignored a court order, the person asking for the finding of contempt must follow these standards closely:

- The request for a finding of contempt must be served on the person personally, not through a lawyer.

- The conduct complained of must be clearly wilful. Any confusion will prevent a contempt finding.

- All the facts must be disclosed to the court at the outset.

- Contempt must be proved beyond a reasonable doubt—as if a crime was being alleged.

- There must be no other appropriate way of punishing the conduct.

This power is used rarely and only to protect the administration of justice as a last resort.

Jail sentences and fines are rarely appropriate in family cases and are saved for the most blatant conduct. Judges, however, have an equally effective method of controlling the process when relatively smaller types of misconduct occur: they can refuse to let the offending person do anything else in the case until the conduct complained of has been remedied. For example, if a husband undertook at the discoveries to produce copies of his income tax returns for the previous three years but has failed to do so, then the court can deny him any court orders until he has produced the income tax returns as promised. If he still refuses to produce them, the court can strike out his case completely (claims and defences) and simply give his wife judgment for her claim. In this way, the court controls the case before it.

CONCLUSION

As you can see, obtaining the family law judgment is sometimes less than half the battle. Enforcement can be just as time consuming and just as expensive. An essential early step in any family law case is the discussion with one's lawyer about the likelihood of recovery and the best methods of recovering any final judgment. Don't let someone tell you, "We'll cross that bridge when we come to it." Orders that cannot be enforced are of no value. Concrete plans can be made right at the outset of a case to ensure compliance with any order that is finally made by the court.

CHECKLIST

1. Do you understand the difference between criminal law and civil law enforcement of custody orders?

2. Are you aware of how to contact Child Find (Canada) if you need them to assist with an abduction?

3. If your child is abducted internationally, will you remember to consult with a lawyer to determine whether the countries involved are participants in the Hague?

4. If you are travelling with a child after separation or divorce, do you have that child's birth certificate and/ or passport as well as a letter of permission from the other parent?

5. If you have an access order that provides for only "reasonable access," have you considered consulting with a lawyer to have the access terms made more specific to improve your chances of enforcement?

6. Do you understand the limited connection between the court's power to suspend child support payments and a custodial parent's denial of access?

7. Have you discussed with your lawyer the role of a provincial enforcement agency in the enforcement of your support order?

8. Have you anticipated at the outset the possibility that there may be problems in enforcing a property judgment? Would a restraining order with respect to property be appropriate?

9. If your personal safety is in danger, have you considered obtaining a restraining order and do you understand the methods by which these restraining orders are enforced?

13

GRANDPARENTS AND "OTHER INTERESTED PERSONS"

Every year for the last 20 years, I have happily accepted an invitation to speak on a Sunday afternoon to the Toronto Chapter of the GRAND Society. The society is a support group for grandparents who wish to maintain contact with grandchildren after their own children have divorced or in some cases where they have been denied access to grandchildren who are members of an intact family.

Most afternoons I estimate the number in attendance to be approximately 30 to 40 people. They come from all across Ontario and some from as far as the United States. Their stories underscore the sometimes forgotten consequence of marriage breakdown, the ending of common-law relationships or sadly in some cases the death of their own children. If we remember that there are approximately 100,000 divorces a year affecting nearly 75,000 children, we can safely estimate that there are hundreds of thousands of grandparents who are affected in some way by family breakdown. Many more are drawn into conflict over their grandchildren as a result of death, substance abuse and other personal tragedies.

Grandparents, of course, are not the only ones unexpectedly caught in the legal difficulties of couples separating or other tragedies—aunts, uncles, brothers, sisters and others all can be drawn into the dispute over children.

In this chapter, I would like to examine a special aspect of family law, which although it is really a part of custody and access considerations, merits separate treatment because of its importance to Canadian families.

GRANDPARENTS

The special role of grandparents in a child's upbringing has long been a vital component of Canadian society. Unfortunately, it is taken for granted, and only recently have Canadian courts begun to grasp the importance of a grandparent to grandchildren. No doubt, the role of grandparents has changed over the years with the increasing mobility of families, the frequency of divorce and the impact of other tragedies, but their special status remains.

It is not uncommon to see grandparents having a regular role in their grandchildren's lives. In many families, they are the daycare providers. Grandparents are often an important source of heritage and continuity to a family. Sadly, however, some grandparents have found themselves cut off from their grandchildren by divorce, by tragedy or by some other family dispute. A grandchild can become a chattel that is wielded as a prize to be withheld or granted if the grandparents "behave properly" and comply with their adult children's demands. I have seen cases where families have actually extorted so-called "loans" from their own parents by withholding access to a grandchild. Many lawyers have seen cases where grandchildren are caught in a crossfire between grandparents and sons and daughters-in-law. What seems like invaluable help one day can suddenly be seen as meddling and interference on another day. Grandparents who are considered a valuable part of a grandchild's life can suddenly have a door slammed in their faces without explanation.

This is not to suggest that all grandparents have some divine right to be with their grandchildren. There have been cases of grandparents who have attempted to use access to a grandchild as a means to disrupt their own children's marriages. Whatever their personal axe to grind, these grandparents have placed their children in a position of choosing between an ongoing relationship with their parents and looking after their own children.

In my experience, the problems that grandparents encounter fall into one of three categories:

1. Where their children are divorcing or separating after the end of a common-law relationship or perhaps where a child has died and the surviving spouse has custody of the grandchildren. In such situations the grandparents are justifiably nervous about the significance of this development to their relationship with the grandchildren.

2. The situation of an intact family where the mother and father of the child decide, for whatever reason, that the grandparents should not have a significant role in the upbringing of the grandchildren.

3. Situations in which grandparents end up in disputes with third parties, such as the Children's Aid Society (CAS), where their grandchildren have been taken into care perhaps on an emergency basis. In such circumstances, the grandparents wish to have the grandchildren taken out of foster care and placed with them. What seems an obvious choice to many may not seem obvious to the CAS.

Divorcing, Separating or Death of a Child

The federal Divorce Act and various provincial family laws acknowledge this issue by permitting persons other than the parents themselves to start or participate in legal proceedings affecting a child. Depending on whether the family is undergoing a divorce or is intact, different rules will apply. Let's first consider the situation of a couple divorcing where custody and access to their child is in dispute.

It can be difficult to watch from the sidelines as a son's or daughter's relationship goes sour. This is particularly so if the parents had doubts about the "wisdom" of the union in the first place. Rarely does the problem surface suddenly; more often than not, the marriage's difficulty is known to everyone in the family circle, well in advance. Opinions and advice may already have been offered, with parents being drawn into the dispute and being asked to take sides.

If the couple is acrimonious and a custody dispute looms, the grandparents may be on pins and needles wondering whether their role with the grandchild can be maintained and whether picking any sides, other than the child's, is advisable. Special questions occur to grandparents: What if the son-in-law gets custody and moves back west? What if the daughter-in-law gets custody, remarries and the child has a new stepfather? Will there be stepgrandparents? A new world may await the child and adjustments for the family circle will be inevitable.

The Divorce Act, as we have seen, applies only when a legally married couple is divorcing. It does not apply to "intact" families or separating common-law spouses. The Act provides for persons other than the parents to apply for custody or access to a child of the marriage in the divorce action itself. It does not use the word "grandparent" specifically, but the words "other person" clearly include grandparents. So, any person, including a grandparent, may apply, but the Act also provides that they must first get the court's permission to intervene. This means that if a couple separated and filed for a divorce the grandparents could, with the help of their own lawyer, apply for permission to intervene in the divorce action. If permission is granted, the grandparents may ask for custody of or access to the child.

In deciding whether to grant permission, the court will examine the past connection between the child and the grandparents. Is there a real connection between them? Why is the grandparent applying to intervene? What is in the child's best interest? Once permission is granted, the request for custody or access is decided like any other, by asking simply: "What is best for the child in this family?"

A special consideration will be the obvious constraints on the child's time. There is only so much time to be parcelled out to the parents, the grandparents (both sides) and any others who have an interest in this child's life. The issue becomes how much time, realistically, this child has for all of these people. The court will strive to maintain as much continuity in the child's life while the parents try to build new lives for themselves.

Where the child of a grandparent has died and the surviving parent is looking after the grandchildren, no divorce proceeding will be under way, so there will be no action in which a grandparent can intervene. In such a circumstance, the grandparent will have to initiate a court action pursuant to the provincial custody law.

Intact Families

What if the family is not divorcing? Perhaps the marriage or relationship is intact but the grandparents are being denied contact with the child for a particular reason. The problem could be one of remarriage. In this situation, the Divorce Act would not permit an opportunity to intervene. However, most provincial family laws offer some recourse to grandparents in this position.

Provincial custody and access laws also contemplate "other persons" applying for an order with respect to children. These laws do not necessarily speak in terms of marriage breakdown or divorce and may thus be used by a grandparent faced with an intact family or a common-law relationship that has ended.

Ontario's Children's Law Reform Act, for example, provides that a parent of a child or "any other person" may apply to a court for an order respecting custody or access to a child. This provision has been used by grandparents seeking access to children in intact families. Again, the best-interests test applies and the court considers all the needs and circumstances of this particular child. In Ontario, the best-interests test includes a consideration of the relationship by blood between the child and each person who is party to the application.

In a British Columbia decision, the judge commented that "any person" might include blood relatives, relatives by marriage, grandparents, aunts, uncles (including in-laws), babysitters, foster parents or daycare workers who have developed some relationship with the child.

Attitudes vary from province to province about the degree of latitude in use of the provisions, and a lawyer should be consulted to determine whether or not a particular province's law has been applied on behalf of grandparents. Grandparents can obtain access to or custody of grandchildren. Dozens of successful cases have been reported right across Canada.

A word of warning, however. Occasionally, grandparents have applied for access to their grandchildren and lost. The court will only do what is best for the child, and there has been one highly publicized case in Ontario where the grandparents came under considerable criticism by the court as being completely unsuitable for contact with the grandchild. In that case, these grandparents were ordered to pay their son's legal costs in defending their weak claim for access to a grandchild.

In April of 2001, the Ontario Court of Appeal gave a decision in a case involving a grandparent. This case, known as Chapman v. Chapman, concerned a situation where a 77-year-old grandmother was attempting to maintain a relationship with two grandchildren who were ages eight and 10. The Chapmans were an intact family who were uncomfortable with the amount of access the grandmother wanted to the grandchildren. They were prepared to allow her to have, at most, six visits per year. The grandmother stated that this was not adequate and the situation deteriorated.

At trial, the judge ordered that the grandparent could have 44 hours of access to be exercised over six to 10 visits. The parents were uncomfortable with this and appealed. The Ontario Court of Appeal considered a number of cases, including some that had been decided by the Supreme Court of Canada. The Court of Appeal stated that the test was not about what was best for the children in theory, but rather what was in the best interests of the particular children before the court. The court went on to state that a relationship with a grandparent can and ideally should enhance the emotional well-being of a child. When positive relationships are imperilled arbitrarily, as happens when there is a divorce or other re-organization of the family, the court may intervene to protect the continuation of the benefit of the relationship to the children.

Importantly, the court stated that, generally speaking, if parents were behaving in a way that demonstrated capability of looking after the children, then their right to make decisions and judgments about the children's best interests would be respected. This included decisions about who the children would see or not see. Generally, the parents will be allowed to make these decisions; however, the court will intervene if it is only a poor relationship between a grandparent and a parent that is causing the denial of access to the grandchild. Where there is an established record of the grandparents being interested in the child, the court is also more likely to award access. There is almost a presumption that it is best for a child to maintain contact with those who would bring the child's heritage forward. There is a delicate balancing act between the parents' rights and the possible contribution of the grandparents.

In one New Brunswick case, the court suggested that four questions be posed when considering these problems:

1. Are the concerns expressed by the custodial parent for denying access reasonable?

2. Is the access that is being denied important to the child's well-being?

3. Is it possible that the denial of access to the third party may have a long-term negative impact on the child?

4. Will the access to a third party have a negative impact on the custodial person's relationship with the child?

I expect that we will see ongoing judicial and court interpretation of grandparents' rights vis-à-vis their grandchildren. A significant case was decided recently by the United States Supreme Court. This case, known as Troxel v. Granville, dealt with the situation of grandparents trying to maintain a relationship with their grandchildren after the children's father committed suicide. The mother did not want them to have access. The United States Supreme Court took a different approach to that situation and reaffirmed the presumption in U.S. law that fit parents act in the best interests of their children.

There may be a tendency to interpret this decision from the U.S. Supreme Court and the decision from the Ontario Court of Appeal as inhibiting the ability of the grandparents to apply to the courts for custody of or access to their grandchildren. I do not agree with that interpretation and would suggest that any grandparent who can demonstrate that an ongoing relationship with the child is in that child's best interest should certainly consider a court application as a possible option. Remember, there are many cases in Canada that have been decided where grandparents have been given custody of their grandchildren or access to them.

A few years ago in Toronto, a senior panel of judges and lawyers considered grandparent access problems. There was near unanimous agreement that where a grandparent has a positive contribution to make to a child's life, access will be ordered. Consult your lawyer about your rights under provincial law.

Grandparents Fighting Third Parties

In other situations, the grandparents may find themselves pitted against a CAS. If the parent of the child is suddenly faced with a trauma—jail, a drug overdose, a mental breakdown or has simply disappeared—the CAS may be called to intervene on an emergency basis. The child could be placed in emergency foster care before the grandparents are even aware of the problem. Once notified, they may find themselves trying to convince the CAS to release the child into their custody. Remarkably, in such cases the CAS officials will ask the parent what he or she thinks about the grandparents having custody. If the relationship has been strained, they may say no and leave the child with CAS. Such struggles can be heartbreaking for grandparents as they realize they must use provincial law to obtain custody of their grandchildren from the provincial authorities.

STRATEGIC CONSIDERATIONS

This raises some important considerations for grandparents—the advisability of legal proceedings, alternatives to court and the expense of legal proceedings.

The advice in Chapter 3—Taking a Look at the Process, about hiring a lawyer who specializes in family law, applies equally to grandparents who are considering such an application to the court. The commencement of legal proceedings should be seen as an absolute last resort. If the relationship between the grandparent and the child is beyond the point of no return, the court will do little if anything to salvage it. I recommend family counselling in such cases and, if possible, the use of mediation to sort out the underlying problems that have created the barrier to contact between the child and grandparent.

Legal fees can be considerable in these proceedings and should be reviewed, in detail, with the lawyer at the outset. Discuss the likelihood of success based on cases that have been undertaken like your own. If there are none, you may find that you are the test case and much depends on your individual circumstances.

I think a reasonable place to begin is a private conversation between the parents of the child and the grandparents in the absence of the grandchildren themselves. The purpose of the meeting should be to assure the parents who are in question about the following:

- that you as grandparents do not sit in judgment on either their decision to separate or their parenting abilities,
- that you as grandparents have had a role in the grandchild's life that has been positive and that you want that role to continue and
- that the overriding consideration should be what is best for the child and that you want to develop a plan that allows you to contribute to the child's life.

Be patient in approaching these matters. It is certainly advisable to take the long view. It may be that contact with the child will have to be established in small increments. I am familiar with one case where a grandparent painstakingly re-established contact with his granddaughter by submitting to two years of supervised visits. In other words, he had a third person from the local CAS present whenever he had access to his granddaughter. He did not feel that the supervision was necessary and, in fact, felt that it was a little insulting, but he complied in any event. Within that two-year period, the CAS became convinced that he was a very positive influence in the granddaughter's life and recommended the end to his supervision. Later, the granddaughter herself suggested that there was no need for anyone other than her and her grandfather to schedule and arrange meetings and they resumed a normal granddaughter-grandfather relationship. The grandfather was extremely patient and everyone benefited. (After all, aren't grandparents famous for their patience?)

The point of this private conversation should be to let the parents of the child know that you want to understand their decision to exclude you from the child's life and why they think that this decision is best for the grandchild.

Do not threaten to sue, withdraw financial support, eliminate inheritances or penalize the couple in any way. To do so suggests, perhaps proves, that you are not actually acting in the child's best interests after all. If you feel strongly about inheritances and other financial relations between you and the couple, you are free to make whatever arrangements you wish, but I believe it is a mistake to connect them to spending time with the grandchild.

If the meeting is refused or is unproductive, you should seriously consider obtaining legal advice from an experienced family law lawyer about your likelihood of success in a court application under either the Divorce Act or provincial family law. The proceedings may take several months and cost over $10,000. Certainly, family relations will worsen, but most grandparents in such circumstances realize they have no choice. Many grandparents have been successful.

"OTHER PERSONS"

As I mentioned at the outset, there may be more than just the grandparents interested in the children at marriage breakdown. Across Canada, dozens of cases have tested the applicability of the expression "other person" in custody and access applications. Consider the following who have applied—not always successfully—for custody of, or access to a child:

- a man who claimed he was the father of a child but whose paternity had not yet been established,
- a child's stepfather,
- a former common-law partner of the child's mother,
- a grandmother and an aunt together,
- the child's biological mother after she had given the child up for adoption,
- the child's biological father after the biological mother had given the child up for adoption,
- a former adoptive father,
- a babysitter,
- foster parents,
- a stepsister and her husband and
- an adult family friend.

I have seen cases where the paternal and maternal grandparents fought each other for custody of the grandchild and a case where a maternal grandmother fought a great-aunt for custody. The same considerations with respect to the advisability and cost of legal proceedings apply for anyone in these categories.

These cases, whether they involve grandparents or other family members, serve as a serious reminder of the ripple effect of divorce and marriage breakdown. More than the child's parents and the child himself or herself are affected—the child's whole world has an interest.

More and more of these cases will be brought forward. I have noticed that many of the grandparents seeking custody of or access to grandchildren are younger and more and more able to fight to maintain a role in their grandchildren's lives. I have also noticed a genuinely sympathetic attitude among judges when dealing with grandparent cases. (Is it because most of the judges are grandparents themselves? Who knows.)

CHECKLIST

1. What has caused the underlying dispute between you and the parents of the grandchild?

2. Have you considered the emotional stages described in Chapter 1—Taking a Look at Ourselves?

3. What steps can be taken to solve any underlying emotional or psychological problems between you and the parents of the grandchild?

4. Have you considered family counselling?

5. Have you considered using a neutral third party to mediate?

6. Have you considered the possibility that commencement of legal proceedings may place you in a position of having to choose between the grandchild and your own children?

7. Are you taking the long view and are you prepared to patiently rebuild a relationship with a grandchild through incremental steps?

8. Are you being asked to submit to blackmail in return for time with the grandchild? If so, consult a lawyer immediately.

9. Have you reviewed the chapter on custody?

10. Have you reviewed the chapter concerning hiring a lawyer and the costs of proceedings?

14

DOMESTIC VIOLENCE

A Problem that Just Won't Go Away

Many years ago I was working in my office when a new client, an older woman, arrived for some advice about a separation and a divorce. When I walked into the reception area, I saw her sitting there with three of her daughters. The mother had obviously been beaten up and looked very sad. With the help of her daughters, she got into my office where she explained that her husband of 25 years had beaten her up and thrown her out of the family home. The husband was still back at the house drinking.

I was in shock. As a young lawyer, I had never seen such a case. My initial shock got worse as the woman told her story. I was not the first lawyer that the woman had consulted. The previous week, she had gone to the lawyer who handled the purchase of her home. He was not a family law lawyer and was very busy with real estate work. After talking to her for a while, he suggested that she go home and try to work things out. Court was expensive and slow. Did she really want to separate after all? Her husband had done crazy things before and it had all blown over. Why overreact now? In fact, she was tempted to go back but she didn't. Her daughters persuaded her to see another lawyer and after a lot of work I was able to obtain for her an order for custody of the children, support and possession of the home. We also obtained a restraining order prohibiting the husband from contacting the family, and she was able to re-establish a normal life when she had extracted herself from the violence in that home.

Now, 26 years later, I continue to be horrified by the violence that goes on undetected in many Canadian homes. Everyday the papers are filled with stories of spouses who murder, children who are caught in the cross-fire and the seeming inability of our justice system to help these families.

I would like to examine in this chapter the ugly secret of violence that affects thousands of families every day in Canada. Perhaps it has occurred in your neighbour's home or even in your own home.

What do we mean by "domestic violence"? Other terms are used from time to time—"wife beating," "wife battering," "wife assault" and "wife abuse." I have used the term "domestic violence," because it captures two important aspects of this issue—it generally occurs in the home and the term does not leave the impression that it only happens to married women. We are talking about violence by men against women and children and in some cases violence by women against men. Even same-sex couples fall prey to domestic violence.

One definition that captures the elements of this conduct is as follows: Domestic violence involves the intent by a husband or wife to intimidate, either by threat or by use of physical force on the other person or property. The purpose of the assault is to control his or her behaviour by the inducement of fear. Underlying all abuse is a power imbalance between the victim and the offender.

Examples of physical abuse abound but consider the following: slapping, punching, kicking, shoving, choking and even pinching. Shelter workers report cases of women being burned, beaten with belts, stabbed and even shot—sometimes with fatal consequences. Domestic violence can include sexual assaults, humiliation, forced and unwanted sexual acts or such things as being forced to watch pornography.

It need not be just physical assaults; psychological abuse can often achieve the desired effect. I recall from my own practice a woman who had been hit "only" once, but it was enough to make her feel that one false move would bring a reign of terror against not only her, but also her children, her family and her friends. She dared not jeopardize anyone else, because her spouse could make his threats real. She suffered for years thinking that her "walk on eggshells" was actually protecting others. It justified her miserable life. She saw her clothes destroyed and her personal photos burned, suffered humiliations and was forced to beg for money. Threats against the victim, family, children, property or pets can be quite effective.

Her abuser rivalled another husband who responded to his wife's suggestion of marriage counselling with a promise to cut her wedding ring finger off with a pair of tinsnips. She got the message—and so did her daughters. Like others I had met, she described a pattern to the terror in her home—first a period of growing tension, an explosion of violence often triggered by some minor event and then the "honeymoon" when the repenting man becomes the charming person she used to know. Apologies then flow with gifts and lavish attention—until the next period of tension and the cycle repeats itself.

I mentioned the woman whose daughters learned a lesson from seeing their mother assaulted. The lesson was in how to be a victim. Girls who witness violence against their mothers pick up a message about how women are supposed to relate to men. Similarly, young boys who see their mothers being beaten learn that this is how men treat their intimate partners, their future wives and the mothers of their children. The emotional trauma these children experience is well-known and has a lasting, damaging effect on them.

In this book, I cannot undertake any proposed cure-all. I would rather deal with the violence on a more practical level and look at how to identify the pattern of domestic violence, the victims and perpetrators and, most importantly, provide some advice about how to deal with it, should it happen to you or to someone you know.

VIOLENCE: THE MYTHS

Experts in this area have identified nine common myths about domestic violence. The prevalence of these popular misconceptions has allowed the secret of domestic violence to be kept so long.

1. People who assault their partners are mentally ill.

   Not necessarily. Many function quite well at work and among their friends. This violence is not caused by mental illness.

2. People who assault their partners are drunk.

   Not necessarily. Studies have found that the violence can occur whether alcohol is consumed or not. It does sometimes contribute to the violence, but it is not a cause.

3. Domestic violence occurs only among the poor.

   Dead wrong. Money cannot buy protection from this violence. The spouses of lawyers, doctors and successful businesspeople are all victims.

4. The victim does something to provoke it.

    Yes, something like breathing. The violence has no connection to conduct. Victims who were sound asleep have been beaten.

5. The victim actually enjoys it.

    This is a particularly disturbing myth, because it not only minimizes the violence and blames the victim, but also suggests that the violence is desired. The stream of women and children flocking to shelters should be proof enough that this is simply not true.

6. If the victim didn't like it, he or she would speak up or leave.

    As in the way that hostages on airplanes complain to terrorists that they don't like the way they are being treated? The syndrome that develops from the domestic violence is an invisible cage that keeps the victim from leaving.

7. Abusers who do this are a danger to the rest of the community.

    Maybe in the long term, but day by day they function well and can appear quite charming and friendly to everyone outside the home. They only beat their partners and children because they know that they can get away with it.

8. At least nothing will happen while she is pregnant.

    On the contrary, pregnant women are frequently victims, with blows deliberately aimed at their abdomen.

9. It happens to other people.

    You should be so lucky.

WHY ARE WOMEN ASSAULTED?

It is a complex combination of things that have put women in this position. I hope the following is not too much of an oversimplification.

- Our society conditions women to be dependant, to be victims. Many have seen and learned to accept the violence at their parents' knees.

- The privacy of the home allows it to occur out of sight.

- There is pressure to preserve the family. Reporting violence in the home may break it up.

- Those who do report it have found that they are blamed—"What did you do to provoke him?"

- There has been, until recently, little community support when victims of domestic violence finally leave the home.

- Society has not thought it necessary, until recently, to punish the offenders.
- In many cases, the woman and child have been so financially dependent on the male provider that they could not afford to leave.

These factors combine to mould a woman who is afraid and feeling helpless, who blames herself, who feels ambivalent about her life, who has no self-esteem, who prays for a change and who feels inferior to everyone around her. These factors form themselves into a syndrome of domestic violence that keeps her from leaving.

WHY DO MEN DO IT?

Again, a complex combination of elements of our society have contributed to this problem.

- Society has tolerated it over hundreds of years. Men think it is acceptable to beat those with whom they are angry.
- Given the prevalence of this type of violence in the home, it is likely that thousands of men have learned this behaviour from their own parents.
- Society has also been quick to blame the victim rather than the offender. Why should a man change when "it's not his fault?"
- Men who are violent with their wives and children generally have poor impulse control and an inflexible method of dealing with frustration.

These factors, coupled with poor self-esteem, produce a man who denies he is violent, blames everyone else, is highly emotionally dependent on his partner, is very traditional in his views of male-female relations and handles life in one of two ways—everything is okay or he is furious. This is a man who is emotionally isolated and who lashes out at easy prey—his family.

I was involved in a case recently where the husband/father was particularly abusive. He had been charged and convicted of assault. Part of his probation included taking an "anger management" course. When I did background research on this fellow, I learned that he had been through a previous marriage and a common-law relationship. We located the court files and read the affidavits and allegations that had been made by his previous partners. They were almost identical to the records in my case.

My client was number three. While the proceedings were under way he met, lived with, abused and left three more women! This fellow was unemployed for most of the three years I dealt with him. He was not particularly good-looking. He had no driver's licence and no property. He could, however, be quite charming and sought out single women with children.

How can you avoid this kind of person?

If you meet someone who talks about previous relationships that went sour, try to find out what happened. Do a little research. If someone has a conviction for spousal assault, then draw your own conclusions. If you see evidence of the cycle I mentioned, avoid this person. You are placing yourself and your children in danger.

WHAT CAN BE DONE?

As frustrating as this situation appears, there are some things that can be done on a practical level and a legal level.

On the practical side, consider the following suggestions:

- Get out. It won't be easy, but it's possible. Others have done it and so can you. But rather than just walking out, have a plan. You put your life and the lives of your children at risk by staying.

- Protect yourself and your children at all costs. Do not fight back, but do practise self-defence. Be alert to the building tension and stay out of the line of fire if possible.

- Call the police. Press charges. Follow through. One study found that when the police laid charges, the probability of violence was reduced by half.

- Have a friend available for support.

- Tell your doctor about the violence. Don't make excuses; listen to suggestions and accept support.

- Investigate the availability of shelters in your community. Not every community in Canada has shelters for battered women, but many do. Unfortunately, even when they are available, demand far exceeds available space. In Toronto, for example, shelters are reported to have only one space available for every six requests.

- Keep a record of the abuse and any resulting visits to doctors.

- Develop an escape route for emergencies. Discuss it with the children if necessary. Ask a neighbour to call the police if trouble occurs.

- Set aside some extra money for a cab in an emergency.

- Leave a supply of extra clothes for yourself and the children at a neighbour's house. Have extra keys made for the house and car.

- When you go, take all your identification: Health insurance numbers, passports, personal I.D., birth certificates. You will need them if you apply for public assistance.

- Check the availability of social assistance in your community in advance.
- Consult a lawyer about your plans. Check out the availability of legal aid in your community. Some legal aid plans will expedite a request for legal aid where violence is involved.
- Don't wait for him to change. He won't and you know it. In all my experience, I have never seen a person like this change. Courses, books and so on make no difference. Abusers must take responsibility for changing themselves. You cannot do it for them.

As you can see, a great many steps can be taken in advance. Little by little, step by step, you can plan an escape from an abusive home.

On the legal side, consider the following options:

- Press charges. This assault is like any other in that it is a crime and police intervention is necessary. Many forces now have special training for those responding to such calls.
- Every province has a procedure for obtaining a peace bond. This is a relatively straightforward procedure that requires the abusive husband to post a bond subject to certain conditions. If the conditions (e.g., keep the peace, stay away from the home) are breached, the bond or money (e.g., $500) is forfeited or he may be rearrested.
- All provincial family laws contemplate a court order restraining a spouse from having any contact with his family or, in some provinces, limiting the contact to certain days and certain times. These are called restraining orders.
- Check the availability of legal aid.
- All provincial family laws allow for "ex parte" motions to the court. Ex parte means that the court is asked to make the order without notice to the other side of the court appearance. It is used under limited circumstances but is well-suited to a situation where a woman fleeing an abusive relationship would be at risk the moment her abusive partner received notice of going to court.
- If your children are at risk, apply for custody of the children as soon as possible. The court will likely grant custody, but may also consider some form of access for the other parent if it will not endanger the children. Ask your lawyer to consider your own risk at the time your husband has access to the children. It is possible to arrange access in such a way that the parents do not have to deal with each other.

If you have been assaulted and injured, consider the availability of compensation from two sources:

1. A civil law suit for damages: Essentially, you sue your partner for damages. Damage awards have been made for victims injured by an assault, but relatively few people sue.

2. An application to a provincial Criminal Injuries Compensation Board: All provinces consider the cases of victims of domestic violence applying for compensation.

A number of lawsuits against abusive partners have been successful and I think that people who have been abused or assaulted in their marriage or relationship should sue. I know that someone in this situation has more than enough to think about, but a claim for damages will help the abuser and society get the message—damage has been done.

It is not going to be easy, but with organization, planning, support and the right timing, a person and his or her children can escape an abusive relationship. If you are in that position, a lawyer will be absolutely necessary, especially if the full force of the law is to be exercised in your favour. Good luck.

STRATEGIC CONSIDERATIONS AND DOMESTIC VIOLENCE

Lawyers have now been trained extensively to try to recognize the symptoms of domestic violence. It's fair to say that we continue to be shocked by what we learn about other people's intimate lives. In this brief section, I want to add some strategic considerations on family violence.

Sometimes it's impossible for a couple to split up and move into separate residences. For financial reasons or for strategic reasons, the couple stays under the same roof. The tension can be unbearable and in some circumstances explosive. All family law lawyers have seen situations where couples call the police to deal with these explosions. The police have been trained to be sensitive to these complaints about domestic violence. Laying the charge can set in motion a series of events over which both spouses lose control.

The police must lay the charge if they are satisfied that there has been evidence of violence. In some cases, the violence has been by both spouses or at least it has been alleged by both spouses. In such circumstances, the police lay charges against both the husband and the wife. These charges are then passed on to a Crown attorney who must go forward with the charges and will push for a trial. Crown attorneys have little, if any, discretion now to withdraw charges of domestic violence. This is because policy makers wanted to ensure that wives who were subjected to violence were not threatened by their spouses to have the charges withdrawn. As a result, it was thought to be better to take the matter out of the hands of the spouses and leave it with the Crown attorney. The result is that a Crown attorney must go forward with a domestic violence charge.

Once the matter gets to court, each spouse will give evidence in relation to the specific charges and convictions may be obtained, restraining orders may be granted and peace bonds will likely have to be posted. This process takes many, many months. In the meantime, a court may be trying to sort out who should have custody of the children. With criminal charges for alleged domestic violence hanging over one's head, it can be difficult to convince a court that this person should be given custody of the children.

I mention this because allegations of domestic violence have now become strategically important in custody disputes. The vast majority of complaints of domestic violence are legitimate. Unfortunately, there have been individuals who have abused the police and the Crown attorney and made allegations of domestic violence in inappropriate circumstances in an attempt to affect the custody determinations. Both men and women have been guilty of this. It is particularly infuriating because it undermines the legitimate complaints that have been made by true victims of domestic violence.

I never thought that I would have to add some additional comments in this fourth edition about growing abuse and criminal charges in the area of domestic violence, but we have something of a crisis developing in this area. I am not the first person to point out that the Canadian justice system does not do nearly enough to adequately protect victims of domestic violence. Over the last few years, there have been numerous incidents of abusers who are subject to restraining orders still managing to viciously attack and, in some cases, kill their spouse. In some particularly horrific situations, attackers have killed their children, as well. This is an ongoing problem in Canadian society. Not enough is being done about it. Increasing protection for victims of violence should be a top priority.

Having said that, it is particularly galling to see the limited resources of our police and our justice system squandered on what can only be characterized as false allegations. The problem is not being tracked or monitored, but based on anecdotal experience, it is clear that many spouses have discovered that false or exaggerated allegations of domestic violence can provide a considerable advantage at the time of separation and divorce.

I am personally aware of some terrible incidents of false allegations. In one case a man was in attendance at the same movie theatre as his wife. He did not know that she was in the movie theatre. Both of them were in attendance with new partners. The wife contacted the police and alleged that she was being stalked. The husband was arrested and spent two terrifying days in jail before being released. He was ultimately acquitted, with the judge observing that the charges should have never been laid in the first place.

In another case, a wife struggled to forcibly remove a child from a car. The car rolled two or three inches, but no one was injured. The police were called, however, and the husband was charged with attempting to run over the wife with his car. In another case, the husband tapped on the window of the family minivan to remind the wife that he needed the car seat in the van. The wife called 911 and tried to have the husband arrested for domestic violence.

A wife came home from work late one evening and was taunted by her husband. Pushing and shoving ensued, the wife receiving the worst of it. The husband called the police and both of them were charged with domestic violence. These are not the kinds of situations in which the scarce resources of our police and justice system should be wasted.

In yet another case, a wife accused the husband of attacking her. She presented herself at a police station with wounds. These were later determined to have been self-inflicted. The husband was acquitted—after 17 court appearances and a very large legal bill. Other false allegations were made, and the woman making them ultimately lost custody of her child to the father because the woman had so damaged her credibility with false allegations that no one knew what to believe.

I mention this developing problem for three reasons. Firstly, it is depriving genuine victims of domestic violence of the protection they need and deserve. Secondly, it is undermining the credibility of legitimate victims of domestic violence. And thirdly, it is unjust for people to be falsely accused of crimes. It undermines the credibility of our justice system and will cause people to lose respect for it.

It has become my practice to urge courts to deal punitively with those who make false allegations. I urge fellow lawyers to refuse to act for a client who has made a false allegations and I add this caution for any reader who may be tempted to think that they can make a false allegation and get away with it: I recently appeared before a judge on a hearing concerning a number of false allegations that had been made by a party to a divorce proceeding. The judge looked at the individual who had made the false allegations and explained to them in the coldest possible terms that if it turned out that their allegations were false, nothing—and the judge repeated it for effect—"*nothing* you say from this point forward will be believed."

I caution all of my clients who are living separate and apart under the same roof or who are coming into contact on a regular basis with a spouse where there is a great deal of tension. It is in everyone's interest that you avoid violent confrontations. It is, of course, in the interest of your own safety and in the interest of your children, but strategically avoiding violent confrontations is in the interest of everyone trying to advance their case.

Policy makers are discussing new and more powerful ways to deal with the scourge of domestic violence in Canada. I do not want my comments in this section interpreted in any way as discouraging the reporting of legitimate domestic violence. If you are a victim of violence, then reporting it will contribute to an end to the violence and offer you and your family more protection.

CONCLUSION

Domestic violence, unfortunately, is still a reality for the area of family law. I wish that I could say I had seen improvements in this area in terms of enforcement. It is certainly an area that requires more resources and by that I do not just mean more shelters. Sadly, the rise of false allegations of domestic violence is making this a more complicated area than it needs to be.

For those of you experiencing domestic violence, make a plan to exit safely and get support and you will very likely escape your nightmare. For those of you who are faced with false allegations, you may simply be left with no option but to leave your trust in the criminal justice system and pray that you are ultimately acquitted and that in the interim, your interest in the separation and divorce have not been harmed irreparably.

CHECKLIST

1. Do you understand the meaning of domestic violence?
2. Have you advised your lawyer of domestic violence that may be present in your case?
3. Do you understand the consequences for your children of witnessing violence?

(Continued)

4. Have you reviewed the myths about violence against women? Do you understand why women become victims and why men engage in this behaviour?

5. Do you think you can identify a potentially abusive partner?

6. If you are a victim of violence, have you reviewed the list of practical suggestions for dealing with it in a way that is safe for you and your children?

7. Do you understand the strategic considerations that flow from reporting domestic violence to the police?

15

MARRIAGE CONTRACTS AND COHABITATION AGREEMENTS

~

Managing Your Relationship—Contractually

In this chapter, we will examine two other kinds of domestic contracts, the Marriage Contract and the Cohabitation Agreement.

Marriage Contracts and Cohabitation Agreements have a different purpose than the most common type of domestic contract, the Separation Agreement (which we studied in Chapter 9—Settling Your Differences). Separation Agreements are designed to settle disputes that have arisen over property, custody, access and so on at the time the relationship ends. Marriage Contracts and Cohabitation Agreements are designed to avoid disputes in advance by setting out the couple's agreed intentions about important things like property division or support.

Marriage Contracts and Cohabitation Agreements are for people of different legal status. Marriage Contracts are for those who are married or intend to marry, while Cohabitation Agreements are for those who are living together or intend to live together.

In looking at these areas, we should never lose sight of the fact that these arrangements are contracts, pure and simple, designed to deal with a specific issue the same way a contract to purchase a car or house is a written record of an agreement that has been reached.

Every province's family law contemplates couples making such agreements, and the technical requirements are not difficult to meet. Just as in the case of a Separation Agreement, these contracts must be written, signed by the parties and witnessed. They can be signed before or after the marriage or cohabitation commences.

With this in mind, let's examine each type of contract in more detail with a view to seeing why they are needed, how they are made and how they are broken.

MARRIAGE CONTRACTS

A Marriage Contract is an agreement entered into by a man and a woman (or same-sex couple) who are married to each other or intend to marry (in which case it is sometimes called a pre-nuptial), in which they agree on their respective rights and obligations under the marriage or on separation, annulment or dissolution of their marriage or on death.

No one is quite sure how many couples are turning to Marriage Contracts as a planning device for their marriage, but one thing seems clear—more couples are exploring the possibility and in some cases actually signing them. Lawyers report often being consulted about them, although many contracts are left unsigned when the issues touch nerves within the relationship.

The need for a Marriage Contract seems to arise in two circumstances, in anticipation of the marriage or after the marriage has taken place and some new circumstance has arisen. Each can produce dramatically different situations for the couple.

I know of an incident where a bride-to-be was presented with a Marriage Contract at her wedding rehearsal. She was told rather sheepishly by her fiancé to take the contract to a lawyer and have it signed—before the wedding. The message was clear, if not spoken—if it's not signed there will be no wedding. This is probably the best example of the worst way to handle a Marriage Contract. In fact, weddings have been cancelled or, worse, contracts have been signed under circumstances of virtual blackmail. What a way to start a marriage!

In negotiating a contract before the wedding, people are usually attempting to do one of two things: Exempt some specific property (a home, pension, business) from division in the event of separation and divorce or they are completely opting out of the province's scheme for division of property and providing their own scheme. Rarely will you see a couple opt out after the marriage has taken place.

In discussing the proposed exclusion of an asset from division, it is fair to ask why this asset should not be shared. Is there some emotional, financial or other reason to exempt this asset? The most common example would have to be the case of the person entering a second marriage and bringing a home. Perhaps the home was inherited or is the chief asset from the property division after the first marriage. These concerns may be quite legitimate and can probably be met with some creative alternatives.

If the goal of property division at the end of a marriage is to ensure that the fruits of the marriage are shared equally or that one spouse is not left disadvantaged because the other spouse holds all the property, then special assets can be protected through the provision of some alternative security. Perhaps the spouse with the home can take out an irrevocable life insurance policy payable to the other spouse, or some other asset will not be divided equally in order to provide balance. The possibilities are limited only by the assets available and your imagination.

Perhaps one of the most difficult Marriage Contracts to negotiate is where the need for it arises after the marriage has taken place. For example, in Ontario all assets, including business interests, are shareable on divorce. This means that if a person's marriage fails, his or her interest in a company, a partnership or other business is at risk of division in the family property dispute. Business partners or the bank may not wish to expose themselves to the risk of the business being tied up or devalued by the dispute. In such circumstances, business partners have sent each other home to obtain Marriage Contracts from the spouses. In such a contract, the spouse is asked to release any claim he or she may have to an interest in the business. This may be necessary to obtain a line of credit at the bank or other form of financing.

Sometimes the release can be obtained by substituting a full interest in some other equivalent asset. For example, the wife releases the husband's business and he releases any interest in the matrimonial home or her pension. Naturally, values would need to be fairly equivalent. If a separation occurred, he would keep the business and she would keep the house. This example is relatively simple. Situations can be more difficult if the business is the only asset.

Another matter that is often provided for in Marriage Contracts is spousal support. In the contract, the couple agrees in advance with respect to how support would be handled if a divorce took place. They may simply agree to not ask for support from each other if the marriage ends, or they may agree to an actual monthly amount and a fixed term, depending on how long the marriage lasted and the need.

On a scale of lesser importance, some spouses have felt the need to provide for the division of household cleaning and childcare responsibilities. Personally, I feel that if you need to put such things in a contract, you have bigger problems than you think. However, there is no legal restriction against including such provisions. I'm not sure how they can be enforced, but if putting it in helps, why not? At least expectations are clear.

On the other side of the coin, there are some things that one cannot put in a Marriage Contract—or if you do put them in, they will not be binding on anyone or the court. For example, a couple may not provide for custody of or access to their children in advance of separation. The child's best interests cannot be ascertained in advance, so such provisions are not binding. Similarly, attempts to set the amount of, or to avoid altogether, child support are not binding.

It is permissible to agree to "child-rearing methods" such as method of education, religious instruction and so on. So, parents could agree in advance of marrying that any children born will be given, for example, a Catholic education or a bar mitzvah.

At the time of separation, legally married spouses are given special rights to ask for possession of a matrimonial home, regardless of ownership of the home. Any attempt to give up the right to ask for possession in a Marriage Contract is not binding. This is designed to protect people from putting themselves in a very vulnerable position without knowing what circumstances they could face when separating. The spouse can give up the right to ownership of the matrimonial home but cannot give up the right to ask for possession of it at the time of separation.

It should be clear by now that these contracts can have important consequences for one's entitlement to support and property at the end of the marriage, so they should not be entered into lightly or in the absence of independent legal advice. Circumstances will change. Children may be born. Career choices may be made, property may be sold, illnesses may develop and so on. Couples who simply agreed to have separate property at the outset of the marriage have found themselves in an awkward situation 15 years later when one has given up a career to raise children. The contract is still binding on them and may only produce a patently unfair result for one of them.

The courts have been more than willing to enforce and uphold these contracts. Where they have been set aside, it has been because the agreements were grossly unfair.

Just a few years ago, the Supreme Court of Canada dealt with a case called Hartshorne v. Hartshorne. In that case, the couple signed the Marriage Contract in between the wedding ceremony and the reception. Both had had independent legal advice. The wife's lawyer had told her that the agreement was unfair and should not be signed. The wife signed it anyway. Years later, the couple separated and the wife asked to have the Marriage Contract set aside because it was unfair. The court upheld the Marriage Contract, in part because the wife had received independent legal advice and signed it even though she had been advised not to. I think the court took particular interest in the fact that both the husband and the wife were lawyers and perhaps should have known better.

In short, when negotiating a Marriage Contract be cautious, be fair, get legal advice, and think about your future and the need for the contract. An unfair contract will haunt you both.

COHABITATION AGREEMENTS

A Cohabitation Agreement is a contract entered into by a man and a woman (or same-sex couple) who are cohabiting or intend to cohabit and who are not married to each other, in which they agree on their respective rights and obligations during cohabitation or on ceasing to cohabit or on death.

Like Marriage Contracts, we have no accurate estimate of how prevalent these contracts are among cohabiting couples. Based on my discussions with lawyers, they are still relatively rare. Many more people consult lawyers about them than actually sign them.

The purpose of the Cohabitation Agreement with respect to property is to provide a property division scheme where none exists. You will recall from Chapter 8—Common-Law Spouses that one of the difficulties a common-law couple faces when their relationship ends is the reconstruction of their financial or other contribution to property that they jointly acquired. It is necessary for them to prove who acquired which property for what purposes and with whose money. A Cohabitation Agreement can avoid that type of historical review of the relationship by providing for a particular method of division. Options include:

Separate Property Scheme

This method involves each spouse keeping what he or she acquired in his or her own name. If something is registered in his name, such as the car, it is his. If a piece of property is not registered in any way (furniture), then whoever paid for it keeps it.

Community of Property Scheme

This is actually the opposite of the separate property scheme, because under this scheme all property regardless of registration or source of payment is divided equally. In effect, the couple agrees to treat their property as if they were married.

Family Asset Scheme

In this scheme, the couple identifies types of property that will be considered "family assets" and therefore divided equally regardless of registered title or source of payment (home, savings, furniture, vehicles, cottage). Other property (business, pensions, personal investments) would be divided on the basis of a separate property scheme.

Provincial Property Scheme

In this method, the couple simply opts to be treated as if they were legally married and therefore covered by the provincial family law for property division, whatever it may be. Alternatively, they may select a particular jurisdiction's scheme. If they moved to Canada from France, they may want to follow that country's rules.

These are the general options available, but the couple is free to develop whatever scheme they wish. Cohabitation Agreements may also provide for spousal support in the same way as a Marriage Contract. That is, the individuals may waive support or set an amount depending on their wishes.

The same restrictions discussed with regard to Marriage Contracts apply to provisions dealing with custody, access and child support in Cohabitation Agreements. The court never considers itself bound where children are affected. However, as in a Marriage Contract, the couple can agree to educational and religious training of the child in advance of cohabitation.

Other matters of importance include the following:

- Marriage will turn a couple's Cohabitation Agreement into a Marriage Contract.

- Amendments to either a Marriage Contract or Cohabitation Agreement are made the same way the contract itself is made (written, signed, witnessed).

SETTING ASIDE DOMESTIC CONTRACTS

No matter how good one's intentions or how clever one's lawyer, these contracts (and here I include Separation Agreements) can be set aside by the court. Why enter into them at all if the court will just set them aside? While the court has the power to set them (or provisions in them) aside, it will not use that power lightly and will, therefore, do so in very limited circumstances.

The court may set aside a valid domestic contract for the following reasons:

- One person failed to disclose an important asset or liability.
- One party did not understand the nature of the contract.
- Any other reason acceptable in the general law of contract.

Let's consider briefly each one of these reasons.

Failure to Disclose

Since the key to the domestic contract is more often than not financial or property arrangements, everything related to the calculations or property division scheme must be revealed. Most lawyers will not allow clients to sign domestic contracts unless each person provides a sworn financial statement setting out all of their assets and liabilities.

The court will usually set aside an agreement where the failure to disclose relates to a significant asset or liability that existed when the contract was made. The meaning of "significant" will vary from case to case depending on the full asset liability picture for the couple. The court looks to see if one spouse is trying to take advantage of the other spouse. Are they being unfair? Is one preying on the other?

The failure to disclose need not be a deliberate attempt to mislead; accidental failures are still valid grounds to set aside the whole agreement or just parts affected by it.

Failure to Understand

If one of the people signing the domestic contract did not understand the nature or consequences of the agreement, the court may set it aside. This ground is very difficult to establish if both people have received independent legal advice and have signed statements to the effect that they understood what they were doing and were doing so voluntarily. You will recall the affidavits and statements signed at the end of a Separation Agreement that set out the fact of the lawyer's independent legal advice or the availability of it. These same affidavits are attached to Marriage Contracts and Cohabitation Agreements if they have been prepared by a lawyer.

In one case, a man had his wife sign a handwritten summary of how they would like to have a Marriage Contract prepared. In it they summarized their assets and liabilities and exempted some of his property from sharing if they split up. They both signed it and had a friend witness it. When the husband took it to the lawyer, he was told that technically it was already a Marriage Contract. The wife thought that it would be used as a starting point for negotiating between the lawyers. She didn't appreciate that this was a contract (its nature) and that she was giving up property rights (its consequences). The lawyers eventually agreed that the court would probably set it aside, so they started over.

Contractual Failures

You will recall my statement at the outset that domestic contracts are just that, contracts. The general law of contract, therefore, applies to them and any available ground for setting aside a contract will apply to a domestic contract. These grounds include such things as mistake, fraud or public policy reasons. If the couple makes a serious mistake about the law or their assets when negotiating the contract, the court may set it aside. For example, if the couple thought that neither of them was entitled to support after their common-law relationship ended, they would have both made a mistake about the law that likely affected their agreement.

If one deliberately deceived the other to the extent that the contract was actually an attempt to defraud the other, the court will intervene. In one case, a young man moved in with an older woman and, over time, tried to defraud her of her life savings. He had an agreement prepared that he asked "a friend" to witness for them so he could have control over some of her assets. It was a form of a Cohabitation Agreement. No lawyers were involved—until the woman's family found out and stopped the fraud.

There is general ground available in contract law that allows the court to ignore contracts or parts of them that are "against public policy." This means that if the court considers a particular term offensive, it will ignore it. For example, if a woman promised never to have children for the rest of her life or if someone agreed to be a virtual slave to another person, the court would refuse to enforce it. The meaning or extent of "public policy" can vary as society changes.

Religious Barriers

Ontario's Family Law Act and the Divorce Act have unique provisions concerning Jewish divorces. These provisions are designed to deal with a curious and unfortunate practice that had arisen within the Jewish community when marriage breakdown occurred.

Briefly, in order for Jews to divorce, the husband must give and the wife must receive what is known as a "get." It amounts to a contractual release from the religious marriage. Without it, Jews cannot remarry within their faith. The husband is under no obligation to provide it and in some cases it is used to unfairly pressure women into inappropriate settlements. Typically, the subject of the "get" would arise during the discussion of the Separation Agreement. The husband would give the "get" only if, for example, the property was divided in his favour or if he was given custody or generous access rights, etc.

The new laws have short-circuited this process by giving the court the power to set aside any agreement in which the giving of the "get" was a factor. The language of the provision in the Family Law Act is general and does not refer specifically to the "get." It speaks in terms of "the removal by one spouse of barriers that would prevent the other spouse's remarriage within that spouse's faith."

The application to non-Jews is considered to be minimal or non-existent, but should be considered by all faiths as possible grounds for setting aside domestic contracts.

CONCLUSION

More and more couples are consulting lawyers about Marriage Contracts, particularly where it is a second or third marriage and the couple wished to protect assets that they have managed to preserve from their first divorce or perhaps after the death of a spouse. No statistics are kept, but my own estimate based on anecdotal experience and discussions with other lawyers suggests that less than 10 per cent of Canadians who are marrying or co-habiting enter into Marriage Contracts or Cohabitation Agreements. This is a shame, because not only is a couple passing up an opportunity to design their own method of resolving difficulties that may arise in the marriage or its separation, but they are also passing up an opportunity to do financial planning and potential estate planning. Sometimes it is possible for a couple to not only sign a Marriage Contract or Cohabitation Agreement, but to also do their wills and Powers of Attorney at the same time. I hope we continue to see more couples using Marriage Contracts.

CHECKLIST

The following checklist is designed to flag some of the important questions that should be asked when dealing with Marriage Contracts or Cohabitation Agreements.

1. Do you really need one? What event has prompted the discussion of a contract?

(Continued)

2. What are your rights and obligations without the contract? Why change?

3. Are you being pressured to sign? Is there time to discuss this thoroughly?

4. What are the alternatives to a contract? Not marrying? Not cohabiting?

5. What effect will the discussion have on the relationship? Can it withstand the negotiations?

6. What are your expectations—and your partner's—if there was a death or separation?

7. Have you considered and do you both have access to independent legal advice?

8. Has there been full financial disclosure?

9. Is the proposal fair? Will one side resent the agreement?

10. Do you both understand the nature and consequences of this contract?

11. Since a contract is being discussed, is there anything else that could be added that does not relate to property?

12. How will assets acquired in the future be covered?

13. Have you considered a contract that will expire by its own terms on a certain date?

14. Have the technical requirements been met?

15. Do you have a copy of the contract in a safe place?

16. Again, have you considered independent legal advice?

16

FAMILY LAW AND YOUR WILL

In this chapter, I would like to examine briefly some considerations when making a will in the context of family law. It is not my intention here to provide you with a blueprint for will making or estate planning—for that you can consult the bestselling *You Can't Take It With You: The Common-Sense Guide to Estate Planning for Canadians*, fourth edition, by Sandra Foster (published by John Wiley & Sons). However, there are some special considerations that should be kept in mind when making a will or when separating or divorcing.

MAKING A WILL

The most valuable piece of advice I may be able to offer in this chapter is simply to make a will. Thousands of people avoid this essential bit of financial planning; however, the fact remains the same—if you care about your hard-earned money and about protecting your family, then you should make an appointment with a lawyer who has experience with estate planning and have a will prepared.

Not having a will means that your estate would be considered an "intestacy," which will mean considerable delay, the hiring of lawyers and the wasting of your estate's resources by needing to find someone to distribute the estate for a fee. All law offices have computers that will produce the necessary clauses for making a will, and the whole exercise takes very little time. In fact, it is one of the most inexpensive pieces of legal work available from a law firm.

The point of making a will is to plan the distribution of your property after your death. The vast majority of wills provide simply that the property goes entirely to the surviving spouse or to the surviving spouse and the children of the marriage in particular portions.

I strongly urge that when you consult a lawyer about the making of a will, you consider the preparation of two forms of Power of Attorney. A Power of Attorney permits you to appoint a trusted person to make decisions on your behalf with respect to your personal care and/or your property if you're incapable or unable to do so.

Usually lawyers will prepare a separate Power of Attorney for each requirement so you will have a Power of Attorney for personal care, which allows the person to make decisions about your health, personal needs, and, for example, housing; and a second Power of Attorney for property. This second Power of Attorney permits the person you have appointed to manage your bank accounts, real estate investment and the payment of bills.

I strongly recommend that when you consult your lawyer about a separation and divorce, a Marriage Contract or Cohabitation Agreement or any family problem, you should also have your lawyer prepare the full package containing a will and Powers of Attorney. Once they are prepared, put them in a safe place and let the person know where they can find that authority if it is needed.

When clients meet lawyers to discuss their wills, two common concerns are expressed from a family law perspective. First, the possible effect of family law property division rules on the planned distribution of the estate and second, the effect of a child's marriage breakdown on an inheritance that the child has received during his or her marriage.

In Ontario, the Family Law Act provides a unique Canadian solution to the potentially inequitable treatment of one spouse after the death of the other spouse as opposed to at separation. As we have seen, family law provides for the equitable division of property upon marriage breakdown and divorce. Is there any reason why a spouse who survives the other spouse should receive less simply because he or she survived as opposed to separated? It strikes most people as patently unfair that a husband, for example, could upon his death leave everything to his children, but if he had separated he would have had to share the property with his surviving spouse. In other words, why should separating spouses be treated more fairly than widows and widowers?

Ontario sought to address this problem by providing the surviving spouse with a choice (called an election) if the other spouse died. The survivor could either take the inheritances in the will or take what they would have received had they separated. If they elected to take what was given to them in the will, then the estate would be distributed as planned. However, if they chose to take what they would have received if they had separated, then the estate plan would be thrown into turmoil. For example, if the will left the surviving wife only 10 per cent of the total property value in the estate when she would have received 50 per cent upon separation, then the transfer of the extra 40 per cent will upset the other gifts in the will. Everyone else will have to accept less. In most cases, these beneficiaries would be the testator's children, perhaps children from a previous marriage.

At present, most provinces have provisions in their family laws that state that the death of a spouse has an effect on the division of family property. It is a little different in each province, but the point is a simple one for our purposes—when making a will, it is now necessary to keep in mind the possible effect of provincial family property division rules upon the estate. An estate plan that is turned upside down by an unhappy surviving spouse is worthless.

This has led to lawyers using Marriage Contracts and wills together. The estate plan actually comes in two parts—the will, which sets out the intended inheritances to beneficiaries, and the Marriage Contract, by which the spouses release any interest in particular pieces of property and agree to accept the will without challenge. The releases are often given in exchange for the substitution of some other property or something else of value. In many cases, the spouses make what are known as "mutual wills" and "mutual Marriage Contracts" by which they simultaneously agree to honour each other's wills and develop a joint estate plan through the use of their wills and Marriage Contracts.

A second aspect of wills in the family law context concerns inheritances and children and the effect of a child's divorce on the inheritance. It is not uncommon for a person, when giving a lawyer instructions for a will, to ask whether the inheritances given to his or her children can somehow be protected from that child's spouse in the event of the child's marriage breakdown. For example, a father may wish to leave the family business to his son but wonders whether the business would be jeopardized if his son's marriage broke down. These concerns are not unlike those mentioned by parents who wish to give large wedding gifts to their children but only so long as the marriage works out.

Most provinces have provided in their family property division rules exemptions for gifts and inheritances. Generally, a person who receives a gift or inheritance during the marriage will not have to share that asset with the other spouse at marriage breakdown. In some cases, such as in Ontario, any income earned by the gift or inheritance after it is received can also be shielded from division with a spouse. However, the inheritance must specifically state that the income is not to be shared. This means that in Ontario, if a father wishes to pass on a family business, then it will be critical to also state in the will that income earned by the business is not to be included in the son's family property should the son's marriage break down.

Therefore, when consulting a lawyer about a will, two important considerations are

1. the ability of the surviving spouse to set aside the estate plan if he or she is dissatisfied with the inheritance in the will and

2. the advisability of protecting a child's inheritance from his or her spouse in the event their marriage should break down after the inheritance is received.

DIVORCE AND YOUR WILL

Assuming you had the foresight to have a will prepared but now find yourself divorcing or separated, an important consideration is the effect of your Separation Agreement on your will. Most Separation Agreements have standard form releases by which the husband and wife release any interest in each other's estate. (See the Separation Agreement in Appendix A.) This may mean a direct contradiction between the will and your Separation Agreement. Making a new will with a new beneficiary should be undertaken at the same time as the drafting of the Separation Agreement.

Another consideration at the time of separation or divorce is whether any support orders made in the context of the divorce will be binding on the estate of the person paying support. Several provinces now provide that the support will continue to be paid by the support payer's estate. This should be specifically discussed at the time a Separation Agreement or court order for support is drafted.

An important consideration at the time a spousal or child support order arises is the possible impact that order might have on a person's estate plan should they die. Imagine, for example, a man who has consulted a lawyer and carefully prepared an elaborate will and estate plan that parcels out gifts and inheritances to very specific individuals, including family members and children. If that person had a child support or spousal support obligation at the time he died, it would become a charge upon his estate. This means that assets and money from the estate plan would need to be diverted in order to pay the child and spousal support on an ongoing basis. All estate planning may be down the drain. In such circumstances, lawyers and clients have turned to insurance to ensure that a separate fund exists if a death occurs, and that fund will pay the child or spousal support obligation. In some cases, the person paying support simply designates that his or her life insurance policy will be made irrevocably payable to the person in receipt of the support. This means that the person receiving the support will receive a lump sum payment that could, in some circumstances, far exceed the actual child or spousal support obligation. However, the payment of that life insurance protects the estate. An alternative that has developed is a specialized form of insurance that replaces the monthly payment as opposed to providing a lump sum. In other words, if the person paying support dies, this form of insurance kicks in and replaces the monthly payment until the child is no longer in need or until the spousal support obligation ends. For more information, contact the Family Law Insurance Centre, 701 Evans Avenue, Suite 406, Etobicoke, Ontario, M9C 1A3. Or check out their website at www.familylawcentre.com/FLIC2.html. They provide quotes Canada wide. To my knowledge, they are the only company providing this service. I have used them on a number of cases and found the service to be of great assistance to both the person paying and the person receiving the support.

At the first meeting with a client who is consulting a lawyer about a separation and divorce, some important questions arise with respect to wills that have already been made, death benefits, survivor benefits, beneficiary designations on RRSPs and life insurance policies. It can be a difficult conversation. The individual who has consulted the lawyer has separated or is about to separate. The lawyer must ask this person whether they want their current spouse to inherit or benefit from such things as insurance policies or beneficiary designations.

In some cases, the client is horrified to think that the person they are about to separate from may, for example, inherit under their existing will or be the beneficiary of their RRSPs if they die before the separation and divorce is concluded. Usually the client will say, "You mean if I die on the way home from this meeting, he/she will get everything?" The answer is yes, because if, for example, the home in which they live is owned as joint tenants, the surviving spouse will obtain full title to the home. If the spouse is the beneficiary of a life insurance policy, they will receive the proceeds. Similarly, if they are the beneficiary of designations of RRSPs, pensions and other death benefits, they will also receive those funds. In many cases, lawyers must tell clients to go directly to their human resources department or their insurer or their pension administrator and change their beneficiary designations—at least until other arrangements have been made through the separation and divorce. A husband who has taken the wife off his insurance policy as a beneficiary may end up changing it back to her if that life insurance is used to secure the husband's obligation for child and/or spousal support.

I mention these considerations because some couples concentrate so much on issues of custody, access, property division and spousal support that they forget these other details. Make sure you review these issues with your lawyer when you are at that first consultation. Most lawyers have heard stories of husbands and wives separating and one of them dying before an agreement is concluded. The survivor may get it all!

CONCLUSION

In conclusion, while the above is not a detailed overview of all the aspects of estate planning for a family, there are a number of considerations both at the time a will is drafted and at the time of separation that are of special interest to Canadian family law issues.

CHECKLIST

1. Do you have a will? If not, why not?
2. Do you have a Power of Attorney for personal care and a Power of Attorney for property?
3. Remember that not having a will causes an intestacy, meaning delay and expense. Do you want your hard-earned money to go towards paying for lawyers for relatives who are fighting over your money?
4. Does your province's family law provide a surviving spouse with a choice between the family law division and the estate that you have provided?
5. Does your will leave at least 50 per cent of your estate to your surviving spouse?
6. Have you considered a Marriage Contract that would work in conjunction with your will?
7. Are you worried about leaving an inheritance to a child whose marriage is in trouble?

8. Have you discussed making a will that exempts the gifts and inheritance to your child from division in his or her subsequent divorce?

9. Do you know that your divorce affects your will, especially with the releases in a standard Separation Agreement?

10. If you have separated, have you made a new will?

11. Have you made a new will for your post-divorce life?

12. Have you discussed the fact that support orders both for spousal and for child are binding on an estate?

13. Did you know that insurance policies can be purchased to fund the payment of support to protect your estate plan?

14. Did you know that a marriage revokes a previously made will? If you plan to remarry, make a new will.

17

SELF-HELP ADVICE

~

Going It Alone?

In this chapter, I want to focus on three ways in which you may be able to help yourself when going through marriage breakdown: complaining, researching and representing yourself.

HOW TO COMPLAIN

My guess is that despite all of the advice, forewarning and caution set out in this book, you will still probably be disappointed in some way by a part of the system, the people in it or the outcome of your case.

Experience tells us that one or more of the following things may give you cause to complain:

- If you are unhappy about your lawyer's conduct or competence. Contact your provincial law society.

- If the judge mistreated you. For federally appointed judges, contact the Canadian Judicial Council in Ottawa; for provincially appointed judges, contact the appropriate provincial judicial discipline body for judges in your province. All complaints should be made in writing.

- If the court system let you down. Contact your provincial Ministry of the Attorney General.

- If the mediator didn't do a good job. Forward your complaint to the appropriate provincial association and also send a copy to Family Mediation Canada.

- If the children's lawyer didn't help. Contact your province's Attorney General's Department.

- If the law needs to change. Contact your provincial Attorney General or the federal Minister of Justice.

- If your spouse let you down again. How should you complain about your spouse? You already know how to do that.

One of the most difficult aspects about complaining is that it is time-consuming and forces you to continue to think about a part of your life that you would just as soon put behind you. In many situations, your complaint may not change the outcome of your own case. So, why do it?

Complaining is hard work—but it's often worth it.

HOW TO DO YOUR OWN RESEARCH

It may be hard to believe, but for all the details we have covered in the preceding chapters we have only scratched the surface. You may want to do further reading on the various subjects I have covered and I encourage you to do so. In this chapter, I have collected a list of materials and resources you may find useful.

Some of the books will be available at the local public library, some are available in university or law school libraries and some are available free from the provincial, territorial or federal governments. A great deal of material is available on the Internet.

Before going any further, I want to add a short note for those who might be adventurous enough to try a law school library. Every province has a law school (Ontario has six) and you should feel free to use them—your tax dollars have paid for every one of them. Having said that, you should note that law students can be a tense bunch—especially around exam time. I know, because I have taught at Osgoode Hall Law School, the University of Ottawa Law School, Carleton University's Department of Law, as well as Ryerson University, and some days it was just better to steer clear of law students—they have a lot on their minds! I have always found the staff at the various libraries, on the other hand, to be very cooperative. They will be more than happy to help you use the indexing system now computerized at all schools and locate the appropriate book. Once you have located the book, find a nice quiet spot away from the fuss of studying students and settle in for a read. You cannot remove books from these libraries.

Law books often contain case citations—codes to help locate actual reported decisions in cases that have been to court. These cases are likely located right there in the library and can be found with a little help and some digging. Not all cases are reported, but the most significant ones are routinely published. (Remember those "Reasons for Judgment.")

The following are the more popular sources of actual family law cases as reported:

- *Ontario Reports* (O.R.) and other provincial series, such as the *Manitoba Reports* (MAN.R.) or the *Western Weekly Reports* (W.W.R.)
- *Reports on Family Law* (R.F.L.)
- *Dominion Law Reports* (D.L.R.)

A typical case citation would be as follows:

Pettkus v. Becker   (1980), 117 D.L.R. (3d) 257 or
                         (1980), 19 R.F.L. (2d) 165.
Gordon v. Goertz   (1996), 19 R.F.L. (4th) 177 (S.C.C.)
Contino v. Leonelli-Contino [2005] S.C.C. 63

The names are the names of the people involved, and the year refers to the year in which the case was reported (not necessarily the same as the year in which it was decided). The next number is a reference to the volume of the particular services (e.g., Vol. 117 of the *Dominion Law Reports* or Vol. 19 of the *Reports on Family Law*). These volume numbers are printed on the spine of the book near the name of the reporting service. The next bit of information describes which edition of the service carries the case. All editions are filed chronologically. Be careful you don't pick up the right volume number but the wrong edition. The last number is the page reference.

Usually, but not always, the case names are the same, e.g., Brown v. Brown, Porter v. Porter and so on.

Try locating the following volumes if you want some experience in a law library locating family law decisions:

- Andris v. Andris (1984), 40 R.F.L. (2d) 315 (Sask.)
- Brockie v. Brockie (1987), 5 R.F.L. (3d) 440 (Manitoba)
- Moss v. Moss (1916), 5 R.F.L. (3d) 62 (Nfld.)
- Chapman v. Chapman (2001), 15 R.F.L. (5th) 46 (Ont.·C.A.)
- Walsh v. Bona (2002), 4 SCR 325

Note: When asking for a case, describe it as "Andris and Andris," not "Andris versus Andris."

There are other terrific resources available in the law library. For example, track down a book called *Ontario Family Law Practice* by Justice Craig Perkins, Justice David Steinberg and Esther Lenkinski. This book, published by Butterworths, is an exhaustive collection of laws and cases related to family law in Ontario. A similar publication exists in each province, whereby the province's laws are collected along with cases that interpret them. I have published a book for lawyers and law clerks called *Family Law in Ontario*. It is published by Canada Law Book and is available in many law libraries and law firms. I am not recommending that you purchase these books, as they are very expensive, but by all means, you should use them for research purposes.

Good luck—it can be a lot of fun in a law library. If you get bored with family law cases, try the Canadian Criminal Cases (C.C.C.)—you won't want to go home until you have registered for law school!

Internet Resources

The Internet and other technology have dramatically changed the availability of legal information to the average person. Virtually everything is now available online. Some of it is free and some of it requires subscriptions. For your purposes, more than enough is available absolutely free.

Many law firms have websites. These "electronic brochures" at least allow you to get a sense of the firm without actually going to the office. Check my firm's website at www.rickettsharris.com.

Larger law firms maintain very elaborate websites. They often publish papers on those websites to demonstrate their expertise in particular areas. These papers are written by experts and are often very readable, as the lawyers have sometimes written the papers for their clients. This information is excellent and it is reliable, so by all means, go to law firm websites. You will more often than not find a menu item called "Members of Our Team." On that team you many find one or more family law lawyers. Under their names you may find articles they have written, which can be of use to you and your case. Remember, these articles should not be filed with the court as proof of the law, as judges generally only want to hear about other court decisions or the actual provisions of the law. The articles, however, can assist you in understanding how certain areas of the law are intended to work, and it's all absolutely free.

There are a variety of websites containing family law information. The best one by far belongs to the Family Law Centre (F.L.C.) at www. familylawcentre.com/. This website was created by Joel Miller, an Ontario lawyer. By coincidence, in 2001, Joel joined the same firm that I am at and our firm website and the F.L.C. website are now linked. Other good websites include the very impressive www.divorcemag.com, which provides not only legal information but a variety of emotional, psychological and practical tips for couples who are going through divorce. See also www.canadianparents.com, as well as the two government sources, www. canada.justice.gc.ca and www.ontariocourts.on.ca. They also have links to other sources.

In the area of self-help information, I need to add a little caution. There are some services available in the marketplace that sell books, tapes, access to lawyers and tips on family law. Our firm works in conjunction with the Family Law Centre. The material is in the form of workbooks and videos and it is quite good. However, there are some other sources out there that have very weak materials and have caused some general harm to consumers. Some of these other services tend to have an "angry" aspect to their marketing, and their pitch is often gender-focussed. I recommend that you steer clear of them, as I can tell you that I have had to fix up more than one mess created by some very bad advice. In two cases, the mess that had been created cost more to fix than the actual service that was required in the first place. In conclusion, by all means use self-help and use free resources, but be very careful when somebody asks for your cash or credit card. Avoid anyone who seems to be hawking angry or spiteful advice. You need help, not fuel for the fire!

HOW TO REPRESENT YOURSELF:
EYES WIDE OPEN

I have to admit that I thought twice about including this new section. After all, the purpose of this book is to equip you to hire and work effectively with a good lawyer. I know from personal experience, though, that our court system is filled with people representing themselves either for financial reasons or because they simply don't trust lawyers anymore. It can be tricky for the judge if one side has hired and is paying good money for a lawyer but the other side is "self-represented." The judge must be neutral and will want to be fair, but he or she cannot stop every five minutes to explain the rules or why something can or cannot be done. Unrepresented people and self-represented people present a real challenge to our justice system right now. There are so many unrepresented people showing up in courtrooms that judges have been given some guidance on how to deal with the problem.

If you absolutely cannot hire a lawyer, the following are suggestions to make your life—and everyone else's—a little easier. I'm sorry you are not using a lawyer for whatever your own reasons. I'm also sorry if the following tips sound a little harsh, but I would be letting you down if I gave you the impression that the family law system was going to welcome you with open arms. Remember, the system sees you as a problem. Brace yourself.

- Be reasonable. Self-representation can be frustrating. You will be tempted to lash out. You're going to be asking people to help you. Do not turn around and be difficult the minute you think you can take advantage of them. What goes around comes around in the justice system, just like in real life.

- Do not expect everyone in the "system" to ignore deadlines, paperwork requirements, rules and legal procedures simply because you are unrepresented. To be frank, the "system" does not like self-represented people. You slow things down, you make it harder for everyone, you ask too many questions, you expect favours. Self-represented people are a nuisance as far as the "system" is concerned. Don't expect anyone to do favours for you and you won't be disappointed.

- Don't be surprised if the lawyer on the other side is reluctant to talk to you. When lawyers and law office staff from opposing firms talk to each other, there is an understanding about certain things being "off the record" and "without prejudice." This understanding allows us to work more freely, but it cannot be extended to self-represented people. We as lawyers have to assume that anything we say or do to a self-represented person will end up in front of a judge somehow. Lawyers live in constant fear that they will be in front of a judge and a self-represented person will stand up and tell the judge something totally in breach of the Rules of Evidence and Rules of Procedure. The statement usually begins "Yes, Your Honour, but Mr. Cochrane said that I should . . ." I may or may not have said it, it may or may not be accurately repeated by the person, it may or may not have been understood by them in the first place, it may or may not be in compliance with the Rules and it most importantly may or may not jeopardize what I want the court to do that particular day. So for a lawyer in my position, it is simply better to deal with self-represented people as little as possible. Certainly lawyers will avoid discussing the case on the telephone with self-represented people.

I personally ask for all communication to be in writing or by e-mail so there is at least a record that can be shown to the judge. So don't be surprised if the lawyer on the other side is reluctant to talk to you. You make the lawyer's work harder and more expensive.

- Do not tape telephone calls with lawyers and your spouse. No one will ever listen to them and it just makes everyone very reluctant to talk to you. Judges are rarely impressed when they hear about telephone tapings or videos being made.

- Be polite and respectful with everyone. Outrageous letters, faxes and e-mails will all come back to haunt you. Foul language and tough talk will get you nowhere. If something important needs to be said, put it in a short, but to the point, letter or fax.

- Save copies of everything. Keep your own file as if you were a lawyer representing a client.

- Be patient. The system involves waiting. Very few things happen when they are actually scheduled. If the court is scheduled to start at 10:00 a.m., be there at 9:50 a.m. and be prepared to wait until 11:00 a.m. before you are dealt with in the most preliminary of ways.

- When in court, remember the judge knows very little about you. He or she may or may not have read the file. Their gut reaction is one of caution in dealing with you. You are a problem, remember? Every minute that a judge must spend explaining procedures to you is a minute not spent on cases that require his or her decision as opposed to his or her advice.

- Call all judges "Your Honour" and refer to the lawyers in the case as Mr. or Ms. and use their name. The courtroom may be filled with people and the judge needs to know to whom you are referring.

- Remember, when you are given an opportunity to speak at some point in court, it is not a chance to tell your life story or try to convince the judge how awful your spouse has been. Make your points and offer to answer any questions the judge may have. Tell the judge what you would like to have happen. Most unrepresented people show up in court not knowing what they want. Try to have a plan and ask the judge to assist you in implementing it. I must add at this point, though, that I have seen some self-represented people do an absolutely fantastic job in court. I saw a man in court make a clear, articulate, fair and well-reasoned presentation. I was shocked to discover that he was representing himself and was, in fact, a recently laid off business executive. On that day in court he got the job done very effectively.

- Don't get fancy and think that you are "as good as any lawyer" simply because you have accomplished one or two steps in a proceeding. I saw a self-represented person get very full of himself in court. He was referring to rules and evidence and was really going out of his way to try to make life difficult for the lawyer and for his spouse. He was being unreasonable and the judge saw right through it. Within a few minutes, he had been cut back down to size and had really hurt his position. Re-read my first point.

- Be prepared to be physically and emotionally drained. Even lawyers who go to court often get drained after a day there. There is a lot of waiting, it is stressful and courthouses are not known for their stimulating environments. I have seen more than one person get sick from the stress and the wear and tear on their nerves. Over the course of a divorce case, there may be multiple court appearances and proceedings and things can get quite drawn out. It can be a difficult burden to carry when your own life, your property and the happiness of your children is on your shoulders. Remember the old saying that lawyers are taught in first year law school, "A lawyer who represents himself has a fool for a client."

- Try not to think of things in terms of "winning" and "losing." It doesn't really work like that. Rarely is someone a clear winner in the family law system. Focus instead on goals, have a plan, be flexible and don't get lost in the details that may not really matter in the long run. Keep your eye on the ball.

- Consider consulting with a lawyer from time to time to see if you are on the right track. It may cost a little, but it could save you in the end.

- Be prepared to compromise. Offer to settle and put it in writing. If the offer is only available for a limited period, then say so. For example, an offer to settle might be available for acceptance until Thursday at 5:00 p.m., after which time it is withdrawn.

- Re-read this book from time to time. I have heard many readers say that they had to read a chapter in the context of what was actually happening to them in order to fully appreciate some of the information.

Being an informed consumer doesn't stop the minute you find the right lawyer. Continue your own research as your case goes forward. You and your lawyer will benefit from your contributions. Be ready to make decisions.

CHECKLIST

1. Are you afraid to complain if you do not feel that you have been well-served by any part of the family law system?

2. Are you doing your own research?.

3. Have you re-read the tips I have set out in this chapter?

4. Are you prepared to be an informed consumer throughout the whole case?

APPENDIX

Some Important Paperwork

Mountains of paper will be exchanged in family law cases, everything from letters between lawyers, faxes, copies of e-mails, pleadings, evidence, offers to settle and affidavits, to Separation Agreements and divorce judgments. I wish I could provide you with an example of each one, but space considerations simply won't permit it. Instead, I have selected three key documents for your consideration: a Retainer Form, a Separation Agreement and a Client History Form. Before each one, I have provided a brief annotation about its purpose and where in the text you can find more information about its role.

Please note: In the following sample documents, [   ] means you should insert name, address, geographical, age or title information, if not otherwise specified.

THE RETAINER FORM

This is your contract with your lawyer. In it, he or she should describe the work that will be done on your behalf and the estimated (or maximum) cost of the work. Retainers vary from lawyer to lawyer, but they should have, as a minimum, the amount of detail contained in the following example. You should always have a written retainer with your lawyer. For more information on retainers, read Chapter 2 and see the definitions in the Glossary.

Sample RetainerForm

I, [client's name], of the City of [city name] in the Regional Municipality of [municipality name] hereby retain and employ Messrs. Cochrane & Cochrane, [City/Province] as my solicitors and hereby authorize them to [purpose] and to take such actions and conduct such proceedings as they may consider necessary or proper for the conduct of such action on my behalf.

DATED this   day of   , 2007.

Witness: _____

_____

[Signature of client]

Sample Fees and Disbursements Policy

For the information of clients, the firm's policy in regard to fees and disbursements is as follows:

1. All services performed by lawyers and students on behalf of a client are ordinarily recorded on a time-occupied basis and charged against the client on that basis at rates ranging from $500 per hour down to $75 per hour. The hourly rates are reviewed on an annual basis. Time in court may be charged in certain cases at rates in excess of $5,000 per day depending upon the nature of the case, its complexity, and the lawyer or lawyers involved.

2. Most matters require the disbursement of money by the firm on the client's behalf. These disbursements will be billed regularly to the client as they are incurred on an interim statement of account entitled "Disbursements Only."

3. GST will be billed as a separate item and fee quotations do not include GST.

4. In most litigious and other matters, clients will be requested to provide an advance on accounts of fees and disbursements, which sum

will be held in the firm's trust account to the client's credit to be applied towards such disbursements and fees incurred in connection with the matter.

5. It is recognized by this firm that many clients are unfamiliar with the manner in which lawyers bill and, further, are unfamiliar with the amount of fees that may be owing from time to time during the course of a particular proceeding. In the circumstances, clients are encouraged to discuss fees at any time with any representative of the firm and, in particular, to discuss the method of billing when the firm is originally retained.

Sample Note to Litigant

In view of the fact that [lawyer's name]'s practice involves a great deal of court work, he/she may be out of his/her office, or on occasion, out of the City and thus sometimes unavailable on an immediate basis for appointments or reception of telephone calls. On those occasions, his/her secretary and other members of the firm who are familiar with your case will be of as much assistance to you as possible.

[lawyer's name] will, of course, attend to your problem at his/her earliest opportunity.

Note: Fees (exclusive of GST and disbursements) will not exceed $ without prior written authorization.

Barristers & Solicitors
City
Telephone Number

Note: Whether the lawyer's preprinted form includes it or not, I recommend placing a limit on the maximum fee that could be incurred without prior authorization. Write it in by hand if necessary.

A SEPARATION AGREEMENT

The Separation Agreement is the most common of the three types of domestic contract (the other two are Cohabitation Agreements and Marriage Contracts). All three contracts must be written, signed and witnessed. A Separation Agreement acknowledges that the parties are living separate and apart and intend to do so from now on. It sets out important details about their background, their marriage, children and so on. It then describes, in as much detail as is required, the terms upon which the parties will end their marriage. It can deal with all or only some of the outstanding concerns. It may describe who will have custody and access, who will have which pieces of property, possession of the home on an interim or permanent basis, responsibility for family debts, life insurance, etc. The agreement can be final or interim (temporary).

The following example of a Separation Agreement is not a complete document, but shows a selection of typical provisions and some alternatives. Law offices have draft clauses and agreements in their computers. Legal secretaries prepare a first draft by filling in the blanks. While the following is not necessarily a model agreement for your situation, it will help you to understand how comprehensive an agreement can be.

Sample Separation Agreement

THIS IS A SEPARATION AGREEMENT MADE ON [day/month/2007].

BETWEEN:
[husband's name]

– and –

[wife's name]

1. INTERPRETATION

1. In this Agreement,
    (a) "husband" means [name], who is one of the parties to this Agreement, whether or not the husband and the wife are subsequently divorced;
    (b) "wife" means [name], who is one of the parties to this Agreement, whether or not the husband and the wife are subsequently divorced;
    (c) "child" means [child's name], born on [date], or, [child's name], born on [date], both of whom are the children [   ] or who is the child [   ] of the husband and the wife [   ];
    (d) "cohabit" means to live together in a conjugal relationship, whether within or outside marriage;
    (e) "matrimonial home" means the buildings and lot located at [address];
    (f) "cottage" means the buildings and lot called [address];

(g) "Family Law Act" means the Family Law Act (or relevant provincial law);

(h) "property" has the meaning given by the Family Law Act.

2. An Act of the Legislature or Parliament referred to by name will mean that Act in force at the material time and includes any amendment or any successor Act that replaces it.

3. The proper law of this contract shall be the law of [appropriate province], and this contract shall also be deemed to be valid and enforceable in accordance with the law of any other jurisdiction. The parties intend all of their affairs and property to be governed by this contract and the law of [appropriate province].

4. The parties agree that the contract is valid and enforceable in [appropriate province] and that they intend it to be a domestic contract in accordance with the Family Law Act, and that it is legally binding.

2. BACKGROUND

This Agreement is entered into on a basis of the following, among other facts

1. The parties were married at [location], on [date].

2. The parties have [   ] child [   ], born on [   ], and [   ], born on [   ].

3. The parties have no children.

4. The parties are living separate and apart from each other since [date], and there is no reasonable prospect of their resuming cohabitation.

5. The parties desire to settle by agreement all their rights and obligations that they have or may have with respect to:

   • the custody of, and access to, their child [   ],

   • the support of their child [   ],

   • possession, ownership and division of their property and

   • support of each other.

3. AGREEMENT

Each party agrees with the other to be bound by the provisions of this Agreement.

4. DOMESTIC CONTRACT

Each party acknowledges that this Agreement is entered into under s. 54 of the Family Law Act [or appropriate provincial law] and is a domestic contract, which prevails over the same matters provided for in the Act or its successor.

5. EFFECTIVE DATE

This Agreement will take effect on the date it is signed by the last of the husband or the wife.

6. LIVING SEPARATE AND APART

The parties will live separate and apart from each other for the rest of their lives.

7. FREEDOM FROM THE OTHER

Neither party will molest, annoy, harass or in any way interfere with the other, or attempt to compel the other to cohabit or live with him or her.

8. CUSTODY AND ACCESS (SOLE CUSTODY/ACCESS)

1. The wife will have custody of the child, subject to reasonable access by the husband on reasonable notice to the wife of his intention to exercise such access.

2. The husband will have access to the child [   ] as follows:

    (a) (Be very specific: days, times, holidays, special events, total number of days per year, make-up times.)

    (b) The husband and the wife each acknowledge that it is in the best interests of the child [   ] for [   ] to have frequent contact with [   ] father and to spend time with him. Accordingly, the husband and the wife will each use their best efforts for the child to have frequent and regular periods of access with the husband, consisting of a combination of both daytime and overnight visits appropriate to the needs and stage of development of the child.

    (c) In making plans for access, the husband and the wife will give the needs and convenience of the child primary importance and will give their own needs and convenience only secondary importance.

    (d) The parties will keep each other fully informed of all matters touching the interest of the child and they will confer as often as necessary to solve any difficulty raised by or on behalf of the child.

8. CUSTODY (JOINT)

(a) The child [name] shall be in the joint custody of the husband and the wife. The child shall have [his or her] primary residence in the home of the [   ].

(b) The husband and wife each acknowledge that the other is a devoted and loving parent. The [   ] acknowledges that it is essential to the welfare of the child [   ] that [   ] have as close communication and contact with the [   ] as is reasonably possible, commensurate with the best interests of the child [   ].

(c) The husband and wife agree and undertake that in all matters relating to the custody, maintenance, education and general well-being of the child, the child's best interests and wishes shall at all times be paramount.

(d) The husband and wife shall conscientiously respect the rights of one another regarding the child. The husband and wife shall continue to instill in the child respect for both of the parents and grandparents, and neither the husband nor wife shall by any act, omission or innuendo, in any way tend or attempt to alienate the child from either of them. The child shall be taught to continue to love and respect both parents.

(e) The husband and wife shall have the right to communicate with the child by telephone and letter at all reasonable times, provided that such telephone communication shall not interfere with the private life of either the husband or the wife.

(f) The husband and wife agree that there shall be full disclosure between them in all matters touching the welfare of the child, and they agree that they shall confer as often as necessary to consider any problem or difficulty or matter requiring consideration touching the welfare of the child.

(g) The [   ] shall have generous and regular access to the child. It is acknowledged that the kind, frequency and duration of such access should be established in advance, and made as certain as existing circumstances permit, in order to enable the child, the husband and the wife to make plans for their day-to-day living.

(h) If special occasions, holidays, excursions or other presently unforeseeable opportunities become available to the child, neither the husband nor the wife will unreasonably insist that visiting arrangements be adhered to without exception. On the contrary, the husband and the wife shall at all times maintain a reasonable and flexible position respecting the visiting arrangements with the child, and at all times, the best interests of the child shall prevail.

(i) In any matter of contention between the husband and the wife that the husband and wife cannot resolve between themselves by mutual agreement, the parties agree to mediate any such disagreements or differences of opinion through a mediator that the parties may here-after agree upon. If the parties are not able to agree on a mediator or if the mediation is unsuccessful, the parties acknowledge that either one of them may bring an application to a court of competent juris-diction to resolve the outstanding matters between them.

(j) The husband and wife acknowledge that the wife may wish to change her residence from the Province of [Ontario] as a result of remarriage or career opportunities. The husband acknowledges that provided that the wife is leaving the Province of [Ontario] for such reasons, he will not take any action that would prevent the wife from leav-ing the Province of [Ontario] or unduly insist on exercising the ac-cess as set out in this Agreement in order that the wife be prevented from changing her residence from the Province of [Ontario]. The wife agrees to give the husband at least sixty (60) days notice of any intention to change her residence from the Province of [Ontario] for the reasons set out in this paragraph so that the parties may make alternate arrangements with respect to access to the children, or

(k) Neither party shall move more than thirty (30) km from the city of [   ] without the consent of the other.

(l) Neither shall change the child's name without the consent of the other.

9. FINANCIAL PROVISION (SPOUSAL AND RELEASE)

1. Both parties accept the terms of this agreement in full satisfaction of all claims and causes of action which he or she now has or may in the future acquire against the other for support whether under the *Divorce Act,* the *Family Law Act,* the *Succession Law Reform Act,* or otherwise, under presently existing legislation or future legislation whether in this jurisdiction or any other jurisdiction and releases the other from any such claim. They each intend this agreement to be forever final and non-variable.

2. Each of the parties, and "w" in particular, releases all rights to claim from the other or obtain from the other, and releases the other of any obligations to provide support, interim support, maintenance, or interim maintenance, or alimony for himself or herself pursuant to any statute or law or the common law.

3. This agreement has been negotiated in an unimpeachable fashion and fully represents the intentions and expectations of the parties. Both parties have had independent legal advice and all the disclosure

they have asked for and need in order to understand the nature and consequences of this agreement and to come to the conclusion, as they do, that the terms of this agreement, including the release of all spousal support rights, constitutes an equitable sharing of both the economic consequences of their relationship and its breakdown.

4. The parties agree that the terms of this agreement substantially comply with the overall objectives of the *Divorce Act* now and in the future and the parties' need to exercise their autonomous rights to achieve certainty and finality. In particular, the parties acknowledge that they have taken into consideration the factors and objectives set out in section 15.2 of the *Divorce Act* and applied those considerations to their current situation.

5. The terms of this agreement and, in particular, this release of spousal support reflect their own unique particular objectives and concerns. Among other considerations, they are also depending upon this spousal release remaining in full force and effect upon which to base their future lives. As a result, each party recognizes that the other party is relying upon the provisions for spousal support not being changed from as set out in this agreement and will be arranging his and her affairs accordingly.

6. The parties acknowledge that they have been advised of the significance of the decision rendered by the Supreme Court of Canada in the case of *Miglin v. Miglin*. They have applied their minds to the negotiation of this agreement as they understand a married couple should do when separating. In that regard, they each specifically acknowledge and confirm that this agreement was prepared with the advice of experienced family law lawyers acting for both parties and in circumstances without any kind of pressure or undue influence from the other. There was an ample period of time for each party to receive full and complete legal advice and each party has sought and obtained that advice.

7. "h" and "w" do not want the courts to undermine their autonomy as reflected in the terms of this agreement, which they intend to be a final and certain settling of all issues between them. They wish to be allowed to get on with their separate and independent lives, no matter what changes may occur. "h" and "w" specifically anticipate that one or both of them may lose their jobs, become ill and be unable to work, have additional child care responsibilities that will interfere with their ability to work, find their financial resources diminished or exhausted whether through their own fault or not, or be affected by

general economic and family conditions changing over time. They each also recognize that the financial circumstances of the other may improve modestly or dramatically. Changes in their circumstances may be catastrophic, unanticipated, or beyond imagining. Nevertheless, no change, no matter how extreme, will alter this agreement and their view that the terms of this agreement reflect their intention to always be separate financially. "h" and "w" fully accept that no change whatsoever in their circumstances, or the circumstances of the other, will entitle either of them to spousal support from the other.

8. This agreement and this section in particular may be pleaded as a complete defence to any claim brought by either spouse to assert a claim for support.

9. FINANCIAL PROVISION (CHILD SUPPORT)

1. Commencing on the [   ] day of [   ], 2007, and on the [   ] day of each and every month thereafter, the husband shall pay to the wife for the support of the child [   ], the sum of [   ] per month (per child), being a total of [   ] for the support of [   ] in accordance with the child support guidelines based on a gross annual income of $[   ], until one or more of the following occurs:

    (a) the child becomes eighteen (18) years old and ceases to be in full-time attendance at an educational institution,

    (b) the child ceases to reside with the wife,

    (c) the child becomes twenty-two (22) years old,

    (d) the child marries or

    (e) the child dies.

2. In clause (b), "reside" means to live in the home of the wife, and the child does not cease to reside in the home of the wife when the child is temporarily away from home to attend an educational institution, to work at summer employment, or to enjoy a reasonable holiday.

3. The parents agree to share the child's special expenses in accordance with the child support guidelines and will divide them annually in proportion to their respective gross annual incomes.

9. FINANCIAL PROVISION (ALTERNATIVE SPOUSAL)

3. Commencing on the [   ] day of [   ], 2007, and on the [   ] day of each and every month thereafter, the husband shall

pay to the wife for her own support, the sum of [   ] per month, until one or more of the following occurs:

(a)   the wife remarries or cohabits,

(b)   the wife dies or

(c)   the husband dies.

4.   The husband and wife agree that the spousal support will be paid each and every month until the [   ] day of   ], 200[ ], at which time it will be reviewed on application to the court [or alternatively that it will be terminated at that date].

10. INDEXING SUPPORT

1.   The amount of support payable under this Agreement for the support of:

(a)   the wife

will be increased annually on the anniversary date of the effective date of this agreement by the indexing factor, as defined in subsection 2, for November of the previous year.

2.   The indexing factor for a given month is the percentage change in the Consumer Price Index for Canada for all prices of all items since the same month of the previous year, as published by Statistics Canada.

10. INDEXING SUPPORT (ALTERNATIVE)

1.   The support payments outlined in paragraph [   ] shall be increased annually in each year commencing in [   ], [year], for so long as spousal [   ] support is payable under this Agreement, by an amount equal to the lesser of the [   ] annual percentage increase in the cost of living of the preceding year and the annual percentage increase in the husband's salary [   ]. The increase shall be calculated according to the Consumer Price Index for Canada for prices of all items since the same month of the previous year, as published by Statistics Canada.

2.   The wife shall deliver to the husband a notice in or about the month of [   ], [year] with respect to the increase in spousal [   ] support based on the cost of living increase. If the husband alleges that his increase in salary is less than the said increase in the cost of living he shall provide such evidence of the salary increase to the wife within thirty (30) days of the delivery by the wife of the notice

to him. If the husband fails to deliver such evidence to the wife, the increase shall be in accordance with the cost of living as set out in paragraph [   ] herein.

11. WAIVER OF RIGHT TO INDEX SUPPORT PAYMENTS

Each party hereby:

(a) waives any right and

(b) releases the other from all claims

that he or she has or may have to require that the amounts or any amount payable for support under this Agreement be increased annually, or at any time, by an indexing factor as provided in the Family Law Act, or by any factor or percentage.

12. MATERIAL CHANGE IN CIRCUMSTANCES

1. The husband and wife intend paragraphs [   ] to be final, except for variation in the event of a material change in circumstances. If such change occurs, the husband or wife seeking the variation will give to the other a written notice of the variation he or she is seeking, and the husband and wife will then confer either personally or through their respective solicitors to settle what, if any, variation should be made.

2. If no agreement has been reached thirty (30) clear days after notice has been given under paragraph (1), variation relating to custody, access and support of the child and wife may be determined at the instance of either the husband or the wife by an application pursuant to the Family Law Act, or the Divorce Act. Any such application by a party shall be deemed to be an application for maintenance or support pursuant to the Family Law Act or the Divorce Act.

13. HEALTH AND MEDICAL EXPENSES

1. The husband warrants that he is maintaining in force for the benefit of the wife and child a plan of insurance established under a health insurance plan to protect them against the costs of health services.

2. The husband agrees to continue this insurance or equivalent insurance,

   (a) in the case of the wife until one or more the following occurs:

      1. the marriage is terminated or
      2. the wife cohabits with another man.

(b) in the case of each child so long as he is obligated by this Agreement to support the child.

3. If the husband fails to maintain this insurance or equivalent insurance, he will pay the costs of all health services that would have been paid by the insurance.

14. DENTAL AND ADDITIONAL MEDICAL COVERAGE

The husband agrees to continue a dental and medical plan for the benefit of the wife and child through his place of employment as long as he is able to obtain coverage for such plans through such employment, for the wife until the husband and wife are divorced and for the child so long as he is required to provide for [spousal or child] support under this Agreement.

15. MATRIMONIAL HOME AND CONTENTS

1. The parties acknowledge that they hold the matrimonial home as joint tenants.

2. The parties agree that the wife may remain in exclusive possession of the matrimonial home until one or more of the following occurs:

(a) five years elapse from the date of this Agreement,

(b) the wife remarries,

(c) the wife cohabits with another man,

(d) the wife ceases to reside on a full-time basis in the premises or

(e) the husband and the wife agree in writing to the contrary.

3. During the period of her exclusive possession of the matrimonial home, the wife will be responsible for paying all mortgage payments, taxes, insurance premiums, heating, water and other charges related to the matrimonial home, and will save the husband harmless from all liability for those payments.

4. The wife will keep the matrimonial home fully insured at her expense to its full replacement value against loss or damage by fire or other perils covered by a standard fire insurance extended coverage or additional perils supplemental contract and will apply any insurance proceeds to reasonable repairs. The insurance will cover both the husband's and the wife's interest in the matrimonial home. If the husband demands it, the wife will produce proof of premium payments and of the policy being in force. The husband and the wife will direct the insurer to send notices of premiums to both of them.

5. The parties will bear equally the costs of major repairs to the matrimonial home, but only if the repairs are undertaken with the consent of both parties. No consent will be unreasonably withheld.

6. During the period of her exclusive possession of the matrimonial home, the wife shall not change the use of the home, shall maintain its "principal residence" status within the meaning of the Income Tax Act, and shall so designate the home (and no other property) pursuant thereto. If the wife, contrary to this Agreement, sublets the matrimonial home, changes her use of it, does not maintain its "principal residence" status for tax purposes, or does not designate it (or other property) as her principal residence, with the result that the husband becomes liable to pay any tax or penalty under the Income Tax Act, then the wife agrees to indemnify the husband with respect to the liability or penalty.

7. When the wife is no longer entitled to exclusive possession of the matrimonial home, it will immediately be sold. Upon the sale of the matrimonial home, the proceeds will be divided equally between the parties. The wife may continue to remain in exclusive possession of the matrimonial home until the closing date of its sale. Any difference between the husband and wife on the method in terms of sale shall be resolved under the section of this Agreement providing for the solution of differences.

8. The husband and wife agree to divide the contents equally between them as they may agree.

(Or)

9. The husband and wife acknowledge that the contents have been divided between them to their mutual satisfaction and that each is entitled to the contents in his or her possession.

16. COTTAGE

1. Each party acknowledges that the cottage was held by the parties as joint tenants until the transfer referred to in subsection (2) was made.

2. Contemporaneously with the execution of this Agreement, the parties have transferred the cottage from themselves as joint tenants to the husband as sole owner.

3. The wife waives any right she has or may have to, or any interest she has or may have in the cottage, and releases the husband from any claim she has or may have to any such right or interest.

17. PRINCIPAL RESIDENCE DESIGNATION

1. For the purpose of the "principal residence" designation provided for in the Income Tax Act, the wife will designate the family residence as her principal residence for the years from the date of acquisition up to and including 2002, and the husband will designate the cottage as his principal residence for the years from the date of acquisition up to and including 2002.

2. Both the husband and wife will designate the family residence as their principal residence for each of the years after 2002 to and including the year in which this Agreement is executed.

3. Neither the husband nor the wife will designate any other residence or property as his or her principal residence in any of the years after 2002 to and including the year in which this Agreement is executed.

18. AUTOMOBILES

(a) (as may be agreed) (identify vehicle specifically)

19. CANADA PENSION PLAN

The wife may apply under the Canada Pension Plan for a division of pension credits.

(Or)

Neither the husband nor the wife will apply under the Canada Pension Plan for a division of pension credits after the dissolution of their marriage.

20. PRIVATE PENSION PLANS

(a) (as may be agreed)

21. INVESTMENTS AND OTHER SAVINGS

(a) (as may be agreed)

22. LIFE INSURANCE

1. Contemporaneously with the execution of this Agreement, the husband has delivered to the wife (a certified copy of) the following policy [   ] of insurance:

   (a) Policy No. [   ] of [   ] Insurance Company, having a face value of $ [   ] and

   (b) Policy No. [   ] of [   ] Insurance Company, having a face value of $[   ].

2. The husband warrants that he has irrevocably designated the wife as the sole beneficiary under the above policy and that he has filed the designation with the principal office of the respective insurer in accordance with the provisions of the Insurance Act. (Ontario)

3. The husband will pay all premiums when they become due and will keep the policy in force for the benefit of the wife as long as he is required to pay support or maintenance for either the wife or child.

4. Upon the happening of any one of the events described in subsection (3), the husband may deal with the policy as he deems fit free from any claim by the wife or her estate.

5. The husband will deliver to the wife, within fourteen (14) days from the date when it is demanded, proof that the policy is in good standing. This proof may be demanded at any reasonable time and from time to time.

6. If the husband defaults in payment of any premium, the wife may pay the premium and recover from the husband the amount of the payment together with all costs and expenses that may be incurred in restoring the policy to good standing.

23. HOUSEHOLD GOODS AND PERSONAL EFFECTS

Each of the parties acknowledges that:

(a) the contents of the matrimonial home, including furniture, furnishings, household goods, silverware, china, glassware, rugs, books, pictures, bric-a-brac and all other household effects have been divided between the parties or have been purchased or the value set off against the value of other property by one of the parties to the satisfaction of each of them,

(b) each has possession of his or her jewellery, clothing and personal effects and

(c) each may dispose of the items possessed by him or her as he or she deems fit.

24. DEBTS AND OBLIGATIONS

1. Neither party will contract or incur debts or obligations in the name of the other.

2. If, contrary to subsection (1), either party contracts or incurs debts or obligations in the name of the other, he or she will indemnify the other from all loss or expense that results from or is incidental to the transaction.

25. NO PROPERTY TO BE DIVISIBLE ASSET

No property owned by either party or by them jointly on the effective date of this contract or at any later time is or will be:

(a) family property or

(b) property subject to division otherwise than according to owner-ship, under the Family Law Act and the laws of any jurisdiction.

26. PART II OF THE FAMILY LAW ACT

Each of the parties releases and discharges all rights and claims he or she has under Part II of the Family Law Act.

27. RELEASE AGAINST PROPERTY

Except as provided in this Agreement, the husband and the wife each acknowledge and agree that:

(a) all their property has been divided between them to their mutual satisfaction,

(b) each is entitled to property now in his or her possession, free of any claim from the other,

(c) each may dispose of the property they now possess as if they were unmarried,

(d) each releases and discharges all rights and claims relating to property in which the other has or may have an interest, including all rights and claims involving:

    1. possession of property,

    2. ownership of property,

    3. division of property and

    4. compensation for contributions of any kind, or an interest in property for contributions of any kind.

(e) This section is a complete defence to any action brought by either the husband or the wife to assert a claim to any property, wherever situated, in which the other has or had an interest.

28. RELEASE AGAINST THE ESTATE OF THE OTHER

Without restricting the other waivers and releases in this contract, and subject to transfers or bequests that may be made, each party

(a) waives all rights and

(b) releases and discharges the other from all claims that he or she has or may in the future acquire under the laws of any jurisdiction, and particularly under the Family Law Act and the Succession Law Reform Act and their successors, entitling him or her upon the death of the other

1. to a division of property owned by the other or to one-half the difference between their net family properties or to any other share of this difference, or to any share of the property of the other,

2. if the other party dies leaving a Will, to elect against taking under the Will in favour of receiving an entitlement equalizing their net family properties, or in favour of any other benefit,

3. if the other party dies intestate, to elect to receive an entitlement in intestacy or to receive an entitlement equalizing their net family property,

4. if the other party dies restate as to some property and intestate as to other property, to elect to take under the Will and to receive an entitlement in intestacy, or to receive an entitlement equalizing their net family properties,

5. to share in the estate of the other under a distribution in intestacy in any manner whatsoever and

6. to act as executor or administrator of the estate of the other.

29. GENERAL RELEASE

1. The husband and wife each accept the provisions of this Agreement in satisfaction of all claims and causes of action each now has including, but not limited to, claims and causes of action for custody, child maintenance or child support, maintenance, support, interim maintenance and interim support, possession of or title to property, or any other claim arising out of the marriage of the husband and wife, EXCEPT for claims and causes of action:

   (a) arising under this Agreement and

   (b) for a decree of divorce.

2. Nothing in the Agreement will bar any action or proceeding by either the husband or the wife to enforce any of the terms of this Agreement.

30. ATTRIBUTION

(a) The parties hereby elect under clause 74(7)(b) of the Income Tax Act that subsection 74(2) (gain or loss deemed that of the transferor) of the Income Tax Act will not apply to a disposition of any property that has been transferred between the parties pursuant to this Agreement, or to any property substituted therefore.

(b) Contemporaneously with the execution of this Agreement, the parties have executed in duplicate a separate form of joint election according to Schedule "A" [not actually attached/ attached] to this Agreement.

(c) Each party authorizes the other to file an executed copy of the form of election completed according to the form in Schedule "A" with his or her return of income for the taxation year in which this Agreement is executed.

(d) The parties will indemnify each other for any tax liability imposed upon one of them by any taxing authority or government, resulting from the transfer of or disposition of property transferred pursuant to the terms of this Agreement.

(e) Specifically the parties agree to indemnify each other with respect to any liability or charge resulting from:

   1. any tax arrears of one enforced as against the property or income of the other and

   2. any attribution of income or capital gains from one to the other after separation.

(f) The parties will not designate any other property except the matrimonial home as their principal residence, for the period up to and including the year of this Agreement.

31. RESUMPTION OF COHABITATION

If at any time the parties cohabit as husband and wife for a single period or periods totalling not more than ninety (90) days with reconciliation as the primary purpose of the cohabitation, the provisions contained in this Agreement will not be affected except as provided in this section. If the parties cohabit as husband and wife for a single period or periods totalling not more than ninety (90) days with reconciliation as the primary purpose of the cohabitation, the provisions contained in this Agreement will become void, except that nothing in the section will affect or invalidate any payment, conveyance or act made or done pursuant to the provisions of this Agreement.

32. AGREEMENT TO SURVIVE DIVORCE

If at any future time the parties are divorced, the terms of this Agreement will survive and continue in force.

33. EXECUTION OF OTHER DOCUMENTS

Each of the parties will execute any document and do all further things, at the cost of the other, that are reasonably required from time to time to give effect to the terms and intent of this Agreement.

34. CONTRACT TO PREVAIL

This contract prevails over:

(a) any matter that is provided for in the Family Law Act [or relevant provincial law], where the contract made provisions for such matters and

(b) any matter provided for in a subsequent domestic contract between one of the parties and another person other than the other party, where the present contract makes provisions for such matters.

35. GOVERNING LAW

This Agreement will be governed by and construed according to the laws of Ontario (or relevant province).

36. GENERAL

1. The husband and wife will each execute any document or documents reasonably required from time to time to give effect to the terms and intent of this Agreement.

2. The husband and wife each warrant that there are no representations, collateral agreements or conditions affecting this Agreement other than as expressed in this Agreement.

3. This Agreement may be amended only by a further instrument in writing signed by the husband and by the wife.

4. The provisions of this Agreement are binding on the respective heirs, executors, administrators or assigns of the husband and the wife.

37. SEVERABILITY

The invalidity or unenforceability of any provision of this Agreement will not affect the validity or enforceability of any other provisions and any invalid provision will be severable.

38. DEFAULT

If either of the parties is in default with respect to the payment of support pursuant to this Agreement, including any provision with respect to indexing of support payments, the other party may register the Separation Agreement in the [name of relevant Family Court] and the parties hereby consent to this Agreement being registered.

39. FINANCIAL DISCLOSURE

Each party:

(a) has fully and completely disclosed to the other the nature, extent and probable value of all his or her significant assets and all his or her significant debts or other liabilities existing at the date of this contract, and in addition to this disclosure,

(b) has given all information and particulars about his or her assets and liabilities that have been requested by the other,

(c) is satisfied with the information and particulars received from the other and

(d) acknowledges that there are no requests for further information or particulars that have not been met to his or her complete satisfaction.

40. INDEPENDENT LEGAL ADVICE

Each of the husband and the wife acknowledges that he or she:

(a) has had independent legal advice,

(b) understands his or her respective rights and obligations under this Agreement,

(c) is signing this Agreement voluntarily and

(d) believes this Agreement is fair and reasonable and that its provisions are entirely adequate to discharge the present and future responsibilities of the parties and will not result in circumstances unconscionable to either party.

41. LEGAL FEES

The husband will pay the wife's solicitor's fees for the preparation and execution of this Agreement.

(Or)

The husband and wife will each bear their own legal fees incurred in the negotiation and execution of the Agreement.

TO EVIDENCE THEIR AGREEMENT, each of the husband and the wife has signed this Agreement under seal before a witness.

SIGNED, SEALED AND DELIVERED   )

     in the presence of:)

)

)

_____) _____

Witness as to the signature of   )   [name]

[wife] [Date]   )   [wife's signature]

)

)

)

_____) _____

Witness as to the signature of   )   [name]

[husband] [Date]   )   [husband's signature]

Caution: Please do not attempt to adapt these contracts to your situation without the advice of a lawyer. Many of the clauses are alternatives to each other and would not necessarily be applicable to every case. This Agreement also has an Ontario emphasis. It is reproduced only as an example or guide. Using it as a drafting guide would be a good way to gather information about your situation.

THE FAMILY LAW CLIENT HISTORY FORM

Many law firms will ask a client to complete a Family History Form. This Form facilitates the collection of family details and prevents people from overlooking important details. The following is a modified Form that you may wish to use as you sort out your own predicament. A completed Form will give any lawyer a big head start on behalf of the client.

Sample Client History Form

Date: _____

Your Full Name: _____

Your Address: Home: _____

Office: _____

Telephone: Home: _____ Office: _____

Fax: _____ E-mail: _____

Date of Birth _____ Place of Birth: _____

Date of Marriage: _____ Place of Marriage: _____

Date of Separation: _____

Your Status Before Marriage: Wife: _____

Husband: _____

Divorced:_____ Decree Available: _____

Surname of Wife at Birth: _____ At Separation: _____

If 2nd Marriage for Either of You, Give Details of Earlier Marriages

_____

_____

_____

When Did You Come to Canada? _____

Length of Residence in Province: _____

Prior Residences in Last Year: _____

Names of Children, Dates of Birth, Grade and School

1. _____

2. _____

3. _____

Special Needs: _____

Surname of Your Spouse at Birth: _____

Surname of Your Spouse at Separation: _____

Spouse's Date of Birth: _____

Spouse's Place of Birth: _____

Name, Address, Fax and Phone Number of Spouse's Lawyer:

_____

_____

_____

SOCIAL HISTORY OF MARRIAGE:

(Includes courtship, cohabitation date, lifestyle, conduct, present status and counselling details. Complete in detail. Use additional pages as necessary.)

_____

_____

_____

ECONOMIC HISTORY OF MARRIAGE:

(Includes education, financial position before marriage, history of matrimonial homes, net worth of both of you, employment records, fitness for employment, contributions by spouses to the marriage. Complete in detail. Use additional pages as necessary.)

_____

_____

_____

CUSTODY AND ACCESS:

(The positions of you and your spouse, the allegations and expected cross-allegations. Complete in detail. Use additional pages as necessary.)

_____

_____

_____

YOUR IMPRESSION OF THE SITUATION:

(Complete in detail. Use additional pages as necessary.)

_____

_____

_____

WHAT DO YOU WANT?

(Complete in detail. Use additional pages as necessary.)

_____

_____

_____

APPENDIX

Canadian Child Support Guidelines

In Canada, we use Child Support Guidelines to calculate the correct amount of child support payable. The amount payable is determined by at least two factors: the annual income of the person paying child support and the number of children. (This is discussed in detail in Chapter 7— Support: Financial Assistance after Separation.) On the following pages you will find examples of some of the typical calculations done by families living in Ontario, for example. The Guidelines were updated in May of 2006 and are slightly different from province to province. To see the full spectrum, visit the website maintained by the Federal Department of Justice, where all applicable Guidelines are set out (see http://canada.justice. gc.ca/en/ps/sup/grl/Pdftab.htm).

Income ($)	Monthly Award ($)					
	No. of Children					
	1	2	3	4	5	6+
75100	681	1099	1434	1708	1936	2129
75200	682	1100	1435	1710	1938	2131
75300	682	1102	1437	1711	1940	2134
75400	683	1103	1439	1713	1942	2136
75500	684	1104	1440	1715	1944	2138
75600	685	1105	1442	1717	1946	2141
75700	686	1107	1443	1719	1949	2143
75800	686	1108	1445	1721	1951	2145
75900	687	1109	1446	1723	1953	2147
76000	688	1110	1448	1724	1955	2150
76100	689	1111	1450	1726	1957	2152
76200	689	1113	1451	1728	1959	2154
76300	690	1114	1453	1730	1961	2157
76400	691	1115	1454	1732	1963	2159
76500	692	1116	1456	1734	1965	2161
76600	693	1118	1457	1736	1967	2164
76700	693	1119	1459	1737	1969	2166
76800	694	1120	1461	1739	1972	2168
76900	695	1121	1462	1741	1974	2170
77000	696	1122	1464	1743	1976	2173
77100	697	1124	1465	1745	1978	2175
77200	697	1125	1467	1747	1980	2177
77300	698	1126	1468	1749	1982	2180
77400	699	1127	1470	1750	1984	2182
77500	700	1129	1472	1752	1986	2184
77600	700	1130	1473	1754	1988	2186
77700	701	1131	1475	1756	1990	2189
77800	702	1132	1476	1758	1993	2191
77900	703	1133	1478	1760	1995	2193
78000	704	1135	1479	1762	1997	2196
78100	704	1136	1481	1763	1999	2198
78200	705	1137	1483	1765	2001	2200

Income ($)	Monthly Award ($)					
	No. of Children					
	1	2	3	4	5	6+
78300	706	1138	1484	1767	2003	2203
78400	707	1140	1486	1769	2005	2205
78500	708	1141	1487	1771	2007	2207
78600	708	1142	1489	1773	2009	2209
78700	709	1143	1490	1775	2011	2212
78800	710	1144	1492	1776	2013	2214
78900	711	1146	1494	1778	2016	2216
79000	712	1147	1495	1780	2018	2219
79100	712	1148	1497	1782	2020	2221
79200	713	1149	1498	1784	2022	2223
79300	714	1151	1500	1786	2024	2226
79400	715	1152	1502	1788	2026	2228
79500	715	1153	1503	1789	2028	2230
79600	716	1154	1505	1791	2030	2232
79700	717	1155	1506	1793	2032	2235
79800	718	1157	1508	1795	2034	2237
79900	719	1158	1509	1797	2037	2239
80000	719	1159	1511	1799	2039	2242
80100	720	1160	1513	1801	2041	2244
80200	721	1162	1514	1802	2043	2246
80300	722	1163	1516	1804	2045	2249
80400	723	1164	1517	1806	2047	2251
80500	723	1165	1519	1808	2049	2253
80600	724	1166	1520	1810	2051	2255
80700	725	1168	1522	1812	2053	2258
80800	726	1169	1524	1814	2055	2260
80900	726	1170	1525	1815	2058	2262
81000	727	1171	1527	1817	2060	2265
81100	728	1173	1528	1819	2062	2267
81200	729	1174	1530	1821	2064	2269
81300	730	1175	1531	1823	2066	2271
81400	730	1176	1533	1825	2068	2274

Income ($)	Monthly Award ($)					
	No. of Children					
	1	2	3	4	5	6+
81500	731	1177	1535	1827	2070	2276
81600	732	1179	1536	1829	2072	2278
81700	733	1180	1538	1830	2074	2281
81800	734	1181	1539	1832	2076	2283
81900	734	1182	1541	1834	2078	2285
82000	735	1184	1542	1836	2081	2288
82100	736	1185	1544	1838	2083	2290
82200	737	1186	1546	1840	2085	2292
82300	737	1187	1547	1842	2087	2294
82400	738	1188	1549	1843	2089	2297
82500	739	1190	1550	1845	2091	2299
82600	740	1191	1552	1847	2093	2301
82700	741	1192	1553	1849	2095	2304
82800	741	1193	1555	1851	2097	2306
82900	742	1195	1557	1853	2099	2308
83000	743	1196	1558	1855	2102	2311
83100	744	1197	1560	1856	2104	2313
83200	745	1198	1561	1858	2106	2315
83300	745	1199	1563	1860	2108	2317
83400	746	1201	1564	1862	2110	2320
83500	747	1202	1566	1864	2112	2322
83600	748	1203	1568	1866	2114	2324
83700	748	1204	1569	1868	2116	2327
83800	749	1206	1571	1869	2118	2329
83900	750	1207	1572	1871	2120	2331
84000	751	1208	1574	1873	2122	2334
84100	752	1209	1575	1875	2125	2336
84200	752	1210	1577	1877	2127	2338
84300	753	1212	1579	1879	2129	2340
84400	754	1213	1580	1881	2131	2343
84500	755	1214	1582	1882	2133	2345
84600	756	1215	1583	1884	2135	2347

Income ($)	Monthly Award ($)					
	No. of Children					
	1	2	3	4	5	6+
84700	756	1217	1585	1886	2137	2350
84800	757	1218	1586	1888	2139	2352
84900	758	1219	1588	1890	2141	2354
85000	759	1220	1590	1892	2143	2356
85100	759	1221	1591	1894	2146	2359
85200	760	1223	1593	1895	2148	2361
85300	761	1224	1594	1897	2150	2363
85400	762	1225	1596	1899	2152	2366
85500	763	1226	1597	1901	2154	2368
85600	763	1228	1599	1903	2156	2370
85700	764	1229	1601	1905	2158	2373
85800	765	1230	1602	1907	2160	2375
85900	766	1231	1604	1908	2162	2377
86000	767	1232	1605	1910	2164	2379
86100	767	1234	1607	1912	2167	2382
86200	768	1235	1608	1914	2169	2384
86300	769	1236	1610	1916	2171	2386
86400	770	1237	1612	1918	2173	2389
86500	770	1239	1613	1920	2175	2391
86600	771	1240	1615	1921	2177	2393
86700	772	1241	1616	1923	2179	2396
86800	773	1242	1618	1925	2181	2398
86900	774	1243	1619	1927	2183	2400
87000	774	1245	1621	1929	2185	2402
87100	775	1246	1623	1931	2187	2405
87200	776	1247	1624	1933	2190	2407
87300	777	1248	1626	1934	2192	2409
87400	778	1250	1627	1936	2194	2412
87500	778	1251	1629	1938	2196	2414
87600	779	1252	1630	1940	2198	2416
87700	780	1253	1632	1942	2200	2419
87800	781	1254	1634	1944	2202	2421

Income ($)	Monthly Award ($)					
	No. of Children					
	1	2	3	4	5	6+
87900	781	1256	1635	1946	2204	2423
88000	782	1257	1637	1947	2206	2425
88100	783	1258	1638	1949	2208	2428
88200	784	1259	1640	1951	2211	2430
88300	785	1261	1641	1953	2213	2432
88400	785	1262	1643	1955	2215	2435
88500	786	1263	1645	1957	2217	2437
88600	787	1264	1646	1959	2219	2439
88700	788	1265	1648	1960	2221	2441
88800	789	1267	1649	1962	2223	2444
88900	789	1268	1651	1964	2225	2446
89000	790	1269	1652	1966	2227	2448
89100	791	1270	1654	1968	2229	2451
89200	792	1272	1656	1970	2231	2453
89300	792	1273	1657	1972	2234	2455
89400	793	1274	1659	1973	2236	2458
89500	794	1275	1660	1975	2238	2460
89600	795	1276	1662	1977	2240	2462
89700	796	1278	1663	1979	2242	2464
89800	796	1279	1665	1981	2244	2467
89900	797	1280	1667	1983	2246	2469
90000	798	1281	1668	1985	2248	2471

A GLOSSARY OF FAMILY LAW TERMS

Access   The opportunity to visit with a child. Under the terms of the Divorce Act, a spouse exercising access rights is also entitled to information about the child's health, welfare and education, unless a court orders otherwise.*

Adultery   Sexual intercourse by a husband or wife with someone of the opposite sex who is not his or her spouse. Adultery is one of the ways marital breakdown can be established.* (Note: Until recently, a gay or a lesbian relationship would not constitute adultery, but as a result of some recent court decisions, the definition of adultery has been "modified" to account for these types of extramarital affairs.)

Adversarial System   Canada's court system is designed to resolve disputes between two opposing parties. The parties present their respective sides of an issue through evidence. The judges acts as an impartial arbiter, weighing the evidence and deciding how the law applies in each specific case.*

Affidavit   A sworn statement, typed and signed by a person involved in a family law matter. It is witnessed by someone, usually a lawyer, and filed in support of a motion.

Alimony   An old expression used to describe spousal support. Now that you know what it is, don't use it. Call it spousal support.

Appeal   When a person affected by a judge's decision believes that the judge has made a mistake, that person can ask a higher level of court to review the decision. The court reviewing the decision can uphold it, change it or send the matter back to the original court for reconsideration. There are strict time limits on this type of review.*

Application   A court proceeding starts with the filing of certain documents with court officers and the serving of copies of these documents on other persons affected. Details of the material to be included in the application, the document format and the filing fees are determined by provincial and territorial rules of court procedure.*

Arbitration   A third party is asked to decide a case for two people who cannot agree. This person acts as a "private judge," with rules and procedures made to the likings of the parties involved. It is not mediation. A decision is imposed because the people agree to be bound by whatever the arbitrator decides.

Best Interests Test   This is the overriding consideration in custody and access matters. The court searches for that which will best serve the child's interests.

Child   The Divorce Act defines a "child of the marriage" as a child of both spouses, a child of one of the spouses towards whom the other spouse acts as a parent or a child towards whom both spouses act as a parent. Biological children, adopted children and children looked after by the spouses may all be considered children of the marriage. The custody and support provisions of the divorce law apply to a child of the marriage who is under 16 years of age or who is over 16 and remains dependent on his or her parents because of illness, disability or other reasons.*

Cohabitation Agreement   A domestic contract signed by a man and a woman who are living together or intend to live together but not marry. In it, they may provide for ownership and division of property, support and any other matter affecting their relationship except custody of and access to children.

Collusion   An agreement or conspiracy to fabricate or suppress evidence, or to deceive the court. If evidence to support a divorce application is the result of collusion, the application can be rejected.*

Condonation   The forgiveness of a matrimonial offence with full knowledge of the circumstances, followed by an acceptance of the offending spouse back into the family. A forgiven offence cannot be revived at a later date as a basis for a divorce. A legal opinion may be necessary to decide if a matrimonial offence has been condoned by the subsequent actions of the other spouse.*

Connivance The marital misconduct of one spouse caused by, or knowingly, willfully or recklessly permitted by, the other spouse. Connivance in creating a basis for a divorce application can result in the application being rejected.*

Common-Law Spouse Almost all the provinces recognize that some men and women live together without getting married. While the precise definition varies from province to province, it means achieving the status of a spouse for some legal purposes, such as support, in the province.

Confidentiality People in certain relationships are protected by law from having to give any evidence in court regarding communications between them. Communications between lawyers and clients have this special protection. A court-appointed reconciliator also has this protection with regard to communications made in the course of attempting to reconcile spouses.

Most professional associations have ethical guidelines regarding the confidentiality of communications between members and their clients. These guidelines form a very important part of the professional relationship; however, they do not necessarily provide protection from disclosure in court.

The laws regarding the relationship between other professionals, such as clergy and their parishioners, doctors and their patients, and their clients vary across the country. These professionals may be called upon to testify in court.*

Consummation of a Marriage The "completion" of a marriage by an act of sexual intercourse by a husband and wife after the marriage ceremony.

Contempt of Court A method the court uses to control its own process. It is willful disobedience of a court order, punishable by fine or imprisonment or both.

Contested Divorce If either the husband or wife disputes the grounds for divorce, or if the spouses are unable to agree on child or support arrangements, a court will have to resolve these matters. A hearing will be held and both sides of the dispute will be entitled to present evidence supporting their view. The judge will consider the evidence presented and impose a solution.*

Corollary Relief   Under the terms of the Divorce Act, people involved in a divorce proceeding can ask the court to make supplementary orders pertaining to financial support for a spouse or child, or for the custody of, or access to, a child of the marriage.*

Costs   Sums payable for legal services. When matters are contested in court, a judge has the discretion to order that the losing party pay a portion of the successful party's legal costs.*

Custody   Control over a child given to an adult by the court. This control generally includes physical care of the child and the responsibility to make decisions regarding education, religion and health care, and to provide food, clothing and shelter.*

Decree Absolute   Under the Divorce Act of 1968, a divorce only becomes final when a court grants a decree absolute. A decree absolute can be granted by the court three months after the day on which the court allows the divorce action. If the parties agrees not to appeal the divorce decision, and if special circumstances existed, the court could shorten the three-month period.*

Decree Nisi   Under the Divorce Act of 1968, the court that allows a divorce grants a temporary order called a decree nisi. The divorce is not final until at least three months later when the court grants a decree absolute.*

Dependant   A person who relies on someone else for financial support. In the context of divorce law, it may include a spouse or child.*

Desertion   The failure of a husband or wife to live with his or her spouse. It must be a unilateral act carried out against the wishes of the other spouse. Desertion was a ground for divorce under the old divorce legislation. Under the current divorce law, it would be evidence of the separation period.*

Disbursements   Out-of-pocket expenses incurred in a family law matter, such as the cost of paying for the Petition to be issued at the court office or the cost of paying someone to deliver it to your spouse. It could also be the cost of a family law assessment.

Discoveries   A step in legal proceedings where lawyers get to ask the opposing client, under oath, questions about things said in the legal proceedings, especially in affidavits and pleadings. It is done in the presence of a court reporter and a transcript of all questions and answers can be prepared.

Divorce   The termination of the legal relationship of marriage between a husband and wife.*

Divorce Certificate The actual piece of paper that officially describes the termination of the marriage. It is needed as proof of the divorce in order to get a marriage licence.

Domestic Violence The intent by either spouse to intimidate, either by threat or by use of physical force on the person or property. The purpose of the assault is to control the person's behaviour by the inducement of fear.

Fees and Disbursements The bill of account. This is a statement you will receive monthly, periodically or in one lump sum at the end of the proceeding. The fee is for the lawyer's time, which is calculated by multiplying the hourly rate by the number of hours worked on the case. Disbursements are out-of-pocket expenses. GST is extra.

Final Order An order that is not interim. Interim orders are effective until the end of the trial. The final order is intended to last indefinitely or until changed by the court.

Garnishee A legal procedure that allows for the seizure of money owing to a person who has not paid a court-ordered debt. A court may order the debtor's bank, employer or anyone else who may owe money to the debtor to pay the money into court to help pay the debt.*

Get A religious divorce necessary for observant Jews. It is needed in addition to a civil divorce in order to dissolve the marriage.

Indexing To increase the amount of a support order or provision in a Separation Agreement by a fixed amount each year. The increase is usually tied to changes in the cost of living index. It is also known as a "cost of living allowance" or COLA.

Interim Orders There may be a considerable period of time between the initial filing of a divorce application and the date on which a court is able to grant a divorce and related support, custody or access orders. On request, a court can make a temporary order for the interim period to stabilize custody or access arrangements or to provide financial support for a spouse or child.*

Joint Custody A mother and father can continue to share responsibility for making major decisions that affect their children, regardless of which parent the children actually live with on a day-to-day basis. Such arrangements require a commitment on the part of both former spouses to cooperate for the benefit of the children. Joint custody does not eliminate the obligations of both parents to provide financial support for the children.*

Joint Petition   A special form of divorce petition that can be used by two spouses who wish to have an uncontested divorce. It is one request for divorce filed by two people.

Judgment   The final decision by the court on any issues put to it during the trial. The formal piece of paper that describes who has been successful or not and on which issues.

Limitations   Time limits imposed by the laws and rules of court. If certain things are not done (claim support, division of property), then the right to claim is lost unless the court grants special permission.

Litigation   Resolving a dispute by using the courts and the adversarial process.

Marriage   The voluntary union for life of two people to the exclusion of all others. In Canada, marriage involves a religious or civil ceremony that complies with the procedural requirements of provincial or territorial laws where the marriage takes place. Marriage creates the legal status of husband and wife and the legal obligations arising from that status.*

Marriage Breakdown   The sole ground for legally ending a marriage under the terms of the Divorce Act. Marriage breakdown can be established in three ways: Through evidence that one spouse committed adultery; physical or mental cruelty; or that the spouses intentionally lived separate and apart for at least one year.*

Marriage Contract   An agreement between a husband and wife outlining the spouses' respective responsibilities and obligations. Some contracts also include agreements as to how property and ongoing obligations will be shared if the marriage breaks down.*

Matrimonial Home   Where the family or legally married couple have resided. Common-law spouses never have them (as recognized in law) because they have no statutory property rights. It is possible to have more than one at a time.

Mediation   A process by which people in situations of potential conflict attempt to resolve their differences and reach a mutually acceptable agreement.

Neutral third parties, or mediators, can often help the parties retain a focus on the problems to be solved and possible solutions, rather than on areas of personal disagreement.*

Minutes of Settlement   A method of settling a case by writing out and having the parties sign an acknowledgement of how they want their problem resolved.

Motion   A request to the court for a particular order pending trial, such as interim custody or support. Filed with an affidavit.

Order   The court's decision on a matter that it was asked to resolve. See Motion, and Affidavit.

Parental Support   A request by the parent of a child for financial support from that adult child if the parent is in need and has provided for the child's upbringing.

Parties   The husband and wife, or anybody else who is named in the case before the court and asking for an order of any kind.

Pension   A fixed sum paid regularly to a person or surviving dependent following his or her retirement. There are both public (Canada Pension Plan) and private (from one's own employer) pensions. Some provinces consider a pension that is not yet being paid at the time of marriage breakdown to be property that must be divided.

Petition for Divorce   The formal document by which one person asks the court to dissolve his or her marriage to another and for corollary relief.

Pleadings   The typewritten description of each person's claims in a family law matter, which must be prepared in accordance with the province's Rules of Court.

Possessory Rights   Some provincial family laws give each legally married spouse an equal entitlement to possession of a matrimonial home upon separation. This right exists regardless of actual ownership of the home by one or the other. The court will fix, or the couple will come to an agreement over, the appropriate period of possession. It usually continues for the period leading up to the trial.

Procedure   The technical rules that lawyers must follow to get a case through the civil justice system. They are contained in the province's Rules of Court.

Questioning   *See* Discoveries.

Restraining Order   An order that prohibits contact between two spouses and in some cases their children. It can be a blanket prohibition or it can provide for specific contact at specific times and under specific circumstances.

Retainer The contract by which you hire a lawyer to take your case. It can also mean the sum of money you give the lawyer to be applied to fees and disbursements.

Rules of Court *See* Procedure.

Separate To cease living together as man and wife, possibly under the same roof but usually not. Done with the intention not to live together again.

Separation Agreement A contract signed by the parties to settle their differences. It can deal with property, custody, access, support and any other matter. A form of domestic contract.

Shared Parenting Another term used instead of custody and access. It describes a sharing of the decision making that usually is given solely to the custodial parent.

Solicitor-Client Privilege The lawyer's obligation to keep secret everything you tell him or her.

Spousal Support An order that one spouse pay the other a sum of money either in a lump sum or periodically for a set period of time or indefinitely.

Spouse A married individual.

Statute A law passed by the legislature of a province or the federal parliament (e.g., the Divorce Act).

Uncontested Divorce If neither the husband nor wife disputes the ground for divorce, and if they are able to reach an agreement regarding child care and financial arrangements, it may be possible to ask a judge to grant a divorce without a lengthy court hearing. In some provinces and territories, it may be possible to get a divorce without having to actually appear in court at all.*

Variation If the circumstances that justified making a particular support, custody or access order change, a person affected by the order can ask a judge to alter the order to make it fit the new circumstances.*

NOTE: The definitions in the Glossary that are followed by an asterisk (*) are from a Government of Canada, Department of Justice publication entitled *Divorce Law for Counsellors*.

INDEX

A

abductions, and custody 206–210
acceptance, as emotional stage 17
access 106–107, 212–213, 305
adultery 60–61, 305
adversarial system, defined 305
affidavit, defined 305
alimony *see* spousal support
anger, as emotional stage 14–15
appeals 54, 188–189, 306
applicant's case 183–185
application, defined 306
arbitration 198–199, 201–202, 306
assessments, and custody 99–100

B

balance of probabilities, defined 42
bargaining, as emotional stage 15–16
beneficiaries, changing 261–262
best interests test 94–95, 306
burden of proof, defined 42

C

Canada Pension Plan, and credit-sharing
    82–83
capital gains, and property division 84–85
case citations 267–268
case conference 53
case management system 47
checklists, children 123–124
    common-law spouses 161
    court alternatives 202–203
    court process 189–190
    divorce 69–70

domestic contracts 255–256
domestic violence 245–246
emotional stages 20–21
enforcement 223
grandparents 234
lawyers 36–38
legal process 55
property division 89–90
self-help 273
settlements 176
support 148–149
wills 262–263
child of the marriage, defined 93–94,
    132–133, 306
child support, amount of 127–132
    and common-law spouses 153
    considerations for 134–138
    eligibility for 132–134
    and enforcement 214–218
    and joint custody 102–103
Child Support Guidelines 127–132,
    299–304
children, response to divorce 114–122
    see also custody; paternity
Children's Law Reform Act 40
child's best interests 94–95, 306
clean-break model, and spousal support
    139
clerks, at court 45
closed mediation, defined 195
cohabitation agreements 160, 251–255, 306
collaborative family law 200–201
collusion, defined 306
common-law spouses, and children 153

and cohabitation agreements 160
defined 151–153, 307
and federal legislation 159
and property division 155–159
and spousal support 153–154
community of property scheme, and
cohabitation agreements 251
compensatory model, and spousal support
139
complaints processes 265–266
condonation, defined 306–307
confidentiality 29–30, 307
connivance, defined 66, 307
consummation of marriage, defined 307
contempt of court 221–222, 307
contested divorces 65–66, 307
contract, with lawyer 27–29
contractual failures, defined 254
convenience, marriages of 67–68
corollary relief, defined 308
costs, defined 308
court file, described 181
court personnel, described 43–47
court process, and appeals 188–189
circumstances of 177–179
and courtroom 179–181
described 47–54
and paperwork 181
and trial process 181–188
court reporters 45–46
court system, described 43
courtroom, described 179–180
credit-sharing, and Canada Pension Plan
82–83
cruelty, physical or mental 61
custody, and common-law spouses 153
considerations for 92–100
defined 308
and enforcement 206–211
strategy for 107–111
types of 100–107

D

decree absolute, defined 308
decree nisi, defined 308
defendant's case 185–186
Deferred Settlement Method, and pension
division 81

denial and isolation, as emotional stage
13–14
dependant, defined 308
depression, as emotional stage 16
desertion, defined 308
disability of child, and child support 134
disbursements, defined 31, 308
discovery 51–52, 308
divorce, bars to 66–68
defined 57–58, 308
grounds for 58–62
and legal fees 68–69
procedure 63–66
Divorce Act 39–41
divorce certificate, defined 309
documentary discovery 51–52
domestic contracts 248–255
domestic violence, causes of 238–240
defined 235–237, 309
escaping 240–242
false accusations of 108–111, 242–245
myths about 237–238

E

emotional stages, and marriage
breakdown 11–17
enforcement, of access 212–214
and contempt 221–222
of custody 206–211
of property division 218–220
of restraining orders 220–221
of support 214–218
exchange of legal documents 49–50
exchange of letters 48–49
exempt property, defined 74–75

F

failure to disclose, defined 253
failure to understand, defined 253–254
family asset scheme, and cohabitation
agreements 252
Family History Form, sample 297–298
Family Law Act 40–41
Family Responsibility Act 40–41
Federal Orders and Agreements
Enforcement Assistance Act 41
fees and disbursements 31–32, 35–36,
68–69, 309
final order, defined 309

Financial Statements, and property
  division 83–84
firing, of lawyer 32–35
fixed date method 181–182
friendly parent rule 96

G

garnishment of wages 215, 309
get, and separation 254–255, 309
grandparents, and access 225–233
grounds for divorce 58–62

I

illness of child, and child support 134
impeachment, defined 185
income security model, and spousal
  support 139
indexing, defined 309
insurance, and support obligations 261
intact families, and grandparents 228–231
interim orders, defined 309
Internet resources 268–269

J

Jewish divorces 254–255, 309
Joint Application for Divorce 65, 310
joint custody 101–104, 135–136, 309
joint petition, defined 65, 310
jointly held property, and property
  division 77
judges, described 43–44
judgments 187–188, 310

L

law libraries, using 266–267
lawyers, and confidentiality 29–30
  contracting with 27–29
  as court personnel 46–47
  handling problems with 30–36
  selecting 23–27
legal aid 26–27
legal documents, exchange of 49–50
legal fees 31–32, 35–36, 68–69, 309
legal process, and court personnel 43–47
  and family law 39–41
  and legal system 41–42
  and rules of court 47–54
legal system, described 41–42

letters, exchange of 48–49
limitations, defined 310
litigation, defined 310

M

marriage, defined 310
marriage breakdown, defined 58–62, 310
marriage contracts 248–251, 252–255, 310
marriage counselling 18–19
marriages of convenience 67–68
matrimonial home 79–80, 108–109, 159,
  310
mediation 192–198, 199, 201–202, 310
Minutes of Settlement 167–168, 311
mobility restrictions, on custodial parents
  104–106
Modernization of Benefits and
  Obligations Act 159
motions 52–53, 311

N

non est factum, defined 174

O

Offers to Settle 165–166
open mediation, defined 195
opening statements 183
oral discovery 51–52
order, defined 311
order for exclusive possession 220
Orders on Consent 168
other persons, and access to child 233

P

parental support 147–148, 311
parties, defined 311
paternity, determining 111–113
peace bonds 221
pensions 80–83, 159, 311
personal restraining orders 220–221
petition for divorce, defined 311
petitioner's case 183–185
physical or mental cruelty 61
pleadings, defined 311
possessory rights, defined 311
Powers of Attorney 258
pre-trials 53
property, defined 73–74

property division, and common-law
   spouses 155–159
   described 71–74
   enforcement of 218–220
   and financial statements 83–84
   and matrimonial home 79–80
   and pensions 80–83
   process of 74–79
   strategy for 86–88
   and taxes 84–86
provincial property scheme, and
   cohabitation agreements 252
psychological parent, defined 95

R

Reasons for Judgment 187–188
reconciliation, and separation 62, 175
Registered Retirement Savings Plans,
   transferring 85
registrars 45
release, of spousal support 145–146
religious arbitration, and provincial law
   199–200
remarriage, and spousal support 144
research, resources for 266–269
residency, and divorce process 63–64
respondent's case 185–186
restraining orders 220–221, 311
retainer form, sample 275–277
retainers, defined 27–29, 312
Rules of Practice, in legal system 47–54

S

sample forms, Family History Form
   297–298
   retainer form 275–277
   Separation Agreement 277–296
self-representation, tips for 269–272
separate property scheme, and
   cohabitation agreements 251
separation, and marriage breakdown 59–60
Separation Agreements, described
   168–175, 312
   sample 277–296
   setting aside 252–255
   and wills 260–262
settlements, circumstance of 163–165
   and Minutes of Settlement 167–168

and Offers to Settle 165–167
and orders on consent 168
and Separation Agreements 168–175
shared parenting, defined 312
siblings, and custody 98–99
sole custody 101, 104–106
solicitor-client privilege, defined 312
special expenses, and child support
   129–131
spousal support 138–147, 153–154,
   214–218, 312
Spousal Support Advisory Guidelines
   146–147
spouse, defined 312
statute, defined 312
step-parents, and child support 134
stepfamilies, and children 121–122
summation 186–187
supervised access, defined 107
support, described 125–126
   and enforcement 214–218
   see also child support; parental support;
     spousal support
Support Enforcement Offices 216–218

T

tax considerations, and property division
   84–86
tender years doctrine 99
transition people, defined 19–20
travelling with child, and custody 210–211
trial coordinators 44–45
trial process 53–54, 181–188

U

uncontested divorces 64–65, 312
unequal division of property 78–79
Unified Family Court 43

V

valuation, and property division 74, 75–78
variation, and support 131–132, 146, 312

W

wills, importance of 257–262
withdrawal from parental control 133–134
without prejudice, defined 166